A Walking Guide to Lawyer's London

Third Edition

Andrew Goodman

Published by Mediation Publishing
St Albans, UK
email: admin@mediationpublishing.com
website: www.mediationpublishing.com

ISBN 978-1-85811-728-7 (paperback)
ISBN 978-185811-729-4 (ebook)
Text © Andrew Goodman 2024
Photography © Clive Berridge
First published 2000

British Library Cataloguing in Publication Data
A catalogue record for this book is available from the British Library.
This publication is protected by international copyright law. All rights reserved. No part of this publication may be reproduced, stored in a retrieval system, or transmitted in any form or by any means, electronic, mechanical, photocopying, recording or otherwise, without the prior permission of the publisher.

Printed and bound in Great Britain

Contents

Foreword to the first edition by the Rt. Hon. Lord Falconer of Thoroton QC	v
Foreword to the first edition by the Rt.Hon. Lord Bingham of Cornhill	vii
Preface: the third edition	ix
Acknowledgements	xi
Introduction	xiii
1 Westminster	1
2 Strand and the Southern Inns of Chancery	25
3 Royal Courts of Justice	47
4 The Temple	75
5 From Fleet Street to Old Bailey	145
6 Chancery Lane	173
7 Lincoln's Inn and the Fields	193
8 Holborn and the Northern Inns of Chancery	221
9 Gray's Inn	235
Bibliography	263
Index	265

To Clive Berridge in memoriam

Foreword to the Second Edition

The law runs through the history of London as powerfully as the river Thames.

And the strength of that history is reflected in the buildings in which the law is housed in the UK's capital.

Parliament Square houses Westminster Hall, where the senior courts in England sat from the 13th to the 19th century. And the new Supreme Court building, where the final court of appeal has sat since 2009. And the House of Lords where the final court of appeal used to sit, in an inaccessible but opulent committee room on what is described as the first committee floor of the House.

Move eastwards from Parliament Square, down Whitehall, where the government departments are based, and the prime minister is housed off to the left, in Downing Street. Through Trafalgar Square onto Strand where, three quarters of a mile to the right, is the Temple, and to the left the Royal Courts of Justice. In the Temple, the barristers' chambers, in the Royal Courts of Justice, the senior courts of the English legal system.

The Royal Courts of Justice is a monument to the unbridled self-confidence of the Victorian era - there was no inhibition in expressing the importance of the law. And the Temple - beautiful, private, dominated by the preservation of history and values.

Back onto Strand and travel east past Chancery Lane, which leads to Lincoln's Inn and Gray's Inn where more barristers' chambers are to be found. But also a lot more solicitors' offices, and the civic grandeur of the Law Society halfway up that thoroughfare.

Travel further down Fleet Street and up Ludgate Hill, and there on the left is the most famous criminal court certainly in the United Kingdom, possibly in the world - the Old Bailey, where perpetrators of the most brutal crimes have been tried.

The architecture and personality of these buildings impacts on those who work in them, but, much more importantly, on those who come to seek advice or to resolve their cases, or indeed their lives here.

The intensity, the history and the power of these buildings is brilliantly exposed to the reader in Andrew Goodman's much needed book. In this second edition he does what no other guide to these buildings does - he explains not just their architecture and their history but their place in the culture of law in London. He is a practising barrister who understands the courts and the part of London inhabited during the long working hours by the lawyer.

The late Lord Bingham of Cornhill, in his introduction to the first edition, said the abiding impression of the book's description of the buildings was continuity. He was right. This book takes the reader on a journey - through the streets of London, and through the development of the law. It's a brilliant travel book. But it is much more than that. It reveals and illuminates a part of London in a way that even Dickens did not attempt in its breadth and its insight.

The Rt. Hon. Lord Falconer of Thoroton KC
London
November 2010

Foreword to the First Edition

In many old cities there are quarters where practitioners of a given craft or trade are found gathered together, be they silversmiths, money-lenders, leather-workers, restauranteurs, carpet-sellers or whatever. But nowhere in the world is there anything quite like the concentration of legal and judicial activity to be found at the southern end of the boundary between the Cities of London and Westminster. Here, within a radius of about a mile, may be found the four surviving Inns of Court and the home of the Law Society; here too were the three Serjeants' Inns and the nine Inns of Chancery, all now defunct, and a number of other bodies which have at some stage of history styled themselves as inns.

If, like shipping offices clustered round the quayside in Piraeus, these institutions had grown up round the formidable battery of civil courts now operating at the Royal Courts of Justice in Strand, or the fewer but perhaps even more formidable battery of criminal courts operating a short walk away to the east at the Old Bailey, this concentration of legal institutions would be readily explicable. But, as Andrew Goodman recounts in this fascinating survey, these institutions flourished for hundreds of years before the Royal Courts of Justice was opened in Strand, and most of them well before criminal sessions were held at the Old Bailey.

So the author begins his journey through Lawyers' London at Westminster Hall, where the common law first found institutional expressions. Now majestically and austerely empty, the Hall must in its legal heyday have resembled a small town on market day, with judicial and other stall holders offering their wares and a crush of participants and onlookers. From this, almost hallowed, place where it all began, we are led downstream, with brief pauses at Middlesex Guildhall and Somerset House, to the heart of what is now Lawyers' London: the Temple, Strand, Chancery Lane, Lincoln's Inn and Lincoln's Inn Fields, Gray's Inn and the Old Bailey.

Andrew Goodman is an engaging guide, not shy to instruct nor slow to digress. Even those who have spent their professional lives working in this area of London will learn much that is new to them. All will enjoy his guidance through scenes rich in historical associations familiar to those brought up in the common law, whether in Britain or the United States, or Australia, New Zealand, India, Sri Lanka, South Africa, the West Indies or other common law jurisdictions throughout the world.

The abiding impression is, perhaps, one of continuity. Not only centuries but light years separate the legal practitioners of early medieval times from the specialised, sophisticated, computerate lawyers of today. But today's practitioner is recognisable as the progeny of his medieval predecessor, and the institutions described in this book, although founded centuries ago, have continued to nourish, enrich and civilise successive generations to the benefit of the law and, one trusts, the public whom they all exist to serve.

Lord Bingham of Cornhill
Royal Courts of Justice
London
2 May 2000

Preface and Acknowledgements: Third Edition

Once again, the impetus for a new edition of *The Walking Guide to Lawyers' London* has been the organised visits of sections of the American Bar Association in the years leading to the 250th anniversary of the Declaration of Independence. In the intervening decade and a half since the second edition was published the legal fraternity felt the full force of a lockdown caused by the covid 19 pandemic, the impact of which perhaps changed people's working lives for ever. Offices, bars, restaurants and other service establishments known to generations of lawyers practising within the area disappeared. Significant mergers, releasing and concentrating the use of office accommodation followed, and while the buildings visited in the last edition remain, their occupants are now very different. Thus, the London of the law has a very different feel to it, much as the changes wrought by the Blitz some 85 years ago. We all fled online, and some of us are only gradually creeping back.

I am greatly indebted to Steve Weisbrot of the U.S. claims management firm, Angeion Group of Philadelphia and London, whose kind initiative in sponsoring this edition enabled us to keep the cover price significantly lower than it otherwise would have been and made possible the format for a real guide to walk with.
I thank the publishers, Mediation Publishing, and their director and editor, Andrew Griffin, for taking the project outside their normal list, with the concomitant effort and marketing which that entailed.

I reiterate my thanks to the original contributors and the assistance of those who helped produce the original and second editions, without which we would have had no base upon which to build.

And as ever, I commend this work with my best wishes to my fellow lawyers and the mediators into which, like me, they eventually mature.

Andrew Goodman
81 Chancery Lane, London.
November, 2024.

Preface to the Second Edition

Ten years have passed since the preparation and publication of Lawyers' London. During that period its print run sold out due in particular to the enthusiasm of visiting American and Commonwealth lawyers for the work, and my old friends at the American Bar Association.

Those years have seen major developments in the legal system of England and Wales, not the least in areas of funding and practice. The UK government has quietly restricted public funding and diminished access to justice. The full impact of the Woolf reforms which created the Civil Procedure Rules has generally made what civil litigation remains far more expensive. We can truly once again say as it was in 1947, that justice is open to all – as is the Ritz hotel.

These minor quibbles aside, there have been changes worth dealing with in a book which looks at the geographical side of legal practice in the capital. A substantial number of buildings, both public and private, have been brought back into pristine condition since the last edition, including the Royal Courts of Justice, Temple Church and much of the Inns of Court. The Temple Bar has been re-erected as new in the precincts of the City at Paternoster Square by St. Pauls Cathedral. And the absence from print of this work has seen Middlesex Guildhall transformed into the new Supreme Court of the United Kingdom.

I wish to extend my warm appreciation to Jonathan Gregory of Nova Law and Finance for making this new edition possible. The first was dedicated to my friends at court, with the Latin legend to be found in Middle Temple Hall beneath the arms of Edmund Plowden. This second edition I dedicate to Clive Berridge whose illness made it impossible for him to contribute additional and updated photography, but whose original work makes this volume what it is.

Andrew Goodman
1 Chancery Lane
October, 2010

Acknowledgements - First Edition

Although I take the blame for its contents, the appearance of this book is very much the product of a team effort. Its overall attractiveness lies less in my words than the striking and atmospheric original photographs of Clive Berridge and additional photographs of Jon Shamah, and design and layout by Mario Bettella at Artmedia.

I am indebted to Alistair MacQueen of Blackstone Press who took on and believed in a project which was outside both the experience and the normal list of his company. The editorial team of Derek French, Ramona Khambatta and Jennifer Strachan put an enormous effort into shaping the manuscript, and my thanks are also due to Trevor Hook who battled with a very tight production schedule, Roy Heywood of Wildy's who read the manuscript and the indexer Moira Greenhalgh.

I am particularly grateful for the kind foreword contributed by the Rt. Hon. Lord Bingham of Cornhill, formerly Master of the Rolls, at the time of its writing the Lord Chief Justice of England, and presently the senior Law Lord. May I thank also those who assisted in my research, notably the Rt Hon. Sir Robert Megarry, His Honour Paul Baker QC, Robin de Wilde QC, the collector and staff of the library of Inner Temple, and the librarians and staff of the libraries of Middle Temple and Lincoln's Inn. For their kind permission to take photographs in the Royal Courts of Justice, Jayne Follett, of the court superintendant's office, and at the Central Criminal Court, His Honour Judge Michael Hyam, the Recorder of London, and at Middlesex Crown Court, John Laverick, deputy court manager.

I was greatly encouraged by the support shown for this project by the members of the ABA 2000 Organising Committee, in particular Lady Helen Otton, Lord Goldsmith QC, Gerard McDermott QC, David Wilby QC and Neil Morrison, and by James Podger of the American Bar Association Journal.

Finally, but most importantly, I wish to pay tribute to my wife Sandra. She has more than enough to cope with, without my taking on additional writing commitments. She is a great strength to me and my anchor, and ensures that whatever I may do, family, house and home all function smoothly.

This book is dedicated to the lawyers themselves, and in particular those who still practice with idealism, and who assist in the development of the law for its own sake; those who give freely of their time to serve on bodies dealing with the reform of the law, to the development of practice and procedure, the preservation of ethical standards, the protection of the liberty of the individual, and of the community as a whole, and the provision of education to both young and mature professionals. In essence it is for those who give back.

Andrew Goodman
199 Strand
London
WC2R 1DR
July 2000

Introduction

This book has a twofold purpose. First, it is intended to provide the visitor to the quarter of London populated since at least the early 14th century by the lawyers, with an insight into their practices, culture and traditions in an environment which was developed by and for their number. It is a story resonant with great men and of a great heritage, sadly now fading. And though the narrative tells of the past, the picture intended is in reality a snapshot of the present, particularly viewing this area of London as it is to be found today and not as it was at the commencement of the Second World War, which to many seems a natural place to halt the tale of the historical development of the Inns of Court. This book celebrates what has been achieved in the 70 years since the Blitz as much as the accomplishments by lawyers over the past 700 years.

The second purpose is to develop the concept of a snapshot as a document of record. This country is going through a period of profound constitutional changes with, among other things, the creation of a Ministry of Justice replacing the Department for Constitutional Affairs, formerly, and for hundreds of years the Lord Chancellor's Office, and the replacement of the Judicial Committee of the House of Lords with a Supreme Court of Justice. Significant changes in legal representation were brought about by the Courts and Legal Services Act 1990, the Access to Justice Act 1999 and the Legal Services Act 2007. Thus, it may be that in not too many years distant, the picture painted of the legal quarter of London as it is today will have receded into memory, with the disappearance of legal traditions which are much a part of the present fabric of English life. It is to be hoped that any changes will prove to be for the better.

The reader may be forgiven for thinking that the history of legal London is confined to the Bar, since it dwells on the great advocates of the past and tends to regard advocacy as the high point of legal practice. That would be an unfortunate presumption, since there are some 118,000 practising solicitors in England and Wales and only 14,000 practising members of the Bar. Solicitors are the bedrock of the legal system upon whom all else depends.

However, it is true to say that by far the majority of the Bar still practice within the area covered by these pages, whereas the solicitors are spread throughout the country. That apart, for three hundred years the story of our split profession in London is one and the same. The English solicitor came into being in the 15th century at a time when a need arose for legal and general business agents, whose work extended beyond the formal clerical staff attached to the courts.

By that time the Bar, who conducted all higher court advocacy, and the attorneys, who undertook procedural steps in litigation, had been separate professions for over 100 years. During the 16th century the courts of equity in particular gave recognition to solicitors as the equal of attorneys, and they came to exist side by side with the same Act of 1728 regulating entry into both professions. Until the end of the 18th century solicitors were members of the Inns of Court, attorneys having been removed in 1574, but they were excluded by the Bar in 1793. By that time, however, they had virtually monopolised the Inns of Chancery.

In 1831 the Law Society of England and Wales, which governs the solicitors, was chartered, and by the mid 19th century regulations under statute were laid down for admission. By the Judicature Act 1873, all solicitors and attorneys became Solicitors of the Supreme Court and thereby officers of the court. The function of the solicitor today is to provide general legal and business advice, negotiate and conduct the sale of real property, draft wills, trusts, settlements and deal with probate, business, company and commercial work, and to instruct counsel. Under the Acts of 1990 and 1999 mentioned above, approved solicitors now have rights of audience in the higher courts in England and Wales.

Legal London has been bracing itself for a period of change, though quite what the change will be is harder to predict. Happily it is beyond the scope of this book to make such a prediction.

The Palace of Westminster

1. Westminster

Earth has not anything to show more fair:
Dull would he be of soul who could pass by
A sight so touching in its majesty.

William Wordsworth in his sonnet
'Upon Westminster Bridge' in September 1802.

Westminster

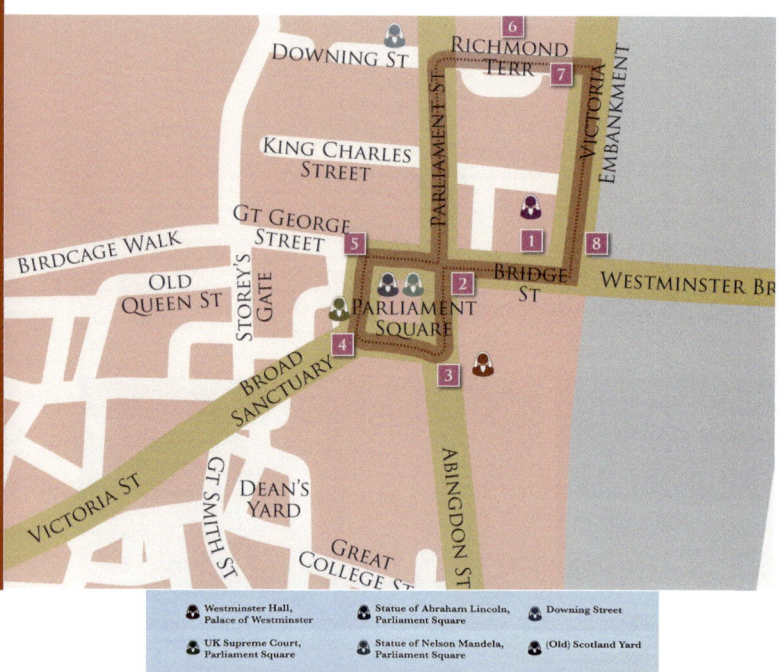

1. Westminster Underground station; circular walk. Allow 1 hour, excluding visits to Parliament, the Supreme Court or the Banqueting House. From Westminster Underground take Victoria Embankment exit 2 and proceed up the steps onto Westminster Bridge.
2. Cross the road, turn right and proceed to the corner of Parliament Square.
3. Proceed to northern end of Westminster Hall.
4. Cross Parliament Square to the north-east corner, at its junction with Victoria Street.
5. Cross over to the north-west corner of Parliament Square outside the Supreme Court building.
6. Proceed around Parliament Square to Whitehall, and pass along the north side of Whitehall to the corner of Downing Street.
7. Cross Whitehall and pass through Richmond Terrace on to the north side of Victoria Embankment. Turn right and proceed along 150 yards (137 m.).
8. Proceed along Victoria Embankment and return to Westminster Underground station.

1. Westminster Underground station; circular walk. Allow 1 hour, excluding visits to Parliament, the Supreme Court or the Banqueting House. From Westminster Underground take Victoria Embankment exit 2 and proceed up the steps onto Westminster Bridge.

The view may have changed since Wordsworth's words above, but not the sentiment. For here, on the north bank of the river Thames, stands the mother of Parliaments: the font of principles of the rule of law, free speech, parliamentary debate and representative democracy which are now seen as the ideal basis for government and politics all over the world. Between the end of the Seven Years War with France in 1763 and the end of the British Empire in the early 1960s, the legal system established by this mother of Parliaments governed the peace and well-being of a quarter of the land surface of the globe, and ruled the lives of one third of the world's peoples. This small area, named 'West Minster' because its minster church, Westminster Abbey, is to the west of St. Paul's Cathedral, and has been a seat of government for well over a thousand years.

Parliament is situated on land named as Thorney Island in a 785 charter of Offa, King of the English. There, Edward the Confessor, who was king of England 1042-66, built Westminster Abbey on the site of an ancient Saxon monastery and put up his own palace nearby. In 1265 Simon de Montfort, Earl of Leicester (1208?-65), attempting to settle the civil war between the barons and King Henry III, summoned to this Palace of Westminster an assembly which, because it was more broadly based than previous assemblies, is often regarded as the first English Parliament. Subsequent Parliaments met in the chapter house of Westminster Abbey until a permanent council chamber could be built on a site adjacent to Westminster Hall. What became the House of Lords met in a hall next to St Stephen's Chapel, known as the Court of Requests, or the White Hall. Henry VIII took this name for his much later, sumptuous palace built some 450 yards (500 m.) from the Palace of Westminster.

Westminster

By Plantagenet times (1154-1485) the area housed 20,000 souls, though many of these were rogues and vagabonds who came from all over England to claim sanctuary in the Abbey precincts. This is commemorated in the street names of the area once known as the rookeries, where there are Little Sanctuary and Broad Sanctuary, and Thieving Lane (long since disappeared) which was a turning used by the authorities to convey felons and so avoid the area of sanctuary.

Those sprawling quarters of Parliament and of government, both ancient and medieval, were lost in a terrible fire in October 1834. Only Westminster Hall, St Stephen's Chapel and the little Jewel Tower remained of the great press of buildings that had grown up haphazardly over the years. The task of rebuilding Parliament was given to the architect Sir Charles Barry (1795-1860), who undertook the work from 1840 to 1857, after much discussion whether the seat of government should remain at the riverside. King William IV had offered Buckingham Palace as a new home. However, the Duke of Wellington, then minister without portfolio in Sir Robert Peel's government and mindful of the

Westminster Hall, interior detail

Elizabeth Tower with Big Ben seen from Parliament Square

The Palace of Westminster with Big Ben seen from St Thomas's Hospital

popular discontent in the country after the Napoleonic wars, wanted a defensible site, should the need arise. So came about Barry's river frontage, 940 feet (287 m.) long, together with the Victoria Tower, 336 feet (102 m.) high, and the clock tower of St Stephen, now called the Elizabeth Tower in tribute to the late Queen's Diamond Jubilee, which is 316 feet (96 m.) high. The clock tower houses a clock built by Dents and a 13.75 tonne bell, which was named Big Ben, probably after Sir Benjamin Hall, the Chief Commissioner of Works at the time of its installation in 1859. The name Big Ben soon came to be used for the whole clock and its tower.

Westminster Hall, interior

2. Cross the road, turn right and proceed to the corner of Parliament Square.

New Palace Yard, that wide expanse in the shadow of Big Ben and Westminster Hall, was enclosed by William the Conqueror, who became king of England in 1066, with a wall and three gates, and subsequently became infamous as a place of ill-use and execution. Here in 1685 Titus Oates, who had used invented stories of Roman Catholic conspiracies against the State to inflame religious strife suffered the indignity of the stocks, before his imprisonment. Another, but much earlier occupant of these stocks was Perkin Warbeck (1474?-99), who, claiming to be the younger son of the deceased King Edward IV, had sought to depose the later King Henry VII, but was defeated in battle. In that corner of the yard to the east of Westminster Hall stood a clock tower, built at the expense of Chief Justice Hengham for offending King Edward I. It contained the Star Chamber, in which the king's council often sat and which was probably named after the design on its ceiling.

William the Conqueror established the Aula (or Curia) Regis, or Court of the Barons of the King's Household. This consisted of the great officers of State and dispensed justice, of which the king was the font, at the Palace of Whitehall, or wherever the royal household was located. From it derived the Courts of King's Bench, Common Pleas (or Common Bench), and Exchequer (each of which existed with a defined sphere of competence by 1272). The system it created suffered much from abuse and corruption by household officials. So much so, that by Clause 17 of Magna Carta (1215) the barons specifically asked for the Court of Common Pleas to be regulated and kept in one place. In 1487 King Henry VII created the Court of Star Chamber as a committee of the royal council. By a statute of that year the Lord Chancellor, Lord Treasurer and Lord Keeper of the Privy Seal, or any two of them sitting together with one lord spiritual and one lord temporal, the Chief Justices of the Courts of Common Pleas and King's Bench, were empowered to call before them and punish the offences of combinations of nobility and gentry supported by liveries, partiality by sheriffs in the selection of jurors, bribery in jurors, riots and unlawful assemblies. The Court of Star Chamber was used as an instrument of repression by which the monarch sought to control the powerful nobility and gentry in the provinces, where the normal judicial system gave him little practical redress.

King Henry VIII (1509-46) went a step further in his political manipulation of the Star Chamber. He used it as a tool, devised by the ingenuity and skill of his sometime Lord Chancellor, Cardinal Wolsey, to tackle the opposition from the peerage to his break with the Church of Rome. In 1529 Henry had added the President of the King's Council to the list of judges. This was a blatantly political appointment. Ten years later, by the statute *Custos Morum*, the king's proclamations on ecclesiastical matters were given the force of law. Offenders against such proclamations were to be tried in the Court of Star Chamber and there face fines and imprisonment. It was this Act that purported to make the Star Chamber the court concerned with guarding the morals of the nation and its subjects. The court was ignominiously abolished in 1640.

3. Proceed to northern end of Westminster Hall.

Nothing in the Palace of Westminster can match the beauty and nobility of Westminster Hall, which is by far the most important building in London to survive intact from medieval times. Westminster Hall and Durham Cathedral are designated world heritage sites by Unesco. The Hall was designed by Henry Yevele who was master mason to Kings Edward III, Richard II and Henry IV, and built the naves of Westminster Abbey and of Canterbury Cathedral. It stands 92 feet (28 m.) high to its 12-bay hammerbeam roof, made of English oak. At 238 feet (72.5 m.) long and 68 feet (21 m.) wide it is the finest example of its kind in the world. It has with great good fortune survived the bombs of two wars, fires at the Palace and an arson attack by the IRA.

Westminster Hall was originally constructed for King William II (William Rufus) from 1097, and was used until the mid l4th century by the reigning monarch, when in London, for coronation festivals, State banquets and the entertaining of foreign guests and ambassadors. Here the King's Champion would ride before the assembled company; and here the Curia Regis met. Subsequently some early Parliaments used the Hall until such time as a council chamber could be built.

Westminster

Reproduced by kind permission of V&A Picture Library

Restored by King Edward II after a fire in 1291, it was King Richard II who ordered alterations to the Hall which were carried out between 1394 and 1401, and which included the raising of the roof by 2 feet (60 cm.) and the addition of the hammerbeams. Accounts of the cost of its construction from 1399 to 1400 were preserved by John Godmaston, the clerk of the works at Westminster, and may be seen at the Public Record Office Museum. Until 1980 this famous old hall was freely open to the public but the strictures of security now make access available only to those who have legitimate business in the House of Commons, or who queue daily to watch or lobby their MPs.

Many great historical events have taken place in Westminster Hall, not least the trials of great men by their peers. Many were condemned to death: in 1305 the Scots patriot, Sir William Wallace; in 1520, for treason against King Henry VIII,

Reproduced by kind permission of National Monument Record Office

Henry Stafford, Duke of Buckingham; in 1551 Edward Seymour, Duke of Somerset, who had been Lord Protector of the kingdom during the minority of King Edward VI; and two years later Somerset's great rival, the Earl of Northumberland. In January 1641 John Evelyn recorded in his diary his presence here at the impeachment for treason of the Earl of Strafford. In May of that same year he witnessed that nobleman's execution on Tower Hill. Other notable trials included those of Perkin Warbeck in 1498 for insurrection, Saints Thomas More and John Fisher in 1535 for their

Westminster Hall - detail of the hammerbeam roof
Reproduced by kind permission of National Monument Record Office

refusal to recognise King Henry VIII as Head of the Church in England, the Earls of Essex and Southampton in 1601 for rebellion, and, in 1606 that of Guy Fawkes and the others who conspired to blow up Parliament and King James I on 5 November 1605. The most regrettable of all English trials was held here in the autumn of 1649 when Charles I was prosecuted to his death, after which England became a Commonwealth with Oliver Cromwell as lord protector. After the restoration of the monarchy in 1660, the surviving 'regicides', those who had signed the death warrant of the king, were brought back to Westminster Hall to be judged themselves. And at that time Oliver Cromwell's disinterred head was raised upon a spike and affixed to a gable at the southern end of the Hall where it rotted for 20 more years.

State trials at Westminster Hall afterwards included the trial of the seven Church of England bishops who protested against King James II's suspension of statutes imposing penalties on Roman Catholics and nonconformists – they were acquitted of seditious libel in 1688; the trial of the Jacobite Lords Kenmure and Derwentwater, who pleaded guilty to high treason following the

1715 uprising which aimed to place the Roman Catholic son of James II on the throne in place of the Protestant King George I; and the extraordinary impeachment of Warren Hastings for his conduct while Viceroy of India which lasted for seven years, 1788-95, and led to his acquittal.

In modern times Westminster Hall has become familiar to those wishing to pay their last respects at the lying in state of the monarch, including our late Queen. In 1965 Sir Winston Churchill was also so honoured.

When the Hall was not being used for formal State occasions, it was divided by a series of low partitions and in its four corners, though subsequently expanding along its walls, sat the courts of superior jurisdiction from 1255 until 1822. They were then transferred to a purpose-built annexe between the buttresses to the west side of the Hall.

The High Court of Justice was established in Westminster Hall in about 1255, nearly 50 years before Parliament started meeting regularly at the chapter house of the neighbouring Abbey. There already existed four legal terms, amounting together to less than 100 days per year, during which the courts sat wherever the royal household happened to be. After Magna Carta the Court of Common Pleas was ordered to remain in London regardless of the king's progress through the shires. By his Ordinance of 1292 King Edward I gave the judges of the Common Pleas the exclusive right to select advocates from each county to plead in the royal courts. Thus was created the independent Bar of England and Wales and the judges retained the exclusive right to regulate those entitled to practise advocacy in the higher courts for 700 years until the passage of the Courts and Legal Services Act 1990, modified by the Access to Justice Act 1999.

Westminster Hall, gargoyle
Reproduced by kind permission of National Monument Record Office

In 1306 the same monarch ordered the Court of Chancery to remain in London, although with no permanent seat. Indeed for half a century from 1300 the Chancery Court was held on an occasional basis in various churches, including Blackfriars, Whitefriars, St Mary-le-Strand, All-Hallows, Barking-by-the-Tower, the Domus Conversorum in Chancery Lane, the Temple Church and Southwark Cathedral. In 1350 its position became fixed as the south-west corner of Westminster Hall, with the Lord Chancellor or his deputy dispensing equitable awards from a marble chair behind a marble table.

By the 18th century, the higher courts all occupied places in the Hall. The Court of King's Bench and that of the Lord Chancellor vied for business, and audibility, with the market stalls that occupied the spaces between them. Criticism of the state of the administration of justice will be familiar to the readers of Dickens's *Barnaby Rudge*, *Bleak House*, *Little Dorrit* or *Pickwick Papers*. A less fictional account was left in 1710 by Uffenbach, a visitor from Holland, who wrote:

> *the three courts of judicature are quite open excepting that in front there are enclosed seats for the barristers. One is allowed to listen to everything, but anyone who does not understand English gabble very well can hear little, being disturbed by the tumult of those who walk up and down and by the fact that there are stalls on both sides where books and all kinds of wares are sold.*

It was not, however, the crush and babble that forced the courts to remove from Westminster Hall. Certainly there was a real need for more space, since the expansion of the High Court of Chancery to include a separate court for the Vice-Chancellor, an appointment newly created in 1813. The motivating factor was more the huge disruption of court business caused by the festivities in the Hall to celebrate the coronation of King George IV in 1820. The partitions between the courts were taken down, and both King's Bench and Chancery had to be removed for several months. As a result the architect Sir John Soane (1753-1837) was commissioned to design a court annexe, which was built between 1823 and 1826. Appended to the Stone Building, a parliamentary annexe created by John Vardy in 1755, Soane's new structure rested cleverly between the buttresses on the west side of the Hall and housed seven courts:

King's Bench, the Court of Exchequer Chamber (an appellate court from decisions of the superior courts), the Exchequer Court, the Bail Court, Common Pleas, the Vice-Chancellor's Court, and the Court of Chancery. Rooms were provided for judges' and barons' clerks (the barons were the judges of the Exchequer Court), masters in equity, serjeants (senior barristers) and the Bar. However, the building lacked a law library, consultation rooms and a separate entrance for the judges.

These were the least of the deficiencies, since before its completion Stone Building was already outmoded. Ventilation was extremely poor. Space was at a premium. During the 1830s separate courts were established for the Master of the Rolls and for Bankruptcy. In 1841 two further posts of Vice-Chancellor were created, each requiring a court. For these, two storage areas were converted into courtrooms; the Bar greeted this development with derision, and referred to the new courts as the 'dog-hole' and 'cock-loft'.

As the number of common law judges increased between 1841 and 1849 so began the exodus away from Westminster and back to the precincts of the Inns of Court. The High Court of Chancery moved to Lincoln's Inn; the Master of the Rolls to Rolls Buildings, his official residence off Chancery Lane; and the Bankruptcy Court moved to a new building at the corner of Carey and Portugal Streets. The two vacant courts in Soane's building were rapidly filled by the High Court of Admiralty, and the Probate and Divorce Court. Having survived the fire of 1834 along with the Hall, this entire building was razed in 1883 and no trace remains today of one of Soane's finest and most utilitarian works.

Beyond Westminster Hall lies the modern Palace of Westminster, housing the two legislative chambers. At the time of writing the House of Lords itself faces an uncertain future as to its composition and role. In its judicial capacity until 2009 the Judicial Committee of the House sat daily during the law terms as the final domestic appellate tribunal for the United Kingdom. The Lords of Appeal in Ordinary were supplemented by peers who had held high judicial office. They sat in the Lords Committee Rooms on the south side of the Lords chamber, overlooking the river. Here, before the horseshoe-shaped bench, counsel in court dress argued the niceties of interpretation before the elders of the legal system, who sat comfortably in business suits. Judgments were delivered as if they were Lords' speeches, in the House itself, where counsel, already apprised of the answer, stood before the bar of the House. There the judges, on the front bench and still in business suits, declared themselves either 'content' or 'not content' on the putting of the motion of the appeal.

4. Cross Parliament Square to the north-east corner, at its junction with Victoria Street.

The most public display of the majesty of the law occurs at the start of every Michaelmas term when a service of thanksgiving for the judiciary and senior lawyers at Westminster Abbey is followed by the Lord Chancellor's breakfast, in the precincts of the Lords. Until recently, the two ceremonies were linked by the famous procession from the Abbey across to the House. Later during the legal year, the Lord Chancellor's breakfast is the venue for the 'silk ceremony', when the newly appointed King's Counsel (who are entitled to wear silk, rather than woollen, gowns in court) accept their royal patents from the Chancellor's hands.

At the head of Victoria Street fast by Dean's Yard stood an ancient tower. Here Sir Walter Raleigh was held incarcerated on the eve of his execution in Old Palace Yard in October 1618. Among other unfortunates to share such accommodation during the English Civil War period were King Charles I's consort, Queen Henrietta Maria, John Hampden, the Parliamentary leader who opposed Charles's ship money tax, Titus Oates, and Richard Lovelace, the royalist poet and soldier.

The broad avenue of Victoria Street was constructed between 1845 and 1851, in a dramatic redevelopment which swept away centuries of small courts and alleyways known as the rookeries. Here the Protestant Huguenot refugees from France first sought refuge in London, and created little, or Petty, France.

Along Victoria Street are the sites of two former prisons. Where now stands the graceful Roman Catholic Cathedral of Westminster, a house of correction was built in 1618. In 1834 it grew into a formidable gaol called Tothill Fields, but was demolished in 1854 to clear the site for its present edifice. A little way to the south, the great Millbank Penitentiary covered a huge acreage extending down to the river, where presently the Tate Britain Gallery stands.

Originally built as a separate women's prison in the 1830s, it grew dramatically in size when it became the national holding centre for those wretches sentenced to transportation overseas. Afterwards it became a military prison, the largest in the Empire.

5. Cross over to the north-west corner of Parliament Square outside the Supreme Court building.

Behind the striking statue of Abraham Lincoln, a copy of that by Augustus Saint-Gaudens in Lincoln Park, Chicago is

Statue of Lincoln by Saint-Gaudens

the Supreme Court of the United Kingdom, housed in the gothic splendour of the former Middlesex Guildhall. Since the Middle Ages there has been a local criminal court in the shadow of Westminster Hall, and here at the Town Court House, Middlesex Quarter Sessions were held until 1752. From then until 1913 that court's business was transferred periodically to the North London Sessions House at Clerkenwell Green. By a stroke of irony the

Westminster

present site of the Guildhall was once occupied by St Peter's Sanctuary, containing the Chapel of the Holy Innocents, into which hunted criminals were given entry without hindrance to claim sanctuary. The chapel was demolished only gradually from 1775, and it was not until 1805 that the Westminster Guildhall was erected on this site, as a sessions house for the City and Liberties of Westminster. The surrounding streets were cleared in the first half of the 19th century to create Parliament Square and Broad Sanctuary.

Work started on the present Guildhall in 1906. Designed by James Gibson, its Edwardian free style was put into Gothic decorative form intended to blend with its neighbours across the Square. This is most apparent from the medieval frieze around and above the central portico.

From 1913 the courts doubled up as council chambers for the County Council of Middlesex, until that council was abolished in 1965. The principal courtrooms were panelled and bear the portraits of famous chairmen of quarter sessions held here, including the novelist Henry Fielding (author of Tom Jones) and his blind brother, John, who helped set up the first London police force, the Bow Street runners, and, within living memory, Ewen Montagu, who devised the famous Second World War ruse de guerre, the man who never was. The entrance hall contained a small exhibition devoted to the Middlesex Regiment, and this remains in the public area of the Supreme Court, together with the war memorial to the dead of the Regiment.

The Constitutional Reform Act 2005 made provision for the creation of a new Supreme Court for the United Kingdom. There had long been a desire by some parliamentarians for the creation of a new independent Supreme Court separating the highest appeal court from the second house of Parliament, and removing the Lords of Appeal in Ordinary from the legislature. Before then the most senior judges, the Law Lords as they are often called, sat not only sat judicially, but were also able to become involved in the debate and subsequent enactment of Government legislation in the House of Lords. This ability created difficulties for the management under domestic law of Human Rights Act cases against the United Kingdom Government, since members of the final court on points of law could have participated in the enactment of that law.

Portico of the United Kingdom Supreme Court

Westminster

The Supreme Court for the United Kingdom assumed the jurisdiction of the Appellate Committee of the House of Lords and the devolution jurisdiction of the Judicial Committee of the Privy Council. As an independent institution, it is presided over by twelve independently appointed judges, known as Justices of the Supreme Court and was officially opened at the start of the legal year in October 2009. The Court's website recounts that to create a suitable home, renovation works at the Middlesex Guildhall were wide-ranging. The focus was on enhancing the historic fabric of the building, and sensitively reversing many of the more recent adaptations that left it feeling gloomy and cluttered. The imposing, adversarial atmosphere of the incumbent Middlesex Crown Court also had to be converted into an environment suited to Supreme Court business: learned discussion of points of law rather than trial by jury.

Additionally the new Supreme Court is a United Kingdom body legally separate from the England and Wales courts as it is also the Supreme Court of both Scotland and Northern Ireland. As such it falls outside of the remit of the Lady Chief Justice of England and Wales in her role as head of the judiciary of England and Wales.

An exhibition area situated on the lower ground floor of our building, is open Monday - Friday. It includes an overview of the establishment of the court, a constitutional timeline of the UK, and various panels explaining how its work affects other lower courts and UK citizens. A further exhibition outside Court 1 examines important principles of law that have been decided by the Supreme Court in major cases over its last 15-year existence.

Westminster

The Supreme Court Building

The first members of the Supreme Court

Court 1 above

New Court 3 above

Court 2 seen from the Balcony

Westminster

Westminster

Nos 8-12
Downing Street

6. Proceed around Parliament Square to Whitehall, and pass along the north side of Whitehall to the corner of Downing Street.

Downing Street is named after its speculative builder, Sir George Downing (1623?-84). One of his assistants, the diarist Samuel Pepys, described him as a 'perfidious rogue'. He managed the dubious distinction of being both one of Cromwell's Treasury officials during the Commonwealth and the recipient of a knighthood from King Charles II after the restoration of the monarchy. In his youth he visited America and attended Harvard University. The large houses contained in Downing Street were owned privately until gradually, during the 18th century, they passed into the hands of the Crown. King George II offered No. 10 as a gift to his prime minister, Sir Robert Walpole, who took up residence in 1735. Walpole accepted with the reservation that the gift should not be personal to him, but should attach itself to his office, which was First Lord of the Treasury, the name on the brass plate to this day. Likewise No. 11 has come to house the Chancellor of the Exchequer, and No. 12 the government Chief Whip.

At No. 8 Downing Street, and around into Whitehall, until August, 2009 when they moved to the Supreme Court building, were situated the offices and chamber of the Judicial Committee of the Privy Council, which still acts upon the residual prerogative of the Sovereign as the font of justice to hear appeals from all her dominions. The Privy Council is the King's private council of ministers, and includes all those who have held Cabinet office, judges of the Court of Appeal and House of Lords, as well as many others. The jurisdiction of the Judicial Committee to hear final appeals from the Commonwealth has been regulated by statute since 1833.

Some 30 former colonial and Commonwealth countries have ceased to accept the jurisdiction of the Judicial Committee as a court competent to interfere with their domestic judicial process. This includes many that still regard the King as titular head of State.

The matters still referred to this court are heard in the courtrooms of the Supreme Court. Here present and retired Justices, together with foreign judges appointed for that purpose, sit in judgment over questions of law arising in the Channel Islands, the Isle of Man, Commonwealth countries in the West Indies and other dependent territories, as well as some domestic matters concerning the medical professions.

7. Cross Whitehall and pass through Richmond Terrace on to the north side of Victoria Embankment. Turn right and proceed along 100 yards (90 m.).

In December 1886, Richard Norman Shaw was appointed architect to design a headquarters for the Metropolitan Police, who were moving out of their old building, which was called Scotland Yard. The new building was christened New Scotland Yard, but the adjective 'New' was soon dropped in detective fiction and popular usage. The 'Met' is the territorial police force responsible for policing Greater London's 32 boroughs. Its name derives from the location of the original Metropolitan Police headquarters at 4 Whitehall Place, which had its main public entrance on the Westminster street called Great Scotland Yard. The Scotland Yard entrance became the public entrance, and over time "Scotland Yard" came to be used not only as the common

Westminster

name of the headquarters building, but also as a metonym for the Metropolitan Police Service (MPS) itself and police officers, especially detectives, who serve in it. The *New York Times* wrote in 1964 that, just as Wall Street gave its name to New York's financial district, Scotland Yard became the name for police activity in London. Similar metonyms are used in respect of buildings housing institutions around the world. For example Sakurada Gate (Sakuradamon) — one of the gates at Tokyo Imperial Palace - is similarly used as a metonym for the Tokyo Metropolitan Police Department (TMPD). Downing Street, as we have seen, is a metonym for the Prime Minister's office, the Cabinet Office and government policy generally; the same is attributed to the Elysee Palace for the President of France, and its foreign ministry at Quai d'Orsay. In 1967 the building was renamed Norman Shaw Building after the police moved to a new New Scotland Yard on Victoria Street. This prestigious and important building, occupying a river frontage close to Parliament, was not put out to competitive tender as was the usual Victorian fancy. Rather the government of the day wanted to have the building completed as quickly and as cheaply as possible. A proposed opera house development had recently been abandoned and the site was acquired at a depressed value. A meeting was convened between Henry Mathews, the Home Secretary, and Sir Edward Ducane, Director of HM Prisons, at which it was agreed that granite would be quarried at Dartmoor by serving convicts, with Portland stone facings to be supplied by government-owned quarries. Shaw managed to convince these reluctant men that the location was too important for London to have the rather drab-looking building then envisaged. He was thus able to introduce the red brick that gives the building its handsome and striking appearance, by using the three different materials in bands.

    New Scotland Yard was built in four blocks around a square courtyard. They give the impression of fortress-like sturdiness, and were constructed to be protected from civil disorder. The ornamental turrets which cap each of the corners of the building are reminiscent of the old-style police helmets, used in 1890 when it opened. The four blocks were divided up by the then Receiver, Alfred Pennefather, into Metropolitan Police headquarters, criminal investigation department, public carriage office, and the lost property office. The building also housed the famous 'Black Museum' of criminal artefacts.

Having moved into the building in 1890 the force had grown in size substantially, now needing more administrative staff and a bigger headquarters. New buildings were constructed and completed between 1906 and 1940, so that New Scotland Yard became a three-building complex. The first two buildings are now a Grade I listed structure known as the Norman Shaw Buildings, and are part of the Parliamentary estate.

In 1967 the Met moved its headquarters to purpose built premises at Broadway, Victoria, and remained there until 2016. In October of that year New Scotland Yard returned to the Victoria Embankment, occupying the Curtis Green Building, a 1940s development immediately adjacent to its former site. There it remains, complete with its iconic revolving sign.

New Scotland Yard

The church of St Clement Danes

2. Strand and the Southern Inns of Chancery

Vast thoroughfare crowded with traffic . . . down which the tide of labour flows daily to the City.
                              Augustus Hare, *Walks in London*, 1901.

Strand & Southern Inns

1. From Temple Underground station turn right along the Embankment for 300 yards (275m.), passing beneath King's College. Turn right and climb the stairs up to Waterloo Bridge and proceed to the traffic lights at the corner of Strand and Lancaster Place.
2. Turn right and proceed along Strand to the main entrance of Somerset House, opposite the church of St Mary-le-Strand.
3. Cross over to the north side of Strand and pass eastwards along Bush House to the corner of Melbourne Place.
4. Cross Aldwych. Turn right into Houghton Street and right again at the London School of Economics into Clement's Inn Passage, passing down the steps and along the western boundary railings of the Royal Courts of Justice complex.
5. Proceed along Clement's Inn Passage towards Strand. In spite of the presence of uniformed security personnel this is a public right of way.
6. Pass over to the island church and around its exterior. Cross to the south side of Strand, on the east corner of Essex Street.

1. From Temple Underground station turn right along the Embankment for 300 yards (275m.), passing beneath King's College. Turn right and climb the stairs up to Waterloo Bridge and proceed to the traffic lights at the corner of Strand and Lancaster Place.

The road called Strand has linked the cities of London and Westminster since the two were remote from each other and separated by open countryside. Curiously this great tideway of commerce appears to have been little used by the lawyers, who much preferred to travel from the Inns of Court to the royal courts at Westminster Hall by water ferry, rather than along the road. This they did for more than five and a half centuries.

Strand takes its name from the shoreline of the river, first mentioned in antiquity as the battlefield where in 1052 Edward the Confessor defeated Earl Godwin. Afterwards it became a more defined highway linking London with the royal palace in Whitehall and the West Minster, though still very much an open track with some few dwellings situated where bridges or fords crossed the streams that ran from higher ground down to the Thames. By royal warrant of November 1353, one John de Bedforde was given the responsibility of paving the highway between Temple Bar and Westminster Abbey, the cost of which he was to defray by the levy of a toll on the goods sold at the Staple Market. Whether that appointment was merely a sinecure, designed to impose a tax on the great wool merchants is not above suspicion for Bedforde failed in his task and the road was not paved until the reign of Henry VIII in 1532.

Afterwards this long, broad street became lined with the town houses of the mighty and the good, the south side having access by private jetty on to the River Thames, and the north gardens running up to the fields of St Martin and the convent garden of the Abbot of Westminster. The great mansions of the aristocracy belonged to, amongst others, Simon de Montfort, John of Gaunt (who was patron to Wyclif, Chaucer and Froissart), Lord Protector Somerset, the Dukes of Buckingham, Northumberland, York, Ormond and Monmouth, and the Earls of Leicester, Bedford, Salisbury, Arundel and Essex as well as the Archbishop of York and the Bishops of Norwich, Carlisle and Durham. Many of these resonant titles are to be found in the local street names of today.

Strand & Southern Inns

It was only after the Great Fire of 1666 that more ordinary people started to move westwards out of the City of London to occupy houses built on the land between Drury Lane and the area by now called Covent Garden. In Regency and Victorian times this became a solid and very pleasant middle-class residential neighbourhood. Strand contained upwards of a dozen theatres, the finest of London restaurants, and the capital's most celebrated night life. Sadly the ebullient and more exhuberant character of the area underwent a significant change in the 1890s with the redevelopment of much of the Strand to widen the approach to Waterloo Bridge, and create the Aldwych and, afterwards, Kingsway. The gaiety that had been Strand at night moved up to Piccadilly and the new Shaftesbury Avenue. Even today, despite the presence of theatres, restaurants and the Savoy Hotel, the road has a feeling of drabness, and of being a backwater of London life.

St-Mary-le-Strand Church

2. Turn right and proceed along Strand to the main entrance of Somerset House, opposite the church of St Mary-le-Strand

Opposite the church of St Mary-le-Strand, on the site of the present Somerset House, stood the London residence of the Bishop of Chester until its demolition in 1549. By 1294 the building was known as Strand or Chester Inn, and had become the marshalling point for the King's justices in eyre to meet prior to leaving on circuit. In front of the building, at approximately the west end of the church, stood an ancient stone cross by Strand Well. Here the itinerant justices sat on their return, administering justice in public, and in the open air. Afterwards, a maypole 100 feet (30 m.) high was erected on the site, and by the turn of the 16th century the little Strand Inn had become an Inn of Chancery affiliated to Middle Temple. Removed by the Puritans in 1644, the maypole was again erected on the instructions of the Duke of York in April 1661. His brother, the restored King Charles II had marched past this point on 29 May 1660, at the head of 20,000 troops under the command of General Monk. The new maypole at 134 feet (44 m.) high became the tallest in Europe, and here it stood until 1718 when the site was being cleared and Sir Isaac Newton had it removed to Wanstead Park as a support for his friend Reverend Pound's telescope.

The church of St Mary-le-Strand, which Sir John Betjemen called 'a baroque paradise', was constructed by James Gibbs between 1714 and 1723. Then called New Church, it was the first of 50 new churches to be built at the request of Queen Anne. By that time across the roadway, the first Somerset House had been constructed. Edward Seymour, Duke of Somerset and lord protector of England during the minority of King Edward VI, had long coveted the riverside site which included Strand Inn. In 1549 he ruthlessly caused the Inn's demolition, and the remaining students were obliged to join New Inn to the north.

The rather undiscriminating Lord Protector also confiscated and removed the neighbouring palaces and houses of the bishops of Worcester, Llandaff, Lichfield and Coventry and the old parish church of St Mary where St Thomas à Becket had been a rector during the reign of King Stephen. Many other buildings made way for this, the creation of the most substantial private palace in London, built between 1552 and 1554. By a cruel stroke of fate, Seymour himself did not live to see its completion. He was executed in 1553.

The building was acquired by the Crown. Under the Stuarts, it became the State apartments of the royal consort. King James I renamed it Denmark House in honour of his wife, Anne of Denmark, and subsequently both Henrietta Maria, wife of King Charles I, and Catherine of Braganza, wife of Charles II resided here. During the Commonwealth the building became the headquarters of the New Model Army; and both Oliver Cromwell and General George Monk lay in state here on their deaths. (After Cromwell's death, Monk supported the restoration of the monarchy and died as Duke of Albemarle.) The same privilege was afforded to both Inigo Jones, who designed court masques for James I and Anne, and Sir Joshua Reynolds, first President of the Royal Academy, which occupied Somerset House.

The present building was constructed over a period of 20 years by the architect Sir William Chambers, from 1776. The site had been cleared over the preceding year and formed a rectangle some 500 by 800 feet (150 by 240 m.). The east wing was added 1828-34, the west wing 1854-6. Formed around a large open rectangular courtyard, it was intended to house a burgeoning civil service and has variously contained the headquarters of the Board of Inland Revenue, the office of the Registrar of Births, Marriages and Deaths, the Probate Registry and Wills Office, and the Principal Registry of the Family Division of the High Court. The north wing, with its Strand frontage, was devoted to the arts. Housing the Royal Society until 1856, it was also the home of the Royal Academy and its annual exhibition until 1837, when the Academy moved to the new National Gallery in Trafalgar Square. In June 1990 the Courtauld Institute moved its collection to the north wing, whose former art galleries were refurbished specifically for the purpose, and Somerset House presently contains one of the foremost collections of impressionist art in Europe, although its cultural heyday was perhaps in the late 18th century when the Society of Antiquaries and the Royal Astronomical, Geological and Geographical Societies all met here at their formation. The east wing was occupied by King's College, London upon its foundation in 1828.

Somerset House, river frontage

The magnificent south wing of Somerset House has a river frontage extending 600 feet (180 m.). The façade is devoted to columns in two storeys of the Corinthian order; it contains moulded ceilings by G.B. Cipriani and the American painter, Benjamin West, both founder members of the Royal Academy. Here Charles Dickens's father John worked as a clerk in the Navy Pay Office, one of several Admiralty departments that overlooked the river terrace. Access was given on to this popular walkway through London's first naval museum, and strolling its length became a popular recreation on Sundays, and a haunt of the novelist George Eliot and her friend the philosopher Herbert Spencer. A Millennium project was to reopen the terrace to the public together with the central quadrangle, a fine open space approximating in size to Trafalgar Square. Since then the quadrangle has housed fountains and cafes, open air cinema and concerts in the summer months, and an ice-skating rink in the winter.

To the east of Somerset House stood Arundel House, formerly Bath's Inn, the town house of the Bishop of Bath and Wells. This was demolished to make way for the construction of a new building for King's College, London and was, like many small properties in this area, given the attribution of 'inn' in the 15th century. It would have provided lodging for the bishop's clerks and scriveners, but is not associated with the lawyers.

Courtyard of Somerset House Photo by Simon Goodman

3. Cross over to the north side of Strand and pass eastwards along Bush House to the corner of Melbourne Place.

From 1860 for half a century this area of London was thrown into turmoil by vast redevelopment. To the east over 400 buildings were demolished to clear the site of the Royal Courts of Justice building; to the west the widening of the approach to Waterloo bridge led to the truncating of Drury Lane and the destruction of the Gaiety Theatre; and to the north a broad avenue was cut up to Holborn, to be named Kingsway in celebration of Edward VII who acceded to the throne in 1901. The point at which these three projects met was a collection of courtyards, nooks and rookeries centred on Wych Street. An area rich in the history of London, it contained three of the ancient Inns of Chancery and had been little disturbed by the passing of the years between the turn of the 15th and the mid 19th centuries. Then Victorian speculators took contol. They moved in and constructed, among other edifices, three famous but jerrybuilt theatres and a hotel. All these, together with Wych and Newcastle Streets and the many courtyard slummeries in and around the vicinity, were swept away for the mighty Aldwych development which stands today. Designed between 1901 and 1906 (but completed much later) as a tribute to commerce and empire, the buildings of that era are Bush House, India House and Australia House. The names of the latter two indicate their business as offices of Commonwealth High Commissioners. Bush House is a Grade II listed building at the southern end of Kingsway between Aldwych and Strand. It was conceived as a major new trade centre by American industrialist Irving T. Bush, and commissioned, designed, funded, and constructed under his direction. The design was approved in 1919, work began in 1925, and was completed in 1935. Erected in stages, by 1929 Bush House was of its time the most expensive construction of any building in the world. Now part of the Strand Campus of King's College London, Bush House previously served as the headquarters of the BBC World Service, formerly the Empire Service, broadcasting from winter 1941 to summer 2012.

The south-west wing of Bush House was also known to generations of solicitors and their outdoor clerks as HM Revenue and Custom's Stamp Duty office until its closure in March, 2021.

Stamp duty in the United Kingdom is a form of tax charged on legal instruments (written documents), and historically required a physical stamp to be attached to or impressed upon the document in question. The more modern versions of the tax no longer require a physical stamp and payments are now taken digitally.

On a site near to the southern end of Melbourne Place a hostelry stood 'at the sign of the lion' from about 1413. At sometime during the reign of Henry V (1413-22) its little triangular courtyard became an Inn of Chancery, affiliated to the Inner Temple who purchased the freehold in 1583. Although small in its proportions, and without a hall until 1700, Lyon's Inn boasted Sir Edward Coke both as a student and, subsequently, as its Reader in 1578. By 1800 this tiny precinct, merely a triangle between Holywell Street to the south, and Wych and Newcastle Streets to the immediate north-east and west, was severely delapidated. Though immortalised in Dickens's *The Uncommercial Traveller*, and as the resort of Captain Costigan in Thakeray's *The History of Pendennis*, it was sold off by its members in 1863 to the Strand Hotel Company, for a speculative development that never came to fruition. Great things did, however, come from the site: there arose two theatres which, because they were so badly built, were known as 'the rickety twins'. They were the Globe Theatre, which opened with H.J. Byron's *Cyril's Success* in 1868, and its neighbour the Opera Comique, which introduced London society to Gilbert and Sullivan's *The Sorcerer* (1877), *H.M.S. Pinafore* (1878), *The Pirates of Penzance* (1880) and *Patience* (1881). The rickety twins were demolished in 1902. A last relic of the old Inn was a corner post, surmounted by a lion's head and paws, removed and now held in the Museum of London.

Lyon's Inn, 1804

Immediately to the north of Lyon's Inn across Wych Street lay New Inn, affiliated to the Middle Temple as the latter's only satellite Inn of Chancery for over 350 years. By comparison with its southern neighbour this was a bustling and industrious place. More importantly its history is well documented, and as a favourite son it produced Sir Thomas More (1478-1535) before he was admitted as a student of Lincoln's Inn.

At some time prior to 1460 a rooming tavern stood on the north side of Wych Street 'at the sign of the Blessed Virgin'. Over the following 25 years that sign became the symbol of Our Lady Inn, an Inn of Chancery fêted by students who had gradually migrated down from St George's Inn, close by the site of the criminal court in Old Bailey. In 1500 the premises were let to Sir John Fineux, Chief Justice of the King's Bench, and a member of St George's Inn, and over the next century a variety of buildings grew up, placed rather irregularly on three sides of an open square which led to the notorious slum Clare Market in the west and Clement's Inn to the north-east. Indeed by 1608, when Middle Temple purchased the freehold of its 'New' Inn, it was only separated by a courtyard from Clement's, where a wrought-iron gateway was placed in 1723 to be closed each dusk. Some historians have placed at that separating courtyard a small Inn of Chancery called Symond's Inn, 1468-1540, although a more likely location is in Chancery Lane.

New Inn, 1804

The original buildings of New Inn had been replaced by the turn of the 19th century. The Inn retained its independent character until very nearly the 20th century, being presided over by its own treasurer and 12 ancients. These, together with the Attorney-General's Legal Education Fund, and the benchers of Middle Temple, were the recipients of a windfall in 1899 when the London County Council compulsorily purchased New Inn for the Kingsway improvement scheme at a price of £157,500. Thus it came about that this small and tranquil seat of learning lies somewhere beneath Australia House.

4. Cross Aldwych. Turn right into Houghton Street and right again at the London School of Economics into Clement's Inn Passage, passing down the steps and along the western boundary railings of the Royal Courts of Justice complex.

The last of the southern Inns of Chancery to be developed in the 15th century became justly the most important, producing much literary as well as legal fame. Between the bustle of the Strand, the slums of Clare Market and the spacious quiet of Lincoln's Inn Fields stood the three courtyards of Clement's Inn. Its buildings dated from about 1480 and scholars have argued whether it was founded then, or earlier in the reign of Edward II. It was located on part of the Templars' old jousting arena, Fickett's Field, which ran from Old Wych (the precursor of Aldwych) to Holborn. Clement's Inn was a satellite of, and affiliated to, the Inner Temple. By the end of the 16th century it had ceased to function as an Inn of Chancery, and was used to provide overflow accommodation for attorneys and lawyers who could not find chambers in the Temple. Thus it attracted many of its famous residents to whom legal practice took second place to having pleasant rooms in a salubrious quarter. Here Oliver Cromwell took rooms whilst a student of Lincoln's Inn. Here also, in fiction, lived Shakespeare's Justice Shallow, as he mentions in conversation with Sir John Falstaff in *Henry IV Part 2* when they recall hearing the chimes at midnight there. Thackeray identified this place as Shepherd's Inn, and Dickens recorded its quietude in *The Uncommercial Traveller*. The dramatist and critic Clement Scott

(1841-1904) described Garden House in Clement's Inn as 'the most delightful *rus in urbe* in our mighty London'. Close by his fellow dramatist Sir W.S. Gilbert (1836-1911), who sometimes used the pen-name 'Bab', had chambers as his career veered between Bar and literature. Writing in the Saturday Review of May 1904 Sir Max Beerbohm reminisced:

> *A decade ago Clement's Inn was not the huddle of gaudy skyscrapers that it is now; and in the centre of it was a sombre little quadrangle, one of whose windows was pointed out to me as the window of the room in which Gilbert had written those poems, and had cut the woodblocks that immortally illustrate them. And thereafter I never once passed without the desire to make some sort of obeisance, or to erect some sort of tablet. Surely the Muse still hovers sometimes, affectionately, there where 'Bab's' room once was.*

In 1868 part of the Inn was sold off, and the rest in 1884. The substantial sum raised, £65,000, was divided among its ruling ancients and ordinary commoner members. Its famous and curious statue of a Moor supporting a sundial by Jan van Ost c.1720 was moved to Inner Temple gardens where it remained until 2022 at the foot of Paper Buildings when it was removed in response to the debate over contested heritage.

5. Proceed along Clement's Inn Passage towards Strand. In spite of the presence of uniformed security personnel this is a public right of way.

Clement's Inn Passage is all that remains of that Inn, name or buildings. To the south, along this way, stood the almshouses by the burial ground of the church, used as the chapel of Clement's Inn, and containing the grave of Harold I (Harold Harefoot) who was king of England 1037-40. The passage ran down to Dane's Court, then emerged on to Wych Street, which once ran along the northern frontage of St Clement Danes. In the early years of the 20th century Clement's Inn Passage became famous as the address of the headquarters of the Women's Social and Political Union, 'the suffragettes'.

6. Pass over to the island church and around its exterior. Cross to the south side of Strand, on the east corner of Essex Street.

The name of the church of St Clement Danes is thought to be derived from a quarter outside the City boundaries where the Danes were obliged to live after their defeat by King Alfred the Great in 886. Alternatively it may be because the Dane Harold Harefoot was buried here. The present church is the third on or near the site, and was built by Edward Pierce under the direction of Sir Christopher Wren in 1682; a tower by James Gibbs in the English baroque style was added in 1719, containing, as it still does, a carillon of 10 bells that were cast in 1693 and restored after the Blitz in 1953. At 9.00 a.m. and 3.00 p.m. each day the carillon plays its famous nursery tune 'Oranges and Lemons'.

In the church, pews were reserved for the members of Clement's Inn and, by coincidence, at that sad time when the Inn was being sold off, plans were announced for the demolition of the church to provide an open view of the new Royal Courts of Justice. Thankfully, the outcry proved too great. St Clement Danes is now the adoptive place of worship in London for the Royal Air Force who have done much to keep it in good repair. Statues of Air Chief Marshal Lord Dowding, Commander-in-Chief of Fighter Command during the Battle of Britain in the summer of 1940, and Sir Arthur Harris, Commander-in-Chief of Bomber Command, 1942-5, stand before it.

The church will always be associated with the lexicographer, Samuel Johnson (1709-84), and a small plaque at pew No. 18 in the north gallery marks his place of worship. To the east of the exterior there is a statue of him by Percy Fitzgerald.

Interior, church of St Clement Danes

Photo by Simon Goodman

The name of Essex Street derives from Essex House, which belonged to Robert Devereux, Earl of Essex, sometime favourite of Queen Elizabeth I. The site is that of the fabled Outer Temple, on ground once occupied by the palace of Walter Stapleton, who was Bishop of Exeter from 1308 to 1326 and founded Exeter College, Oxford. Thus, hereabouts, at some point during the reign of King Edward II (1307-26) stood Exeter or Stapleton Inn. Its residents were not believed to be lawyers. The ground must once have been known as Outer Temple, since a yearbook for Trinity 1425 mentions a serjeant of the Outer Temple; however, the records show that the land never passed from the Knights Templar via the Crown to the lawyers. Essex Street itself was cut through to the watergate of the old Essex House in 1682.

Passing along Strand the imbiber will find the George tavern, occupying the site of George's coffee house 1751-1842. This house is as much frequented by Bar students as it was when recorded by W.S. Gilbert in his essay St. Paul's to Piccadilly published in Belgravia magazine of March 1867.

The George tavern, opposite the Royal Courts of Justice

Next to the ornately tiled entrance to the former Lloyds bank is an office block at 222/5 Strand, marked Outer Temple. It bears only a slim relation to the site of its namesake. However, it leads by a concealed but charming Victorian arcade into Essex Court, Temple.

Until 2005 the former Wig and Pen Club at 229/30 Strand was contained in a house constructed in 1625. Roman tiles found at the property bear witness to the continuous occupation of this site for over 2,000 years, and there are deeds in existence attaching to the Bishopric of London dating back to the 11th century. In medieval times the building was used to house clerics in grace and favour apartments, but during the reign of King James I (1603-23) the building was reconstructed by the City Corporation as a residence for the gatekeeper of Temple Bar, which marked the boundary of the City of London and it remained in that use until 1672. By 1859 a catering establishment was to be found on the premises and in 1908 a private dining (and drinking) club was founded for lawyers and journalists. The ground-floor bar contained Sir Godfrey Kneller's portrait, 1685, of Judge Jeffreys, who presided over the trials of Titus Oates (see chapter 1) and the Rye House conspirators (see later in this chapter) and also over the 'bloody assizes' which took revenge on the followers of the rebellious Duke of Monmouth. Other Wig and Pen bars and restaurants contained many mementoes of well-known members and American well-wishers including three United States Presidents, Richard Nixon, Gerald Ford and Ronald Reagan.

The former Wig and Pen club

At 1 Fleet Street stands the premises of former Child and Co., the second-oldest banking house in London after Martin's in Lombard Street (c. 1558). Trading as goldsmiths 'at the sign of the Marygold' in 1673, Messrs Francis Child and Blanchard appear in the first-ever London business directory published in 1677. More famous were its clients, though they tended to be secret at the time: King Charles II, his mistress Nell Gwynne, his cousin Prince Rupert and the diarist Samuel Pepys all had accounts here. In 1678 the ledgers record a deposit of £50 by the poet John Dryden, and, as would be imagined, a great number of the bank's clientele were lawyers. Child himself was knighted and became respectively an alderman, sheriff and Lord Mayor of the City of London, a benefactor to and president of Christ's Hospital, and eventually member of Parliament for the City. His descendants remained in banking and became directors of the first East India Company. The family estates were at Osterley Park, Isleworth, which is now owned by the National Trust. The premises of the bank expanded in two interesting ways. An oak-panelled room above and within Temple Bar was obtained for storage of the ledgers. It is by this means that the bank can readily be identified as that called Tellson's by Dickens in *A Tale of Two Cities*. Child's is one of two banks in the vicinity, the other being Hoare's, to display cases of muskets used by banking staff to defend their premises during the 1780 Gordon riots which Dickens describes in *Barnaby Rudge*.

The second expansion of the bank may be noted by a blue plaque placed to the left of its doorway. The frontage of the present building was erected during a major reconstruction in 1879, which effectively doubled its size. Before then a row of houses stood behind the bank, opposite Middle Temple Lane, and could only be reached through a tiny passageway known as Child's Place, the doorway to which still exists. It was these that were absorbed into the bank in 1879, and which stood on the site

The musket case in Child's Bank

of the famous Devil's Tavern, 2 Fleet Street, itself demolished in 1787. At this ancient inn the dramatist Ben Jonson (1572-1637) presided over the Apollo Club with poets such as Robert Herrick (1591-1674) and perhaps fellow dramatists William Shakespeare (1564-1616), Francis Beaumont (1584-1616) and John Fletcher (1579-1625). It is said that the satirist Jonathan Swift (1667-1745) dined here with the politician and writer Joseph Addison (1672-1719) and the

dramatist, and later poet laureate, Colley Cibber (1671-1757). In the 1750s the Royal Society held its annual dinner here.

The history of Temple Bar dates back to an agreement of 1183 by which a boundary dispute between the Abbot of Westminster and the City of London was settled. This spot marked the boundary of the Liberties of the City, an area governed by the Corporation but wholly outside the walls and gates of the City proper. The boundary of the Liberties ran directly south from Holborn Bars (on Gray's Inn Road and Holborn) dropping down to Temple Bar, along to Twinings, the tea merchants, through New Court and Garden Court, Temple, to a point where the River Thames met the head of the Old Wych, or creek. In 1293 a patent roll contains the earliest mention of Temple Bar as the *barra novi templi*, then a chain between two rails. A second mention is made in 1301, and by 1315 a muddy and dangerous track is described running from Westminster through 'Charynge' and 'St Clement's' to Temple Bar which was in need of repair. At some point between then and 1381 a stone gatehouse replaced the chain and posts, which had been destroyed during the Peasant's Revolt of 1381 led by Wat Tyler. Afterwards a timber house was erected and formed a barrier across the entire street. The ground floor contained a gateway, since variously over the centuries the City records show that repairs or decorations were made for the coronations of Anne Boleyn as second queen consort of King Henry VIII

(1533), King Edward VI (1547) and Queen Mary Tudor (1553). New gates were affixed in celebration of the latter queen's marriage to King Philip II of Spain in 1554.

Royal progresses from Westminster into the City marked their passage by halting at Temple Bar where the Sovereign meets the Lord Mayor to receive that officer's formal consent to proceed into that small domain so jealously guarded from tyranny by its citizens. Thus here came to a halt Queen Elizabeth I on her way to St Paul's Cathedral to give thanksgiving for the defeat of the Armada (1588); King Charles II upon his restoration as monarch (1660); Queen Anne in celebration of Marlborough's victory at Blenheim (1704); and every sovereign between 1660 and the present day. Indeed even under the Commonwealth, when Oliver Cromwell dined with Parliament at the Guildhall in June 1649, the Lord Mayor met his guests at Temple Bar with the City sword.

In 1636 Inigo Jones had been asked to redesign the arch and produced plans which were never executed. Some 34 years later Christopher Wren was asked by the City to undertake the work, and between 1670 and 1672 during the mayoralties of Samuel Stirling, Richard Ford and George Waterman, a new gateway dressed in Portland stone was erected, some three buildings off the boundary line. Each side contained four Corinthian pilasters with two niches for statuary. On the west or Strand side stood figures of King Charles I and King Charles II, and to the east, Queen Elizabeth I and King James I. The central arch allowed for the passage of vehicular traffic and horses, with postern gates at each side for pedestrians, though these were closed from dusk to dawn until 1753. Over the keystone of the central arch was placed the royal coat of arms, and within the first storey an apartment panelled in oak which was leased to Child's bank for £50 a year.

A set of iron stakes surmounted the top of the archway, and these came to bear the dismembered segments of traitors and rebels. In 1681 a forequarter of the body of Sir Thomas Armstrong, convicted of the Rye House plot to murder King Charles II and his brother (later King James II), was placed over the archway, his head having been impaled at Westminster and various other parts of his corpse being distributed around his

The restored Temple Bar in Paternoster Square

home town of Stafford. James Boswell, biographer of Samuel Johnson, records that during a walk he took with Dr Johnson in April 1773, they saw that the heads of the Jacobites of 1745 still rested above the gateway. Our lasting but medieval penal system was also represented by a pillory situated close to the gatehouse. It was occupied by Titus Oates in 1679, and in

1703 by the writer Daniel Defoe for his satirical pamphlet 'The Shortest Way with the Dissenters'.

Dickens mentions Temple Bar in no less than five of his novels, *Barnaby Rudge*, *Little Dorrit*, *David Copperfield*, *Martin Chuzzlewit*, and *Bleak House* in which he describes it as 'that leaden-headed old obstruction, appropriate ornament for the threshold of a leaden-headed old corporation.'

The monument to Temple Bar

Certainly the novelist was correct in his assessment of the gateway's effect on the passage of traffic along both Fleet Street and the Strand. Pressure for its complete removal came with the clearance of all buildings to the immediate north of Temple Bar for the construction of the Royal Courts of Justice (RCJ) in the 1870s. The architect of that immense project, George Edmund Street, had wanted Temple Bar demolished and Strand considerably widened, so that his masterpiece could be properly appreciated. His wish was granted, but only indirectly: for work on the foundations of the RCJ so affected the roadway that Temple Bar was becoming slowly undermined, and its demolition inevitable. In July 1874 traffic became prohibited from passing to Fleet Street from Strand when a gap, appearing by the west keystone of the arch, became the subject of a hurried shoring up. Bracing timbers were afterwards inserted in 1877. But by then the City's governing body, the Court of Common Council, had voted for the demolition of Temple Bar. It was taken down on 2 January 1878.

The City of London ensured that each stone was numbered and put into storage until it could be re-erected somewhere else. In 1880 Sir Henry Meux, the brewer, bought the stones and made use of the Temple Bar as a gateway to his park and mansion at Theobalds Park, between Enfield and Cheshunt. It was erected in 1889. The mansion is now used as part of a conference centre and Temple Bar stood there alone and unused, surrounded by woods and grass until permission was granted to the Temple Bar Trust for the removal of the Bar from Theobalds Park to Paternoster Square, adjacent to St Paul's Cathedral. The journey to return it to the City of London started in the summer of 2003 with the removal and renumbering of the stones, their repair and cleaning, and the sculpting of new statuary and arms for the restored monument.

On 10 November 2004 Alderman Robert Finch, the Lord Mayor of the City of London, officially returned Temple Bar to the City of London. Accompanied by the Sheriffs and Members of the Court of Common Council, he unveiled a plaque before officially pushing open the gates of Temple Bar, weighing just over 1.2 tons each, helped by 14 of the stone masons who had worked on the project for 14 months. The Lord Mayor said: "It is fitting that the Bar should be placed here as a symbol of London's history together with its modern role. I hope that Temple Bar will continue to bring pleasure to visitors and to act as a symbol of the City's welcome to the world for the centuries to come."

After its removal from the Strand the authorities determined to mark the site of Temple Bar and in April 1880, Horace Jones, the City architect, designed the present tall monument surmounted by a griffin. In classical style, the faces bear iconographic panels depicting a young Queen Victoria's first entry into the City of London as monarch in 1837 and the Prince of Wales's progress to St Paul's Cathedral in 1872 for a service of thanksgiving after his recovery from typhus. Additionally there are full-length figures of Victoria and Prince Albert. Ironically the design of this monument was universally attacked by the architectural journals of the day, and George Street, who had lobbied for the removal of its predecessor, described the new monument as 'a really useless erection in a most inconvenient position'.

3. The Royal Courts Of Justice

"That they and their successors may be enabled truly to do justice within these walls as long as the British name shall endure, that the blessing of the Almighty may rest upon their labours, that the law which they administer may ever be a terror to evildoers and a strength and support to those who have right on their side is the fervent prayer of all the Judges of your Majesty's Supreme Court of Judicature."

Lord Selborne, L.C., 4 December 1882.

The Royal Courts of Justice

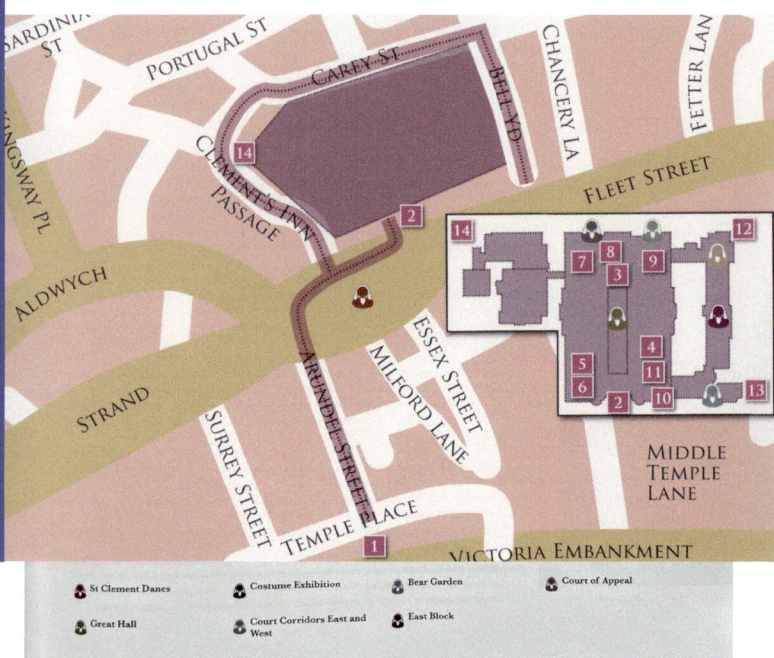

1. From Temple Underground station proceed to the top of Arundel Street, cross Strand in front of St Clement Danes and turn right for the Royal Courts main entrance.
2. Enter the Great Hall through the main entrance on Strand.
3. Proceed under the balcony to the foyer of the Crypt Courts.
4. Return to Great Hall and bear right along wall.
5. Turn right - signpost Citizens Advice Bureau - passing through the Legal Prints Exhibition.
6. Proceed up the circular staircase on the right at the end of the Legal Prints Exhibition.
7. Turn right into Court Corridor North.
8. Turn right at the entrance foyer and proceed inwards to the balcony of the Great Hall.
9. Return to Court Corridor North and turn right, proceeding to Court Corridor East.
10. At the end of Court Corridor East turn left and proceed up the small staircase signposted East Block/Bear Garden. Follow this corridor past the lift shaft and into the Bar Room and Bear Garden.

11. Return down the small staircase to Court Corridor East and turn right to descend the circular staircase by court 9. Pass through the lower corridor exhibition back to the main entrance. Proceed outside and turn left along the southern frontage of the building for a circumperambulation.

12. Turn left into Bell Yard and left again into Carey Street.

13. Turn left down the public footpath around the perimeter of the Courts; this extends from Clement's Inn Passage.

14. Turn left on to Strand by St Clement Danes Church.

1. From Temple Underground station proceed to the top of Arundel Street, cross Strand in front of St Clement Danes and turn right for the Royal Courts main entrance.

Both its variety of function and the pressure of its business had caused the High Court to outgrow its traditional home at Westminster by the last quarter of the 18th century. By the 19th century the rivalry that had existed between the jurisdictions of common law and equity since the middle ages was creating costly and time-consuming delays for litigants; it threw up unfair and unjust anomalies such as those attacked by Dickens in *Bleak House.*

The great reforming ministry of W.E. Gladstone 1868-74 produced sweeping changes which used the need to concentrate the location of all the higher courts in order to rationalise their jurisdiction and procedure. This was a reform that both captured public imagination and was non-contentious, in the sense that when Gladstone left office his otherwise adversary, Benjamin Disraeli, continued the process by completing the Judicature Acts of 1873 and 1876 which established four new Divisions of the High Court of Justice, those being Chancery, Exchequer, Queen's Bench, and Probate, Divorce and Admiralty (the latter quickly attracting the nickname of 'wills, wives and wrecks').

As early as 1845 firm plans for a new concentration of the higher courts of justice led planners to consider building upon Lincoln's Inn Fields. This site, the largest public square in London, was free of buildings and lay close to the Temple. Though the members of the second Commons select committee of inquiry established to find a site were keen to preserve this oasis of greenery on the edge of the City, they accepted that it was necessary to locate the courts near to the rest of 'legal London' (Gray's Inn already being considered too far to the north) with fairly easy access to the River Thames. It came about that the land immediately south of Carey Street and north of Strand came under scrutiny. It then contained a slum extending over approximately 7.5 acres (3 ha.) and the committee, chaired by Charles Buller, Whig MP for Liskeard, felt no compunction about clearing away 400-odd dwellings. The area was steeped in squalor and had neither mains drainage nor sewerage. However, although a recommendation was made, it was slept upon for nearly another 20 years while the debates concerning legal reform left behind the question of accommodation.

Between 1861 and 1865 five attempts were made at passing legislation in Parliament to secure the funds necessary to begin the concentration of accommodation project. The initiative came from Richard Bethell, the Attorney-General, since Lord Chancellor Campbell was not supportive of the idea. Bethell secured for his brother-in-law Henry Abraham, the architect of Middle Temple Library, the position of surveyor and architect to the project. Although his plans for the new courts were not taken up, Abraham's testimony before the select committee of 1861 was most effective in urging the use of the Carey Street site:

> "It is almost impossible to remain for any length of time on some parts, the stench is so dreadful. The condition of the people is, I can use no other word than, terrible; the vice and wretchedness in the young, the decrepitude in those of middle age, and the dreadful condition of those in premature old age is appalling... There are very few work-people in the common acceptance of that term; they are people who gain a livelihood by hawking and letting lodging, and writing occasionally for law stationers; women who wash, and sweeps; in fact a most

Detail of the neo-Gothic façade

extraordinary combination of the most unfortunate characters in the metropolis... I was attacked during my survey, and had a very narrow escape of being robbed near Plough Court. In Shire Lane there are some of the worst houses in the metropolis...of the worst possible description, where the youngest girls are taken in numbers... it is a place of ill-fame altogether...I believe there is no system of drainage at all; I cannot detect any system."

Abraham reported that so far as he could detect there were then approximately 4,175 people living in 343 houses on 7.5 acres (3 ha.). Such was the squalor that an average of 18 persons per house was relatively comfortable. In Robin Hood Court some 52 people shared two houses, and in Lower Serle's Place 189 slept in nine. Three lodging houses accommodated 140 people who found board at 4d per night.

The site took in Shire (earlier Sheer) Lane, a turning opposite Child's Bank, which led away northwards from Fleet Street. Sir Christopher Hatton, who was appointed Lord Chancellor in 1587, recorded that upon Sir Francis Drake's return from his circumnavigation of the globe in 1580 a tavern called the Ship was opened in Shire Lane. Although dingy with squalor, that passageway once housed the Kit-Kat Club (named after Christopher Kat, a pastry cook of Westminster in whose house the club first met), the greatest of social meeting places during the reign of Queen Anne (1702-13). Here came in their time leading polemicists of the day including Queen Anne's physician Dr John Arbuthnot (who invented the character of John Bull as the archetypal Englishman), Joseph Addison, Sir Richard Steele and Jonathan Swift. Thirty-nine poets, wits, nobles and gentlemen formed its active membership including the Whig politician Sir Robert Walpole, the Duke of Marlborough who was commander-in-chief of the nation's armed forces, the dramatist William Congreve, and the dramatist and architect Sir John Vanbrugh. Perhaps only two luminaries of the day were excluded: the poets Alexander Pope, as a catholic, and John Dryden, as a Tory. The club moved in about 1710 to the country house of its secretary, Jacob Tonson the bookseller, at Barn Elms, the now demolished manor house of Barnes, and eventually it was disbanded in 1727, having last met at the Upper Flask on Hampstead Heath.

Shire Lane was reputedly the home of Elias Ashmole (1617-92), the celebrated antiquary, whose collection (which subsequently formed the basis of the Ashmolean Museum, Oxford) nonetheless was kept at his chambers in the Temple, away from his neighbours in 'rogues lane' as Shire Lane had been christened as early as the reign of King James I (1603-25).

This, then, was the neighbourhood to be swept away by the great project. Other casualties were the famed Trumpet tavern and Crockford's eating house; but most serious of all was the removal of Temple Bar, gateway to the City since 1670, as the eventual plans called for the widening of Strand. Additionally, in clearing the site for the great building's foundations, the holy well of St Clement, which had attracted penitents and pilgrims since the reign of King Ethelred (978-1016), was filled in.

In the meantime Parliament directed its attention to ending the anomalies highlighted by Dickens. Gladstone's Whig government set out to remodel the higher judicial system, creating a unified Supreme Court of Judicature and fusing equity and the common law. Since these radical changes were carried on by the Tory Disraeli, both parties saw the need to start on the projected new accommodation. Eventually proposals were adopted into the legislative programme. The Courts of Justice Building Act 1865 provided for three sources of funds with which to purchase and clear the site, and construct, furnish and equip the new building.

Section 3 recited the purpose of the Act 'for...the erecting upon the Site to be acquired under the same Act all such suitable Buildings for the Accommodation of the Superior Courts of Law and Equity, the Probate and Divorce Courts, and the Court of Admiralty, and the various Offices connected therewith, or Offices used for any other purpose of Legal Administration, ...with all proper Furniture and Conveniences, and Accesses thereto'. The funds were subject to an upper limit of £1.5 million and were to be obtained from the sale of all property used for the existing administration of the Courts at Westminster, together with £1 million interest earned on intestate estates held in Chancery and a special tax to be imposed upon the issue of all new proceedings except in the Court of Chancery.

The design for the building was thrown open to architectural competition, to which initially, six leading architects and two reserves were invited to make submissions. These were E.M. Barry (known for the huge Cannon Street and Charing Cross Railway Station Hotels, 1861 and 1864 respectively, and the reconstruction of the Royal Opera House, Covent Garden 1858); Philip Hardwick (new Hall and Library, Lincoln's Inn 1839-45, Great Western

Hotel 1851-3, Charterhouse School 1865); Sir George Gilbert Scott, the most prominent architect of the day (Foreign Office 1868-73, Albert Memorial 1862-3, St Pancras Station 1865); George Edmund Street, the most prolific ecclesiastical architect of Victorian England and, perhaps more importantly, a personal friend of Gladstone; Alfred Waterhouse, winner of the competition for the Manchester Assize Courts in 1859 (Natural History Museum 1873-80, National Liberal Club 1887); and Thomas Wyatt (Devizes Assize Court 1835, Cambridge Assize Court 1840-3, Liverpool Exchange 1863-7). The two reserves were initially Raphael Brandon (Catholic Apostolic Church, Gordon Square, London 1851-5), and Thomas Deane, the architect and surveyor of Clement's Inn, whose buildings were under threat by the entire scheme.

There was considerable political lobbying by the competitors but two things occurred which changed their number. First the competition for the rebuilding of the National Gallery in Trafalgar Square put Street, Barry and Scott in the position of having to consider two of Britain's most important public works at the same time. Secondly, the draft instructions for the competitors contained three clauses that caused dissension: that the designs had to be completed within eight months; that the government had the right to reject the use of all of the submitted designs; and that the winning architect could undertake no other commission for a period of three years after the acceptance of his designs. In view of this, during March 1866, Hardwick and Wyatt declined their invitations to participate and some three weeks later Scott and Barry also withdrew.

The two reserves having been 'promoted', they were joined in the front rank by Henry Garling, winner of the War Office competition, and George Somers Clarke a commercial architect who immediately withdrew in favour of the National Gallery competition. The reserve new faces were John Gibson and John Seddon. This rather farcical situation had caused a storm of debate in the Commons, and by 30 April 1866 Scott and Barry had been persuaded to reinstate their entries after the offending clauses in the instructions were removed. Three further men were now included: Henry Abraham, who originally surveyed the site (Middle Temple Library 1858-61); Henry Lockwood (St. George's Hall, Bradford 1851-2, Bradford Exchange 1864); and William Burges (Lille Cathedral 1855-6, Cork Anglican Cathedral 1862).

John Gibson retired due to overwork in July 1866, and the competitors finally numbered 11. Also in July the government changed from Whig to Tory.

In the autumn of 1866 an extension of the deadline for submitting the designs to 15 January 1867 was granted by the Treasury. During that period a temporary building was erected in New Square, Lincoln's Inn, to house the 250-odd drawings which comprised the competition entries, and to open it to the public. Hangings of such entries had become common since the competition for the Palace of Westminster in the 1840s. Enormous public interest and political controversy had been aroused by this competition, and large crowds came to this exhibition when it opened on 8 February 1867 until its closure in that summer. Here the architects were allowed to supervise the hanging of their drawings each in a 12 feet by 30 feet (3.7 m. by 9.1 m.) skylit alcove. Scott entered 40 drawings, the largest number, followed by Street, Waterhouse and Lockwood; Seddon was the only entrant to put in models of his design.

Extensive coverage of the competition in both the trade and wider press included overt attacks on particular designs, and in March, attacks on both the composition and qualification of the panel of judges. Rumours of political and other bias abounded. Waterhouse and Street were considered the favourites almost from the start. Certainly the committee reports of both the Bar and solicitors favoured the plans of Waterhouse. In any event they recommended the use of a central hall one level lower than the courts. The jury also received reports from independent architectural assessors, George Pownall and John Shaw, which endorsed Barry as first and Scott as second; from the chief officer of the Metropolitan Fire Brigade, Captain Eyre Massey Shaw, which made no positive recommendation except for Deane but severely attacked Scott; and from a Dr John Percy, the government expert on heating and ventilation.

The judges met in five sessions between 29 May and 29 July 1867 and eventually announced a split decision: that no single design was best in all respects, but that Barry succeeded with regard to the plan and distribution of the interior, and Street's design having regard to 'merit as an architectural composition'. William Cowper-Temple (1811-88), the member of Parliament who sponsored and carried the Courts of Justice Building Act 1865, wrote to the Treasury suggesting that the two men be commissioned to act jointly on the project.

Public reaction to the judges' decision was enormously hostile, so much so that the Treasury wrote to the judges asking them to reconsider. It was argued that the instructions required the appointment of a single architect. In any event it was unlikely that Barry and Street would agree with the proposal, and the design costs of both exceeded by far the money available. The judges met again in November and refused to revise their award. Public and Parliamentary discontent continued unabated through to the Spring of 1868. By then Disraeli had succeeded Lord Derby as prime minister and made it clear that none of the entered designs was acceptable. Even were an architect to be appointed from the entrants, the focus of their attention was again directed to consideration of the site, for under review was the idea of a site bordering the Thames, south of Howard Street. In what was very much a surprise move, Disraeli's Chancellor of the Exchequer, George Hunt, suddenly announced on 30 May 1868 that after consultation with the First Commissioner of Works, Lord John Manners, Street was being appointed sole architect to the project. By 10 June Street had received his instructions from the Treasury and within a fortnight he was established in a suite of rooms at the old Insolvent Debtor's Court at 33 Lincoln's Inn Fields. He set about producing three completely new designs and obtained permission for the enlargement of the Carey Street site to 13.25 acres (5.4 ha.). In the meanwhile he produced drawings for the riverside site running down from Howard Street to the Embankment. The decision eventually rested on cost and the fact that the river site, being wide but shallow, would allow insufficient room for future expansion or any necessary office space.

The plans for the Royal Courts of Justice as they are today were executed on 27 July 1870. The basic design called for 18 courts to curtain the central hall. Two were to be substantially larger than the rest, these then being numbered 4 and 18. Each had its own individual design and layout, and was to receive natural light from a variety of skylight sources. The slope of the land running down from Carey Street towards the River Thames was used to enable entrances at ground level from the Strand into the Great Hall and at first, or court floor level, from Carey Street. All of the administrative offices were provided for by housing them in a separate block, containing four floors, to the east of the main building, separated by an open quadrangle.

Initially the flow of visitors to the building was carefully controlled. The current main court corridors were originally intended for the exclusive use of barristers, who entered from the north at Carey Street, and whose suite, comprising robing, smoking and luncheon rooms was immediately by and to the left of their entrance. Judges had, and still have, their exclusive corridor circling the courts to the rear, and one half again the height of the bar corridor. This enabled them to have access on one side directly to the raised judicial dais in each court, and on the other to their private offices. This corridor had its own entrance in Carey Street, and separate entrances on lower floors in the corner of the main block. Unlike today the public were kept entirely away from the personnel of the law. A system of corridors ran along the top of the building, giving access to the public galleries of the courts but not to their wells. Access to these was directly from the street by staircases north of the Great Hall and in the two towers flanking the Strand entrance. Thus the Hall itself was reserved for only those inside the building on official business. It featured as something of use only on ceremonial occasions, and it was never intended by Street that there be any direct access between the south and north entrances of the building.

Ingeniously included in a very complex design were conference rooms, arbitration rooms, jury rooms and witnesses' waiting rooms. Separate stairs had to be provided for jurors and witnesses to enter the courts. Additionally the heating, cooling and ventilation, supply of gas, light and water all had to be considered. A boiler-fed heating system was introduced into the east-block basement in 1877 and afterwards extended to the main courts. This drew in and warmed clean air and, by a series of vents and ducts, passed it around the building at court level. Most ordinary offices, including the judges' chambers, had coal-burning fireplaces until after the Second World War. The lighting for the building was considered only at a very late stage during construction. Gas had been used in principle during the course of building but after a demonstration in April 1881, the Treasury conceded the use in certain parts of electric lighting. It was not until the October, when an exhibition of electric lighting equipment opened at the Crystal Palace, and when the new Savoy Theatre had been successfully lit by them, that 1,500 Swan incandescent lights were installed. Running water was had been successfully lit by them, that 1,500 Swan incandescent lights were installed. Running water was not available in the building until very late. Certainly in 1946 most of the judges' chambers still had chamber pots. A huge underground water tank, placed beneath the great quadrangle and still there, captured water from long lost tributaries of the Fleet river.

The foundation stone having been laid on 7 February 1874, substantial changes in the design were to be a feature of the eight years taken to complete the building. By 1881 it was discovered that the growth of judicial business meant that the number of courts required had to be increased, and the northern Bar rooms were sacrificed to create what is now courts 1 and 2, the first to be the new Court of Appeal. Other delays included the violent strike by the 1,700 members of the London chapter of the Society of Operative Stonemasons, then one of the most radical and militant of trade unions. This lasted through the summer of 1877 and was only resolved by the importation of 529 foreign masons to break the strike. These German workers continued on the building works until 1879, and had to be housed and fed on the site for their own protection.

The masonry for the main building is composed of Portland stone, with fittings and furnishings in hand-carved oak. The decorative carving was undertaken by Thomas Earp, a sculptor who specialised in the carving of pulpits and ecclesiastical devices, and a man who had worked on over a dozen of Street's churches. Earp engaged 20 carvers to work under him, and a boy was employed full-time to sharpen the tools.

Since its opening the pressure of business on the courts has caused substantial redevelopment across the entire site. A building designed to house 19 courts now contains nearly 100, together with more than 700 administrative rooms and 3.5 miles (5.6 km.) of corridor. The RCJ Building passed two world wars relatively unscathed, with the neighbouring Temple taking the brunt of the Blitz. Various court annexes have opened and there are usually temporary courts to be found in the building. The first major extension was the construction of the West Green Building, 1908-12, which attempted to complement the architecture of the main blocks. On 1 October 1968 Her Majesty opened the new Queen's Building. At that rear part of the site more land for building became available and the tower block known as the Thomas More Building, containing companies and bankruptcy registries, opened in the 1970s. In 1990 two more blocks of courts and offices designed to house the Chancery Division were constructed as an extension. However, the principal registries of the Family Division and for probate are still housed outside the immediate concentration of the courts in High Holborn, and another large annexe at the Rolls Building, 7 Fetter Lane, is fully occupied and given over in its entirety to the Admiralty and Commercial, Business and Property Courts and the Technology and Construction Court. It is the largest specialist centre for the resolution of financial, business and property litigation anywhere in the world and a centre of excellence for high value dispute resolution.

2. Enter the Great Hall through the main entrance on Strand.

The Great Hall is some 240 feet (73 m.) long by 80 feet (24m.) high. Floored in a tessellated pavement of marble, it provides access upwards to the main court floor and down to secondary courts in the basement. It also leads to the Crypt Courts and corridors from it give access to the east or administrative block, to the custody area, the advocates robing rooms and public dining and other facilities.

On the immediate right-hand side is the memorial statue of George Edmund Street (1824-81) designed by Arthur Blomfield and sculpted by Henry Armstead. Street's death in 1881 deprived the project of his ever-present supervision and the minutiae of detail that he personally undertook. From his own hand flowed no less than 400 drawings during the period of construction. Of far greater importance was the fact that there was no longer the force of his personality as a bulwark against the official parsimony which he had fought against for so long in order to secure adequate funds for the completion, decoration and furnishing of his masterpiece. It was such a paucity of funds that prohibited the erection of a full-length statue of the architect. Subscriptions to the memorial fund were so slow that work on the monument was not started until December, 1884. It was unveiled by Lord Chancellor Herschell on 24 March 1886, and shows the architect seated with dividers in hand, considering a plan spread over his lap. On three sides of the pedestal are a frieze in marble demonstrating the construction of the building.

It is particularly fitting that the memorial to Street should have been placed here. Between April 1870 and May 1871 he had a long struggle with the Office of Works to keep this hall in the design. The department concerned argued that the hall was an unnecessary expense, and that an open courtyard, canopied or cloistered against inclement weather, would be equally useful.

Beyond the memorial to Street is the large canvas commemorating the opening of the Royal Courts of Justice on Monday, 4 December 1882 by Queen Victoria, although it was on 11 January 1883 that the Courts, or as many as were ready, were opened for business. The Queen inaugurated the building accompanied by the Prince and Princess of Wales, Princess Beatrice and Prince Christian of Schleswig-Holstein, and the Royal Dukes of Connaught, Albany and Cambridge, among whom each of the four Inns of Court was represented by a royal bencher. A throne was placed beneath the gallery at the northern end of the Great Hall, which was otherwise filled with the aristocracy, ambassadors, statesmen, clerics and the senior military. The Lord Mayor and aldermen of the City of London had travelled in state from Mansion House, together with the Lord Chancellor, Lord Chief Justice and the entire bench of judges from Westminster Hall, who processed to a dais set below the throne.

The Queen had been presented with a silver key to the door of the main entrance by the First Commissioner of Works upon her arrival. She handed it to Lord Chancellor Selborne and said:

> My Lord Chancellor – I deliver into your charge, with this key, the care of these courts of law. I trust that the uniting together in one place of the various branches of judicature in this, my Supreme Court, will conduce to the more efficient and speedy administration of justice to my subjects; and I have all confidence that the independence and learning of the judges, supported by the integrity and ability of the other members of the profession of the law, will prove in the future, as they have in times past, a chief security for the rights of my Crown and the liberties of my people.

In proposing the loyal address Lord Selborne replied:

The Royal Courts of Justice

The Great Hall from the main entrance

The Royal Courts of Justice

In the name and on behalf of the assembled judges of your Majesty's Supreme Court of Judicature, I accept the charge which your Majesty has been pleased to lay upon me; and I ask permission to offer to your Majesty the humble expression of our loyal devotion to your Majesty's person and throne, and of our gratitude for the part which your Majesty has been graciously pleased to take in the solemnity of this day. This building, now complete, was authorised by your Majesty with the concurrence of Parliament, in the year 1865, and it has been in progress for more than eight years under the hands of a great architect, to whom it has not been permitted to see this day . . . Man passes away, but his works remain . . .

This building will remain, as we trust, to a remote posterity, one of the most magnificent public works of the time in which we live. These Royal Courts of Justice, stately enough to satisfy even those who are most accustomed to Westminster Hall, will not, like Westminster Hall, recall the memories of Norman or Plantagenet, of Tudor or Stuart

Memorial to George Edmund Street

kings; but they will be for ever associated with the name of your Majesty, and with the glories of a reign happy beyond all which have preceded it in those qualities of the Sovereign which have caused your Majesty to be so universally beloved and revered, in the advancement of all the arts of civilisation, and in the general peace and prosperity of the British people.

Among the legislative improvements which have distinguished your Majesty's reign, not the least has been the consolidation and union of the several branches of the supreme judicature which formerly exercised divided jurisdiction. To give full effect to that great change it was necessary that the different courts and offices should be brought together in one edifice fit for the duties which they have to perform. This has at last been done; and your Majesty, by your gracious presence here today has given a signal proof of your care for that justice which will here be administered in your name. It was, indeed, fitting and worthy of your Majesty that these Royal Courts should be dedicated to their future use by the Sovereign of these realms, whose noblest prerogatives are justice and mercy, and from whom all jurisdiction within the British dominions is derived.

Your Majesty's judges are deeply sensible of their own shortcomings and of their need of that assistance which they have constantly received from the Bar of England and from other members of the legal profession. But, encouraged by your Majesty's gracious approval, and having before them the examples of a long line of illustrious predecessors, they have endeavoured, and will always endeavour, to fulfil the great duties entrusted to them with fidelity to your Majesty, with zeal for the public service, with firmness, impartiality, and integrity, in the fear of God and without fear of man.

That they and their successors may be enabled truly to do justice within these walls as long as the British name shall endure, that the blessing of the Almighty may rest upon their labours, that the law which they administer may ever be a terror to evildoers and a strength and support to those who have right on their side is the fervent prayer of all the judges of your Majesty's Supreme Court of Judicature, for whom, on this august occasion, it has been my privilege to address your Majesty.

There followed the offering up of prayer by the Archbishop of York, after which Sir William Harcourt, the Home Secretary announced, 'I have Her Majesty's command to declare these Royal Courts of Justice now opened.'

The oaken cases in the centre of the Hall contain the daily cause lists which set out the court business for the day. For over 100 years these were printed on an ancient press in the bowels of the east block, each afternoon for the following day. Today the cause lists are published digitally and made available online.

At the rear of the Great Hall is a display case containing artefacts from many jurisdictions around the world donated to and by visiting senior judges and justice ministers as part of the ongoing fraternity of the law, and the fellowship of the judiciary world-wide.

The Royal Courts of Justice: Illustrated London News, 1882

3. Proceed under the balcony to the foyer of the Crypt Courts.

Although for many years the site of both Bar and public dining rooms, this area was converted in November 1983 to three court rooms. The new vaulted brickwork in the immediate foyer is of particular interest and is a rare display of modern craftsmanship.

4. Return to Great Hall and bear right along wall.

Here is the seated statue of Lord Russell of Killowen (1832-1900), the first Roman Catholic since the Reformation to be appointed Lord Chief Justice of England.

The statue of Lord Russell of Killowen by the corridor leading to the basement courts 20-25

Further along the wall hang some fine judicial portraits: Chief Baron Sir Matthew Hale who was one of the 'fire judges' who were appointed to a special tribunal to settle land disputes after the Great Fire of London; Lord Denman who, when Attorney-General, drafted the Great Reform Bill of 1832 and was later Chief Justice of the King's Bench; Lord Hatherley, who was Lord Chancellor in 1868-74 in procession in the House of Lords; and the judges of the Court for Crown Cases Reserved, predecessor to the Court of Criminal Appeal after 1908. This last picture has been placed above the RCJ war memorial.

The windows of the Great Hall are inset with the heraldic devices of Lords Keepers of the Great Seal and Lord Chancellors. At the Strand end of the Hall on the right, stairs lead down to basement courts. These were originally jury rooms which became disused in the 1920s and 1930s as fewer and fewer civil trials required juries for their determination. In the early 1960s the redundant rooms were torn out and replaced by courts currently numbered 20 to 25.

5. Turn right - signpost Citizens Advice Bureau - passing through the Legal Prints Exhibition.

The permanent exhibition of legal prints and manuscripts is a range of materials devoted to illustrating the court system and legal quarter of London from medieval times.

6. Proceed up the circular staircase on the right at the end of the Legal Prints Exhibition.

The main courts floor has changed little since it was opened over 140 years ago. The rectangular circuit is known as Court Corridors North, South, East and West. When the building was first designed it was expected that there would still be a distinction between common law and equity courts. One still has the sense of it in having two rows of courtrooms across the divide of the hall. Differences in the stonework and carving also reinforce this distinction.

Court Corridor West formerly housed the courts of the Chancery Division. No two courts are alike. All have different architectural devices for securing adequate natural light to compensate for the shadow of the Great Hall and surrounding buildings. Thus each has a different ceiling design, for example, court 16 is covered by a flat ceiling with a semi-cylindrical skylight between webs of wooden vaulting. This was one of only two courtrooms to survive changes to the original design.

This corridor contains courts 12 to 18, including court 15, the Lord Chancellor's, and court 16, the Chancellor's, these being intended originally as the permanent benches of the officiants. Outside each courtroom a legal portrait hangs, depicting the great judges and jurists of the past; most are on permanent loan from the National Gallery or National Portrait Gallery. Outside court 12 is a portrait of Lord Chief Justice Sir Alexander Cockburn, who presided over the great Tichborne claimant trial. Outside court 13 is Cromwell's Lord Chancellor Thurlow. Outside court 14 is Lord Brougham who was Lord Chancellor 1830-40. Outside court 15 is a further portrait of Chief Baron Sir Matthew Hale.

*Court 4: The Lady Chief Justice of England's Court
Reproduced by kind permission of the Royal Courts of Justice*

7. Turn right into Court Corridor North.

Court Corridor North contains courts 1, 2 and 19 and the foyer of the Carey Street entrance to the building, originally intended for the exclusive use of the Bar. There is a fine portrait of Mr Baron Huddlestone and busts of Earl Cairns, who was Lord Chancellor 1868 and 1874-80, and of Sir George Jessel who was Master of the Rolls 1873-83. There is also a statue of Sir Edward Clarke QC who represented Oscar Wilde. A fine bronze by Michael Rizzello (1926-2004), winner of the Prix de Rome for Sculpture and noted for a series of heroic bronzes, his work being cast by The Morris Singer Foundry, of Lord Taylor of Gosforth, Lord Chief Justice 1992-1996 stands by the entrance to the antechamber of court 2.

8. Turn right at the entrance foyer and proceed inwards to the balcony of the Great Hall.

A permanent display of legal costume was opened by Lord Chancellor Hailsham in January 1974 and removed to this corridor in 1998. It contains both judicial and advocates' robes, hoods and wigs, together with letters patent and other devices from a variety of jurisdictions, including Scotland, Germany and Italy.

The Royal Courts of Justice

The exhibition represents a virtually complete catalogue of judicial and legal robes, both formal and day dress worn in United Kingdom courts since the 17th century.

A particularly fine example is the black-flowered damask gown, decorated with gold lace worn by Lord Manners, Lord Chancellor of Ireland 1807-27. Such gowns are still worn on ceremonial occasions by the Lord Chancellor of Great Britain, the Master of the Rolls, Lords Justices of Appeal and the President of the Family Division of the Supreme Court. Its design has changed little since 1650.

The gown used by junior barristers is the black stuff woollen mourning gown (with a diminutive vestigial mourning hood hanging over the left shoulder) which was introduced in 1685 for official court mourning on the death of King Charles II. It is worn together with stiff collar, bands and the horsehair forensic tie-wig invented by Humphrey Ravenscroft in 1822 to evade a tax on hair pomade. King's Counsel, who are senior barristers appointed by the Lord Chancellor, are commonly called 'silks' because their proper court dress for over two centuries has been the plain black silk gown worn over court morning suits, and, on formal occasions, over full court dress including breeches and buckled shoes. On such ceremonial occasions they wear the full-bottomed judicial wig. In practice, for day-to-day appearances most 'silks' wear a stuff gown of the same design as a silk robe.

Reproduced by kind permission of the Royal Courts of Justice

The solicitors' black stuff gown was introduced when solicitors, then called attorneys, were granted rights of audience in the county courts upon their creation in 1846. Just after the First World War new violet judicial robes were brought into the county courts, for use by all circuit judges whether sitting in the county court or the crown court.

In October, 2008 a new civil robe was introduced as part of a package of measures to simplify judicial court working dress. The new gown incorporates coloured bands to identify seniority with heads of division and appeal court judges wearing gold bands and High Court judges wearing red. Not received without both criticism and humour (*Star Trek* aficionados would be very at home with the design), the robe was part of a raft of changes announced in 2007 to court working dress in England and Wales, such as ending the wearing of wigs, wing collars and bands by judges when sitting in civil and family proceedings. Circuit judges when they sit as deputy High Court judges and district judges also wear the gown when working in civil and family proceedings.

Other artefacts of interest in the exhibition include a judicial square cap, popularly known as the 'black cap' and much exercised by Hollywood in portrayal of the passing of the British death sentence. Formally this is the proper judicial headdress, since the wig is taken merely to be a substitute for hair. Certainly in pre-Victorian times it was always worn above the wig, or the scarf and coif of the serjeants and certain judges, and used in court whenever judgment was passed. Latterly it became solely associated with the passing of sentence, and afterwards only the death sentence.

Until 1971 the silver oar of the Admiralty was ceremonially laid before the President of the Probate, Divorce and Admiralty Division when trying Admiralty cases. This twelve-inch (30 cm.) paddle-shaped object was the badge of office of the Marshal of the High Court of Admiralty, and a symbol of the authority of Admiralty judges to determine cases which otherwise might have seemed beyond the territorial jurisdiction of the British High Court. The oar bears both the Tudor arms and those of King James II, who held the title of Lord High Admiral from 1660 when he was Duke of York. The central device on both blade and silver loom (handle) is a foul anchor, that is, an anchor which is decoratively but impractically entwined in its own rope. The same symbol is carved in oak on the President's chair in court 33, West Green Building.

An important part of the collection is the Whaddon Hall manuscript which is a set of 15th-century illuminations featuring the only known pictorial representation of superior English courts prior to the Tudor period. They show the courts of Chancery, with the Chancellor presiding over argument by three serjeants; of King's Bench, in which a trial on arraignment before a jury is proceeding before a King's justice; of Common Pleas, featuring the Chief Justice of the Common Bench sitting with six puisne judges hearing a party upon his pleas; and of Exchequer showing a coin being brought into court.

The northern balcony overlooking the Great Hall gives the finest vantage point from which to admire the cathedral like proportions of the building and the marble flooring. An interesting touch can be seen in the witness staircases leading up from the Hall at the southern end: the equity side to the right are semicircular, and the common law side to the left are polygonal.

Admiralty (maritime) law was formally adjudicated in England as early as 1360. A mace in the shape of an oar, made of silver, was used to symbolize the power of the British admiralty courts. It was commonly carried by the court's marshal, and placed before the judge during trials. Vice-admiralty courts were established in several colonial American cities. Some of these courts also used silver oars to symbolize their authority under the British crown. After the American colonies won independence from Great Britain and established their own judicial system, admiralty jurisdiction was placed with the federal district courts and such similar symbolic references were used.

The Silver Paddle.
Reproduced by kind permission of the Royal Courts of Justice

9. Return to Court Corridor North and turn right, proceeding to Court Corridor East.

The eastern court corridor contains the courtrooms of the Court of Appeal, criminal division, including that of the Lady

The Royal Courts of Justice

Court 4 - detail: Reproduced by kind permission of the Royal Courts of Justice

Chief Justice of England and Wales, court 4. It is the largest courtroom in the building and has a flat ceiling supported on knees, with a tall and narrow central monitor that has windows on all four sides. Court 5 is that of the President of the King's Bench Division and court 6 that of the Vice-President of the Court of Appeal (Criminal Division).

The civil division of the Court of Appeal has now been banished to purpose-built courts at the northern end of the East Block. But for over 80 years, court 3 was the bench of the Master of the Rolls. This courtroom is small and cosy, as it always seemed when Lord Denning presided here. It is lit by a skylight set into a raised ceiling borne by coved cornices at both ends of the room.

It will be noticed that each court has a similar layout, with inclined seating facing towards the clerk's tables and bench. The now disused public galleries are stretched across the back of each court, mounted on a masonry balcony. Thus each court is high, with good visibility and little diminution in light and air. However, those who frequent the courts will know that the acoustics leave much to be desired. Electronic amplification was added after the Second World War.

Amongst judicial portraits on this corridor are those of Lord Cowper, who was Lord Chancellor 1707-8 and 1714-18 outside court 8, and Serjeant Maynard at 9.

Courts 10 and 11, which span the main entrance at the southern end of the hall, are smaller than the other original courts, and are covered by wooden vaulting.

10. At the end of Court Corridor East turn left and proceed up the small staircase signposted 'East Block/Bear Garden. Follow this corridor past the lift shaft and into the Bar Room and Bear Garden.

The original Bar Room is the only chamber in the building that was decorated, and sumptuously so. Street himself designed the scheme of painted and carved decoration, and this was completed before his death. The design was restored in 1983, and uses a floral pattern incorporating the royal monogram and fleur-de-lis. An elegant fireplace and much gilding complemented the oriental rugs originally used as a floor covering. The arms of the four Inns of Court, together with the Royal Arms and Queen Victoria's personal cipher are displayed on the upper walls. The windows on the north side overlook the Great Quadrangle, and the orange-red brick of the administrative office block contrasts with the white Portland stone of the main building.

*The Bar Room, antechamber to the Bear Garden
Reproduced by kind permission of the Royal Courts of Justice*

The meeting area where the King's Bench Masters' Corridor runs into the King's Bench Chambers' Appointments is known as the Bear Garden, though the reason for the name is lost in the mists of antiquity. Supposedly it is attributed to a comment made by Queen Victoria about the hubbub she encountered on a visit. On the walls hang drawings of entries for the original architectural competition for the building, not the building as it is or ever was. The writing tables both here and in the anteroom are original to the opening of the Royal Courts having been provided by Collinson and Locke, a then fashionable firm specialising in furniture to complement the revival in Queen Anne style architecture.

11. Return down the small staircase to Court Corridor East and turn right to descend the circular staircase by court 9. Pass through the lower corridor exhibition back to the main entrance. Proceed outside and turn left along the southern frontage of the building for a circumperambulation

The exterior of the building is dominated by a feeling both of ecclesiastical architecture and over-large proportions. The frontage is virtually impossible to photograph complete in one frame. A major cleaning of the exterior, which was undertaken between 1973 and 1976, restored the Royal Courts to their former splendour. The Strand frontage is 470 feet (143 m.) wide, and the finial on the central flèche is 245 feet (75 m.) above the roadway. Street originally asked the Commissioner of Works to widen Strand and demolish St Clement Danes, in order to allow a clear view of his building. Some degree of widening was incorporated within the scheme but fortunately the famous church remained.

Street himself designed the iconographic embellishments to the building, and placed the statuary. The figure of Christ stands on the southern gable of the Great Hall. On two smaller flanking gables stand Alfred the Great to the east, and Solomon to the west. There is no representation of Justice either inside or outside the building. Between the windows of the upper storey the arms of then living jurists were carved, some 40 in number.

An inner frieze over the main portico of the Strand entrance depicts the heads of 24 bishops and scholars of law from the Middle Ages up to the Victorian era. The remainder of the carving is mainly floral, taking medieval designs of British plants in extended friezes across the front of the building and around the stair towers.

At the eastern end of the building is an integral clock tower, 160 feet (49 m.) high. Its inclusion in the finished building owed much to Street's resilience in resisting the Treasury's demands for utilitarian economy. It is easy to see that such official parsimony wore him down over the years. The clock face and casing were designed by Street in 1877, and the clock was itself started on the second

The Janus Clock

anniversary of his death. On the recommendation of the Astronomer Royal the clockworks were constructed by Gillett and Bland, a firm in Croydon which also provided the clock for Manchester Town Hall. The Royal Courts clock is a 'Janus' clock, having a double face and said to be one of only eight in Europe.

Above:
Statue of King Alfred on the east gable of the front entrance

Right:
Bells in the clock tower

12. Turn left into Bell Yard and left into Carey Street.

The northern façade of the building centres, somewhat irregularly, on the rear entrance to the Court Floor, originally the barristers' entrance. The Bar may still cross Carey Street from

Lincoln's Inn in full court robes. High above on the gable over the northern end of the Great Hall is a statue of Moses, holding the Ten Commandments. Beneath were carved the royal arms, those of Earl Selborne and Lord Coleridge, respectively Lord Chancellor and Lord Chief Justice when the building was opened, and the arms of the Inns of Court.

A little beyond the main entrance is a separate entrance designed for the use of the judges. Here the mouldings over the door, now badly weathered, show a dog and cat fighting; perhaps an allusion to the litigants within.

Further back, to the east, is another high corner tower, and clusters of spikes and gables on the rooftops, constructed of orange-red brick in deliberate contrast to the white Portland stone. A closed gateway shows where pedestrians once had access to the great quadrangle, which for the 60 years after the First World War, housed temporary prefabricated courts. Over the gateway is a high and disproportionate roof, reminiscent of a French pavilion.

13. Turn left down the public footpath around the perimeter of the Courts; this extends from Clement's Inn Passage.

On the left are the new office-block extensions of the Royal Courts, housing the Chancery Division and its court offices. The other modern block is the Thomas More Building, containing the companies and bankruptcy registries. Slightly set back is the Queen's Building, in which there are 12 courts.

The West Green Building, opened in 1912, was the long-awaited first extension of the original building and was designed in 1908 by Sir Henry Tanner to house four courtrooms for the new Court of Criminal Appeal. During the post-war years the vast increase in divorce work led to the use of those courts for family business, and in the offices to the south four more small courtrooms were created. On the gable over the southern flank of the building is a statue of King Henry II.

14. Turn left on to Strand by St Clement Danes Church

The exterior of the Middle Temple benchers' rooms

4. The Temple

> *There is yet a drowsiness in its courts and a dreamy dullness in its trees and gardens; those who pace its lanes and squares may yet hear the echoes of their footsteps on the sounding stones, and read upon its gates, in passing from the tumult of the Strand or Fleet Street, 'Who enters here leaves noise behind'.*
>
> Charles Dickens, *Barnaby Rudge*, Chapter 15

The Temple

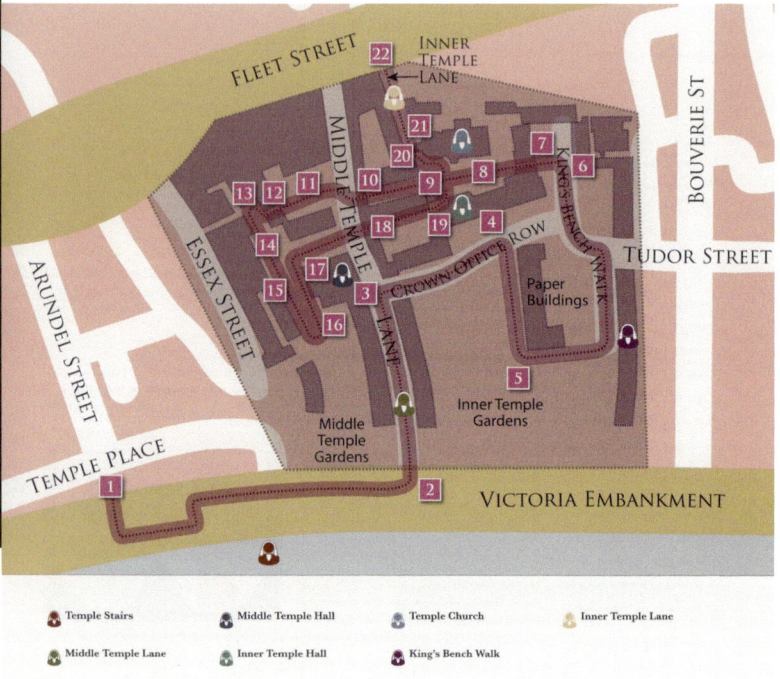

1. From Temple Underground station turn right out of the station on to Victoria Embankment. Cross at the pedestrian crossing on to the riverside and turn left. Proceed to Temple Pier, passing the griffin marking the entrance to the City of London, and up over the lip of the stairs formerly protecting the road against flooding and on to the landing stage marked by the Pegasus and the Lamb and Flag, the badges of Inner and Middle Temple, respectively. Temple Pier Stairs are set immediately behind the war memorial to the submariners.

2. Cross back over Victoria Embankment via the traffic lights to the south end of Middle Temple Lane. Pass up the lane into the precincts of the Temple, passing the little gatehouse erected in 1880 to the archway of Temple Gardens.

3. Turn right. Proceed under the arch along Crown Office Row.

4. Turn right along 2-5 Paper Buildings.

5. Turn left and follow the railings of Inner Temple Gardens.

6. Follow the building line around the corner to 2 King's Bench Walk.

7. Turn right under the archway formed by Inner Temple Library building into Church Court.

8. Proceed across the courtyard towards Cloisters.

9. Pass under Cloisters into Pump Court.

10. Pass through Pump Court emerging back into Middle Temple Lane and turn right.

11. Return down Middle Temple Lane into Brick Court.

12. Proceed under archway between 2 and 3 Essex Court into New Court.

13. Bear right, through Judge's Gate.

14. Return from Devereux Court into the precincts of Middle Temple and proceed down the steps to Fountain Court.

15. Pass down the steps to Garden Court on the right, Middle Temple Gardens and hall on the left.

16. Proceed along the terrace to the end.

17. Return to Fountain Court and turn right.

18. Cross Middle Temple Lane beneath archway into Elm Court.

19. Bear left past the buttery up the steps to Cloisters and cross to Temple Church.

20. From the church turn right, bearing round to the west door and canopy.

21. Proceed up Inner Temple Lane by 3 Dr Johnson's Buildings, then Nos. 2 and 1.

22. Proceed to the head of Inner Temple Lane.

The Temple

1. From Temple Underground station turn right out of the station on to Victoria Embankment. Cross at the pedestrian crossing on to the riverside and turn left. Proceed to Temple Pier, passing the griffin marking the entrance to the City of London, and up over the lip of the stairs formerly protecting the road against flooding and on to the landing stage marked by the Pegasus and the Lamb and Flag, the badges of Inner and Middle Temple, respectively. Temple Pier Stairs are set immediately behind the war memorial to the submariners.

For over 550 years lawyers passed from Temple Stairs to the `watermen's ferry boats standing ready to carry them upstream, around the meander of the Thames, to the courts sitting at Westminster Hall. The little dock, which was called Temple Bridge until the 18th century, was 100 yards (90 m.) or so upstream from the location of the present pier and stairs.

The dock's presence appears in official documents in 1331 passing from King Edward II to the Lord Mayor of London concerning its repair. Since it is known to have been built by the Knights Templar as a landing stage, the existence of Temple Bridge may pre-date that correspondence by upwards of 100 years. Certainly it was used formally upon the king's business and its upkeep attracted royal attention. Such an example was the landing here in 1441 of Eleanor Cobham, Duchess of Gloucester, on a penitential progress along Fleet Street to St Paul's Cathedral, having been accused of using witchcraft against King Henry VI.

In 1541 a conference was held between the two Temple societies to consider liability for repairs. Whatever was resolved it took a subscription of members of the Inns, to which Queen Elizabeth I contributed personally, for the bridge to be repaired. The workmanship may have been adequate for the time being but in 1620 the benchers of the societies ordered a new bridge and stairs to be constructed.

During the great frost of 1683 the River Thames froze from early December 1682 until 8 February 1683. A huge Frost Fair, together with a carnival on the frozen river, was given by the City on New Year's Day 1683, at which booths, tents, shops and even a printing press were established on the ice. Coaches ran from Westminster Pier to the Temple. On 5 February 1683 John Evelyn, the diarist, recorded his crossing the Thames in a coach upon the ice from Lambeth to Horseferry, the point where the river was normally crossed by a horse ferry.

A thriving watermen's business operated on the Thames until it was destroyed by the introduction of steam launches. Prior to that Charles Dickens describes the Temple Stairs in both *Great Expectations* (1860-1) and *The Mystery of Edwin Drood* (1870).

In 1840 gates were erected to lock up the stairs and for the next 25 years the lawyers used Essex Stairs instead. In 1865, on the construction of the Victoria Embankment, the old Temple Stairs were removed and replaced by Temple Pier as it is today. W.S. Gilbert (1836-1911) recounts how he took a twopenny steamer to Westminster Hall during his brief period in practice between 1863 and 1867. Some 20 years later the great advocate Sir Edward Marshall Hall, when a pupil, took the steamer from Temple Pier to that ancient Norman hall to see the last trials ever heard there.

From the stairs on top of the pier the view across the busy road is a broad vista of the Temple, and more specifically from left to right, of Queen Elizabeth Building, the gardens of Middle Temple, Middle Temple Hall, Temple Gardens, the gardens of Inner Temple, Paper Buildings, and the southern end of King's Bench Walk.

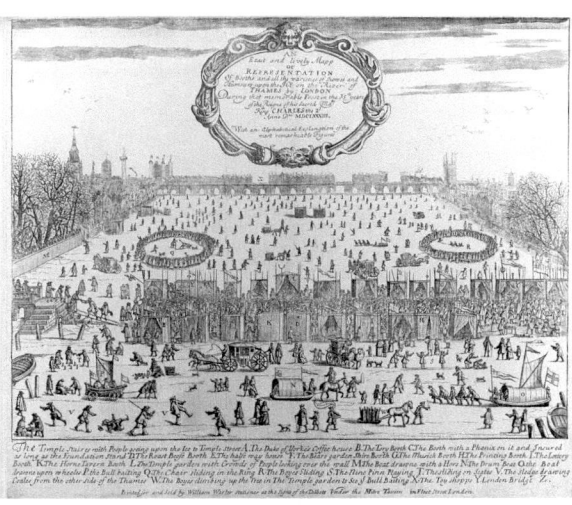

The great frost fair, 1683-4 Reproduced by kind permission of Barnaby's Picture Library

2. Cross back over Victoria Embankment via the traffic lights to the south end of Middle Temple Lane. Pass up the lane into the precincts of the Temple, passing the little gatehouse erected in 1880 to the archway of Temple Gardens.

Until 1865 the river encroached upon the southern boundary of the area known as the Temple, kept at bay by a wall, but susceptible to flooding on a regular basis. With the stabilisation of the land reclaimed after the building of the Embankment, both the Honourable Societies of Inner and Middle Temple, who, among their other functions, own the land and administer the estate, wished to expand their premises southwards. Jointly they engaged Sir Charles Barry (1795-1860), the leading architect of the day, to design 1-4 Temple Gardens, which was completed in 1878-9. With its over-elaborate frontage, balconies and statues, it may fairly be described as an ornate and vulgar expression of the age, totally out of keeping with the surrounding buildings. It does, however, act as the gateway to an intimate and delightful little world beyond. And despite the vulgarity of its river frontage, 3 Temple Gardens contained the chambers of Marshall Hall for most of his practice.

What is striking about the Temple, even today, is that irrespective of which entrance the visitor uses to come away from the bustle of Fleet Street or the Embankment, whether by Middle Temple Lane, Inner Temple Lane, Mitre Court, Tudor Street or through Devereux Court, within 100 yards (90 m.) or so the very peace and quietude of the place are encountered. It is a haven, an oasis which generations of lawyers have been grateful to have as their working environment.

Middle Temple Lane existed before 1330 since an ordinance of King Edward III made in that year and directed to the masters of the New Temple required that the gates to the lane should be kept open to allow free passage for the king's justices and clerks and others who wished to go to Westminster by water from Temple Bridge. The lower half of the lane divides the property of the two societies, the Middle Temple having the buildings to the west and the Inner Temple those to the east. This may be seen by the emblems of the two Inns surmounting the lintels and drain covers of each edifice.

Middle Temple Lane

The Temple

On the right stands Harcourt Buildings, originally constructed in 1703 and named for the treasurer of Inner Temple in that year, Sir Simon Harcourt, who a few years later as Attorney-General, was one of the framers of the Act of Union with Scotland in 1707. As Lord Harcourt he was Lord Chancellor 1713-14. Number 3 contained the chambers of the well-known Victorian judge, Sir Alexander Cockburn, Chief Justice of the King's Bench 1859-1880 and the first officially styled Lord Chief Justice of England. This property was extended in 1878-9 when more building land became available. However, like much of the Inner Temple, the original buildings fell victim to the Blitz in 1940 and 1941 and the present structure was rebuilt to a sympathetic design in 1957-8.

Opposite 2 Harcourt Building is the Middle Temple library surmounted by three crests, the arms of Sydney Turner 1955, Kenneth Macmorran 1956, and James Tucker 1957. These were the three treasurers of Middle Temple holding office during the rebuilding of the war-damaged Plowden Buildings. The present building was designed by Sir Edward Maufe (1883-1974), chosen as Middle Temple's post-war architect responsible for the library, Pump Court and Cloisters, which were opened in 1958 by Queen Elizabeth, the Queen Mother, a royal bencher of Middle Temple.

The enormity of his task is evident from the photographs of the bomb-ravaged Temple from the north of Pump Court down to the Embankment.

Middle Temple library is nearly on the site of the earliest library in the Inn, a very small affair, fitted up in 1625 at Plowden Buildings, then described as being over the kitchens at 2 Garden Court. The library was effectively refounded in 1641 when Robert Ashley, a bencher, bequeathed his collection of books to the Inn and was physically expanded in 1771. It transferred in October 1861 to a purpose-built Gothic Revival building at the foot of the slope south-west of the hall on a site immediately to the rear of the present Queen Elizabeth Building. By the turn of the 20th century the collection exceeded 70,000 volumes, the vast majority of which survived the complete destruction of the Library building by

View of the Temple after the Great Incendiary Raid of 1941

incendiary bombs in December 1940. In reconstructing Middle Temple it was decided to return the library to its former location.

The present building contains a special American law collection, and a standing historical exhibition relating to relevant members of Middle Temple. The Inn has had a long association with the United States. No less than five signatories of the Declaration of Independence were members of this Inn, namely, Edward Rutledge (1749-1800), who became Governor of South Carolina in 1798; Thomas Heyward, Jr. (1746-1809), appointed in 1778 a Judge of the High Court of South Carolina; Thomas McKean (1734-1817), President of Delaware in 1777 and first Chief Justice of Pennsylvania 1777, and Governor of Pennsylvania 1779; Thomas Lynch, Jr. (1749-99) of South Carolina; and Arthur Middleton (1743-87) of South Carolina. Another signatory, William Paca, later Governor of Maryland, was a member of Inner Temple.

A further five members of Middle Temple assisted in the framing of the United States Constitution. These were John Rutledge (1739-1800), brother of Edward and first President of the General Assembly of South Carolina, who chaired the committee of five which drafted the first Constitution and became the second Chief Justice of the United States of America in 1795; William Livingstone (1723-90) the first Governor of New Jersey 1776; John Dickinson (1732-1808) who wrote Letters from a Pennsylvania Farmer 1767-8; Arthur Lee of Virginia; and Peyton Randolph (1723-75), President of the First Continental Congress which met in Carpenter's Hall, Philadelphia. In addition to these other Middle Templars signed the completed Constitution: John Blair (1732-1808), Chancellor and Chief Justice of Virginia 1789-96; Charles Cotesworth Pinckney (1746-1825) who declined an appointment to the initial Supreme Court Bench; and Charles Jared Ingersoll (1749-1822), the first Attorney-General of Pennsylvania.

To mark this association a copy of the American Declaration of Independence, marked up with the Middle Temple signatories, is exhibited at the top of the library staircase, outside the gallery which, most appropriately, houses the American law collection.

On the original library staircase in a poor set of chambers which he shared with Jeffs, the Middle Temple butler, lived the dramatist and author, Oliver Goldsmith (1728-74), who first came to the Temple in 1764 from Wine Office Court. In 1765 money from his writing enabled him to move to a larger set a short way up the lane in what was then Garden Court. He was living there in 1766 when his novel *The Vicar of Wakefield* was published and established his reputation. His second real success, a play called *The Good-natur'd Man*, enabled him to purchase a lease of 2 Brick Court for £400 in 1768.

Opposite 1 Harcourt Building is Middle Temple Treasury, the Inn's administrative centre, housed in 2 Plowden Buildings, above the entrance to which is the crest of Charles Henry Hopwood, treasurer for 1896, surmounted by the Middle Temple arms. The crenellation on 1 Plowden Buildings was added when the block was refaced in 1906.

Plowden Buildings were erected from 1625 onwards but have been called variously through their history Garden Buildings and Garden Court. They were named after the Elizabethan jurist Edmund Plowden (1518-85), the treasurer of

Middle Temple for the extraordinary length of six years, 1561-7. He retained his position whilst he chaired the committee to manage the building of a new hall for the Inn, 1562-1572, and his fellow benchers effectively refused to let him stand down. He was offered the Woolsack by Queen Elizabeth I if he would renounce his Catholicism but, risking the Queen's disfavour, he declined.

In 1626 1-2 Plowden Buildings, then Garden Buildings, housed the Parliament Chamber of the Inn, a large room for the masters of the bench to meet in committee to discuss and approve action to administer its affairs. By 1770 an embankment had been built at the foot of the Temple adding considerably to the land available for building. After that date Plowden Buildings was extended to become Nos. 1-6, with 2 Garden Court renamed as 1-2 Plowden Buildings, and 1 Garden Court renamed Nos. 3-6. In 1896 extensive alterations created the modern-day Treasury building.

Opposite is Carpmael Buildings, housed above the archway under which the roadway passes into Inner Temple. Such an arch has stood here since 1806.

3. Turn right. Proceed under the arch along Crown Office Row.

Crown Office Row is named after the office of the High Court which stood here from the reign of King Henry VII (1485-1508) until 1621 when it moved to 2 King's Bench Walk, where it remained until its removal to the Royal Courts of Justice in 1882. Its precise location at the old 7 Crown Office Row was described in a document of 1523 as being between Fig Tree Court and the Watergate on the eastern side of Middle Temple Lane.

On the corner of the present 1 Crown Office Row is mounted a tablet which reads:

> *Charles Lamb was born in the chambers that formerly stood here 10th February 1775 'Cheerful Crown Office Row (place of my kindly engendure). A man would give something to have been born in such places'.*

The building referred to was No. 2 of a terrace of 10 erected in 1628, replaced in 1707 and destroyed in 1940 by the Germans. The modern neo-Georgian frontage of Crown Office Row was completed in 1959. The famous essayist lived for 20 years at the old No. 6, and the quotation on the memorial tablet is derived from his Essays of Elia in which Lamb writes:

I was born, and passed the first seven years of my life, in the Temple. Its church, its halls, its gardens, its fountain, its river, I had almost said – for in those young years, what was this king of rivers to me but a stream that watered our pleasant places? – These are of my oldest recollections. I repeat, to this day, no verses to myself more frequently, or with kindlier emotion, than those of Spenser, where he speaks of this spot.

> *There when they came, whereas those bricky towers,*
> *The which on Thames' broad aged back doth ride,*
> *Where now the studious lawyers have their bowers,*
> *There whilom wont the Templar knights to bide,*
>   *Till they decay'd through pride.*

Indeed, it is the most elegant spot in the metropolis. What a transition for a countryman visiting London for the first time – the passing from the crowded Strand or Fleet Street, by unexpected avenues, into its magnificent, ample squares, its classic green recesses! What a cheerful, liberal look hath that portion of it which, from three sides, overlooks the greater garden, that goodly pile 'Of building strong, albeit of Paper hight', confronting with massy contrast, the lighter, older, more fantastically shrouded one, named of Harcourt, with the cheerful Crown Office Row (place of my kindly engendure), right opposite the stately stream, which washes the garden foot with her yet scarcely trade-polluted waters, and seems but just weaned from her Twickenham naiades! A man would give something to have been born in such places.

At No. 10 William Makepeace Thackeray was in Tom Taylor's chambers from May 1848 until 1851 and here wrote *Pendennis* in 1849. Thackeray left the Temple in 1851. He had no real intention to practise but at the suggestion of a friend of the family had been called to the Bar in order to secure the position of

Crown Office Row

a London magistrate. Neither realised at the time that the post required seven years' standing in the profession. Taylor was a dramatist and editor of *Punch* (1874-80), who wrote the poem, 'Ten Crown Office Row: a Templar's Tribute to his Old Chambers and his Old Chum'. A good friend of Taylor was Alfred Tennyson (1809-92), afterwards poet laureate and Lord Tennyson, who would meet Thackeray there.

At 9 Crown Office Row were the chambers of Lord Bramwell (1808-92), a highly regarded baron of the Court of Exchequer, 1856-1872 and Lord Justice of Appeal for nine years thereafter. Four doors along at No. 5 two of the great Victorian silks were to be found in practice: Montagu Williams QC and Sir Charles Mathews QC, later chief metropolitan magistrate and Director of Public Prosecutions.

Before the construction of the Victoria Embankment in 1865 the gardens of Inner Temple extended to cover 3 acres (1.2 ha.). This area has been used as a garden since at least the 11th century. No river wall existed until 1528 and the gardens were subject to the tides of the river. On the river bank a path ran from the palace of Bridewell to that of the Savoy, neither of which is still standing. The jetty which was developed into Temple Stairs was put up prior to 1311. A gardener's cottage is recorded as having been on the site of the present-day 10 King's Bench Walk in the l4th century.

The first wall adjoined the estate of the Carmelites at 'the Friar's Wall' and ran from approximately where 11 King's Bench Walk stands today to the south end of Paper Buildings and then south-west to Temple Stairs. It was rebuilt in 1610 at a point some 50 yards (45 m.) north of the present Embankment.

The most famous episode in the history of the garden occurred reputedly in 1430 when a dispute in Inner Temple Hall between Richard Plantagenet, Duke of York, and the earls of Somerset, Suffolk and Warwick led to those great nobles adjourning to the garden and there plucking white and red roses, each to become the symbol and colour of their faction. The Inn's gardens had long since become famous for its roses, Old Provence (the Cabbage) and the Maiden's Blush. The dispute led to that era of violent civil war which became known to history as the Wars of the Roses 1430-1485. The scene was immortalised by Shakespeare in his *Henry VI, Part I*.

Henry Payne 'Choosing the Red and White Roses in the Temple Gardens' Entrance Hall, Inner Temple Treasury

Inner Temple Gardens from the foot of Paper Buildings

The Temple

After 1580 buildings were erected on the site of the present Paper Buildings and what was until then known as the Great Garden was divided up, the smaller area to the east becoming Great Walk, or Bencher's Walk, now the site of 7-13 King's Bench Walk. During the reign of King James I (1603-25) the gardens were developed with extensive new planting and the digging out of a pond enclosed with railings, both of which are now long gone. The accounts of the Inn show the purchase of a new sundial in 1619, the re-turfing of the lawns in 1651 with turf brought down by river on lighters from Greenwich Park, and the greenhouse roofs replaced in 1693. By Oliver Goldsmith's time the gardens were famous for their rookery established by Sir William Northcote, the birds having been brought from Woodcote Park, Epsom.

The filigree wrought-iron gate of Inner Temple Gardens dated 1730, shows the devices of both Inner Temple and Gray's Inn, Inner's ancient ally, and was a gift from Gray's. The sundial at the foot of the steps was acquired in 1707.

The broad gravel walk at the foot of the gardens is mentioned by Shakespeare, Dickens and Thackeray. Not only have generations of lawyers taken a lunchtime stroll there, ruminating upon their afternoon submissions or discussing cases or Temple gossip with their colleagues, but the walk has also been the haunt of 17th-century court ladies playing hoops and 'patches', and of 18th-century young bloods and city merchants. A Dr Dibdin described the garden walks towards the close of the 18th century:

> *Towards evening it was the fashion for the leading counsel to promenade during the summer months in the Temple gardens. Cocked hats and ruffles, with satin small-clothes and silk stockings, at this time constituted the usual evening dress. Lord Erskine, though a good deal shorter than his brethren, somehow always seemed to take the lead, both in place and in discourse, and shouts of laughter would frequently follow his dicta.*

In 1930 a memorial to Charles Lamb was erected in the gardens in the form of a pond with the statue of a little boy holding an open book upon which is written 'Lawyers I suppose were children once'. The words are taken from *Pendennis*. As a Millennium 2000 project the Inn rebuilt the pond and added a fountain.

Inner Temple Gardens and Paper Buildings in winter

The remainder of Crown Office Row contains the frontage of Inner Temple Hall and Treasury with its separate benchers' entrance and common room.

There may have been a communal building in this immediate vicinity as early as the 8th century, and certainly the

Knights Templar or any military monastic order would require on site a hall for communal use in the vicinity of their commandery. In about 1200 the Templars, having been firmly ensconced in this area for nearly 60 years, commenced the construction of a large hall known as the Hall of the Military Knights, situated where 2-3 Pump Court now stand. Both King John and Henry III are known to have dined there. A stone chamber of about 23 feet (7 m.) by 18 feet (5.5 m.) extended west from the present-day Cloisters. It looked like a small refectory and became known as the 'Hall of the Priests'. The ceiling of this smaller hall was supported by groined arches of stone, which have been preserved in the roof of the buttery or promptuarium used by the priests and serving brethren that still stands overlooking Fig Tree Court.

At one stage chambers existed above the buttery known as Hall Chambers. There were also chambers next to the Hall of the Priests known as Chambers under the Hall Stairs, occupied by Sir William Follett in 1825.

The Hall of the Priests had a floor of rushes and was lit by candles and flares. A central wood and charcoal fire was the sole means of heat underneath a smoke louvre in the roof. In 1307, when the Crown seized the property of the Templars, the Hall of the Priests was in disrepair and probably not in use.

By about 1340 the two halls of the Templars were administered by the prior of the Order of St John of Jerusalem from his priory at Clerkenwell. The records of the order show that in 1356 the Temple was an unconsecrated place consisting of a hall, four chambers, a garden and a stable which was let to a body of lawyers, probably the founders of Middle Temple.

In or about 1368 a further group of *apprenticii di banco* left Clifford's Inn on Chancery Lane and took up occupation of chambers in the area west of the Temple Church in present-day Hare Court. These became the Honourable Society of the Inner Temple, at first sharing hall with the existing lawyers of Middle Temple, then constructing a new hall on the site of the old refectory.

The gates to Inner Temple Gardens

The Temple

This was built at some point prior to the death of King Edward III in 1377 since it is known that he attended a serjeants' feast here and the serjeants did not have their own hall.

In the Paston Letters, a unique research archive of the time, the name Inner Temple is first mentioned under the date 1 October 1440. The society obtained partial title to the property they occupied in 1608 and secured the freehold in 1675 for £78. A deed of partition between the two societies was agreed in 1732.

Inner Temple Hall was partially rebuilt in 1606, and restored in 1629. Its northern wall had to be rebuilt in 1680. Further substantial works were required in 1816 when severe cracks to the roof occurred and the wooden cupola containing a bell let in rain. By then the hall contained a Doric screen surmounted by lions and this was extended at the same time to enable statues of Kings Alfred, Edward I and Edward III, all executed by the sculptor Rossi, to be placed in canopied niches at the western end.

King George V and Queen Mary visit the annual RHS Flower Show (before its transfer to the Chelsea Hospital) in Inner Temple Gardens, July 1911.

Reproduced with kind permission of the Honourable Society of the Inner Temple

The substantial growth in the membership of Inner Temple during the 19th century led to the existing hall becoming overcrowded, causing inconvenience with both dining and legal education. The benchers decided to demolish the building and this was undertaken in 1866. A casualty of the removal of the Hall of the Priests was the destruction of an ancient building attached to the buttery believed to have been the Templars' brewery. This structure had to go to make way for new kitchens.

The new hall was built to designs by the architect Sydney Smirke (1798-1877), who had previously 'Gothicised' its predecessor in 1835, and the building was opened on 14 May 1870 by Princess Louise, daughter of Queen Victoria, and Prince Christian of Schleswig-Holstein, Victoria's son-in-law, in the presence of the Lord Chancellor, Lord Hatherley. An inaugural banquet was held four days later in the presence of the Prince of Wales, later Edward VII, and the prime minister, W.E. Gladstone.

On the night of 10 May 1941, Smirke's Inner Temple Hall was reduced by bombing to a smoking ruin along with Parliament Chamber, the benchers' rooms, the Inner Temple treasury and its library. A sad loss to the Inn was that of the picture of Pegasus surrounded by Neptune and the Muses springing from Mount Helicon which was commissioned from James (later Sir James) Thornhill in 1709 and had always hung at the east end of hall. Destroyed, too, were statues of Knights Templar and Knights Hospitaller made by Henry Hugh Armstead in 1875.

The present hall was rebuilt between 1952 and 1955 to a design of Sir Hubert Worthington (1886-1963). It is a spacious high-ceilinged building with half- panelling in oak, upon which shields depict the arms of readers of the Inn dating back to its founding. A minstrel gallery occupies the west end, with a plain screen. The east end of hall has a raised dais for the bench table and a portrait of the late Queen's father, George VI, is directly behind the chair of the treasurer, the annually appointed bencher who is the titular head of the society. By convention in Inner Temple, the treasurership follows directly on from the incumbent's preceding year in the office of reader. This portrait of the King's grandfather is now between two magnificent display cases exhibiting part of Inner's substantial silver collection.

The portrait and silver collection

The Temple

The paintings decorating the walls of hall show a long-standing relationship between the society and the artist Sir Godfrey Kneller (1646-1723), who produced the Inn's portraits of King William III and Queen Mary, King George II and Queen Caroline, Sir Matthew Hale and Sir Simon Harcourt. In addition canvases of Sir Edward Coke by Vansomer, of the Earl of Halsbury, of George, Lord Jeffreys (otherwise known as 'the hanging Judge Jeffreys'), and of the portraits of the four so-called fire judges, Sir John Vaughan, Sir Orlando Bridgman, Sir Thomas Tyrrell and Sir Heneage Finch, which hang in the Hall Gallery, may be seen. These latter paintings were commissioned in gratitude by the Court of Alderman of the City of London for their resolving the numerous boundary and tenancy disputes which had arisen following the devastation caused by the Great Fire of London in 1666.

Stained glass at the west end of Inner Temple Hall. The Pegasus symbol surmounts the arms of Robert Dudley, Earl of Leicester

Inner Temple Hall has been closely associated with the development of English drama for centuries. Commissioned for the Inn's revels and traditional biannual celebrations at Allhallows and Candlemas, for over 350 years plays have been premièred here. Reputedly the first English tragic stage play, the *Tragedy of Gorboduc* by Thomas Norton and Thomas Sackville, was given in hall on Twelfth Night, 1561. Seven years later Queen Elizabeth I attended the première of *Tancred and Gismund* a play partly by one of her favourite courtiers, Sir Christopher Hatton (1540-91), who as a privy councillor participated in the State trial of Mary, Queen of Scots, and who was made Lord Chancellor in 1587, perhaps as a reward. The location of Hatton's town house near Holborn Circus has become one of the most famous of modern London addresses, the heart of its diamond and jewellery trade – Hatton Garden.

Between 1605 and 1640 there were biannual presentations in hall of plays, including the works of the Jacobean dramatists Francis Beaumont (1584-1616) and John Fletcher (1579-1625), but the increasing power and influence of the Puritan movement in Parliament halted this tradition in 1642. It was a further 18 years before revelry was again permitted in the Inner Temple, and a dark time that must have been. Between 1660 and 1688 Restoration comedies were given with great success to the members of the society in hall. And as late as 1890 with a performance of Strafford by Robert Browning the tradition was kept alive.

The members of Inner Temple sitting 'in commons' were famous for their revelry and their independence, particularly of the jurisdiction of the City of London, despite the fact that Inner Temple lies within the City ward of Farringdon Without. Demonstrating the former, the Christmas revels of 1563 lasted for nearly a fortnight of feasting and entertainment in which actors personified the 'Knights of the Order of Pegasus' and created the device of a Pegasus argent on an azure field. Some say that it was this badge, suggested by the Master of Revels, one Gerald Leigh, that was afterwards adopted by Inner Temple as its emblem together with the motto *Volat ad aethera virtus* (He flies with Virtue to the Heavens). However, it is more probable that the symbol of the Pegasus was already linked to the society which had by then been in existence for over 120 years.

The Temple

As for protecting their independence, exactly a century later, in 1669, the reader for that year, Christopher Goodfellowe, invited the Lord Mayor of London, Sir William Turner, to the reader's feast. His guest insisted on being preceded into Inner Temple Hall by his raised sword of office. The students of the Inn took immense offence at this, caused a riot, and physically threw the Mayor and his entourage out of the precincts of the Inn. The City promptly brought a petition before the King, Charles II, for him to determine whether the Temple was within the jurisdiction of the City. He declined to do so. From that date no Lord Mayor set foot in the Temple until October 1939, a period of 270 years.

Interior of Sydney Smirke's Inner Temple Hall 1870 showing the Armistead Knights Templar. Reproduced with kind permission of the Honourable Society of the Inner Temple

Those ancient members of the Society should not be thought inhospitable. In 1568 they gave a celebratory dinner to member Sir Francis Drake and Sir Walter Raleigh. The Inn was a particular supporter of the royal houses of Orange and of Hanover. And, it has been said, on the restoration of the monarchy in 1660 the hall of this Inn became one of the most important social venues in London.

Famous members of Inner Temple include Sir Thomas Littleton, a great jurist of the late 15th century, whose treatise on tenures 1481 was regarded as the first great book on English law not written in Latin and wholly uninfluenced by Roman law. It was repeatedly reprinted until 1903. Sir Edward Coke, called to the Bar at Inner Temple in 1578, was a master of medieval law who wrote the first encyclopaedic legal work. He became recorder of London in 1591, Solicitor-General and Speaker of the House of Commons in 1592, and Attorney-General in 1594, a post he held until 1606. In that office he prosecuted the State trials against the Earls of Essex and Southampton (1600-1), Sir Walter Raleigh (1603) and the Gunpowder Plot conspirators (1605). He was reputedly a savage and vehement prosecutor with a lasting hatred of Catholics. Made Chief Justice of the Common Pleas 1606-13 and Chief Justice of the King's Bench 1613-16, he came into political conflict with King James I over the extent of the jurisdiction of the common law courts and the King's prerogative to interfere with court process. Out of office he became leader of the Parliamentary opposition in 1620, was imprisoned in the Tower in 1623 but afterwards released, and framed the Petition of Right, 1628, which laid the ground for those democratic ideas which would eventually lead to civil war and the removal, 15 years after Coke's death in 1634, of Charles I and of the monarchy.

Sir Heneage Finch, afterwards Earl of Nottingham, was called by Inner Temple in 1645. He was appointed Lord Chancellor in 1675 and took a leading part in passing the Statute of Frauds (1677), becoming regarded as the father of modern equity. Lord Ellenborough was Chief Justice of the King's Bench 1802-18. While at the Bar he led for the defence in the impeachment (1788-95) of Warren Hastings. Lord Erskine was Lord Chancellor 1806-7, and is regarded as probably the greatest advocate ever to practise at the English Bar.

Inner Temple Hall today

The Temple

Two men displayed almost diametrically opposed human traits. The notoriety of George Jeffreys as Common Serjeant (1671) and then recorder of London (1678) drew him to the attention of King James II. He was appointed Chief Justice of the King's Bench 1683 and Lord Chancellor 1685. His management of the trials of Titus Oates 1685 and the Bloody Assizes of the same year, following the Monmouth Rebellion, led him to be characterised as the worst judge that ever disgraced Westminster Hall, drunken, coarse, brutal, unscrupulous, and the exemplar of injustice. Even so his portrait is still hanging in Inner Temple Hall today. By way of contrast in 1888 Inner Temple admitted as a student, and in 1891 called to the Bar, one Mohandas Karamchand Gandhi, the Mahatma, who used Hindu ethics, fasting and passive resistance to bring about the eventual withdrawal of the British Raj, and the grant of independence to India. It is worth noting that Jawaharlal Nehru, the first Prime Minister of India was also a member of this Inn, as was Cecil Rhodes, colonialist adventurer now remembered as a great educational philanthropist. A bronze bas-relief of the Mahatma is mounted on the wall outside the Inn's Ghandi Room, at the foot of the staircase at the west end of Hall.

On the more contemporary scene, members of Inner Temple have, thrught the 1990s and early 2000s, almost monopolised the principal offices of the judiciary, with four Lord Chancellors, Lord Mackay of Clashfern, Lord Irvine of Laird, Lord Falconer of Thoroton (also the first Secretary of State for Constitutional Affairs) and the previous incumbent, Jack Straw (also the first Secretary of State for Justice). The late and much lamented Lord Taylor of Gosforth, was Lord Chief Justice, as was his successor, Lord Woolf of Barnes, who was until June, 2000 Master of the Rolls and architect of the massive civil justice reforms of 1998. Lord Goff of Chievely, formerly senior Law Lord; Sir Stephen Brown and Dame Elizabeth Butler-Sloss, respectively immediate past and present Presidents of the Family Division; and Sir Richard Scott, Vice-Chancellor, a Law Lord from 1 October 2000. This remarkable feat is celebrated in a painting by June Mendoza of five of these judges holding office contemporaneously which now hangs in the benchers' anteroom to hall.

But it is with the advancement of its women members that the Inn has been at the forefront of securing equality in legal practice over the last few years, as also it was the professional home of the first female barrister in 1922. In addition to producing the first Lady Chief Justice in 800 years, Baroness Carr, alone of the four Inns of Court, Inner Temple produced among others the first female Treasurer of an Inn and first female member of the Court of Appeal, the first female High Court Judge, the first female bencher, the first woman judge and President of the International Court of Justice, the first woman Chair of the Bar Council, the first female President of the Queen's Bench Division, the first female President of the Employment Appeal Tribunal, a number of Justices of the Supreme Court, and the first female Advocate General for Scotland.

On the right stands Paper Buildings, running from No. 1 opposite Inner Temple Treasury to No. 5, which protrudes into the gardens. Number 1 stands on the site of Heyward's Buildings, constructed of timber and plaster in 1610 and named for its first tenant, Edward Heyward, who shared chambers here with the great jurist John Selden. It had four storeys, the topmost of which had an open gallery. Selden (1584-1654) was one of the managers of the Duke of Buckingham's impeachment in 1626. He defended John Hampden in the *Ship Money* case of 1627 and famously held down the Speaker in the chair of the Commons for the Holles Protest in 1628. He became the leader of the opposition to the Crown in the Long Parliament but took no part in public life after 1649, and was profoundly shocked by the execution of the King despite his long-standing politics. He died in 1654 and was buried in Temple Church. For much of his time in practice he concentrated on historical research and writing, producing many valuable

Heads of Division by June Mendoza. From left to right: Sir Richard Scott V-C (afterwards a Law Lord); Lord Goff of Chieveley; Lord Woolf of Barnes MR (afterwards the Lord Chief Justice); Sir Stephen Brown P; Lord Mackay of Clashfern, the Lord Chancellor. Overlooking them from the fireplace is a portrait of Lord Taylor of Gosforth, the late Lord Chief Justice.

works on legal history. He had a close circle of literary friends and Samuel Butler (1612-80), Ben Jonson (1572-1637), William Camden (1551-1623) and the cleric John Cotton (1585-1652) became frequent visitors to Selden here.

Also at No. 1 Herbert Henry Asquith was in chambers from 1895. He had been Home Secretary in the Liberal governments led by W.E. Gladstone and Lord Rosebery (1892-5), but returned to the Bar when the Liberals were replaced by the Conservatives. In the next Liberal governments he was Chancellor of the Exchequer (1905-8) and Prime Minister (1908-15) and also led the first wartime coalition government (1915-6). In recent years a cleaning exercise of his old chambers revealed the name board of 1891 on which he appears, and this has been restored and is now preserved under glass.

After a four year multi-million pound redevelopment, the Inn's Treasury building was reopened in May, 2022 by its royal bencher, the Princess Royal. New quarters were provided for the education department, together with a lecture theatre and a suite of seminar and reception rooms, a reorganisation of the library and new kitchens for Hall.

The new Treasury building

The original Paper Buildings, which came to number 14 stairwells, were destroyed in a fire of 1838, and the present buildings were erected between 1839 and 1840 with the Italianate No. 5 being an addition of 1847-8. Dickens referred to these in *Barnaby Rudge*, chapter 15 as 'a row of goodly tenements, shaded in front by ancient trees, and looking, at the back, upon Temple Gardens'. They also merit a reference in *A Tale of Two Cities* and *Our Mutual Friend*.

4. Turn right along 2-5 Paper Buildings

The more well-known occupants of Paper Buildings have included, at No. 6 Edward Law, afterwards Lord Ellenborough, who, as Chief Justice of the King's Bench 1802-18, (other than the Lord Chancellor) was the last holder of a judicial appointment to be included in the Cabinet; Sir William Erle, Chief Justice of the Common Pleas 1859-66; the poet Samuel Rogers (1763-1855); and George Canning (1770-1827), afterwards Foreign Secretary (1807-9 and 1822-7) and prime minister (1827), whose regular visitors here included Charles James Fox (1749-1806) and Richard Brinsley Sheridan (1751-1816).

The ornate entrance of No. 5 with its gargoyle decorations is surmounted by three coats of arms, being those of Thomas Starkie, 1847, and Francis Rogers and George Chilton, 1848. On the ground floor, one pair right, were the chambers of Hardinge Stanley Giffard, afterwards the 1st Earl of Halsbury, Lord Chancellor 1885-6, 1886-92 and 1895-1905, whose name is commemorated in the title of Halsbury's Laws of England of which he was the first general editor. In the same chambers were two great criminal silks, Sir Harry Poland KC and John Lawson Walton KC.

5. Turn left and follow the railings of Inner Temple Gardens.

The earliest known map of London drawn in 1543 by Antonio van der Wyngaerde shows houses on the site of King's Bench Walk with a garden and trees running down to the river with the pathway from Bridewell to Savoy. The earliest buildings on this site were called Black Buildings from 1557 to 1663 and were near the Alienation Office approximately where 3 King's Bench Walk and Littleton Chambers now stand. On the site of Nos. 8-9 'at the Friar's wall', Harrison's Buildings were erected in 1577.

The name King's Bench Walk is derived from the location of the office of the clerks of the Court of King's Bench, near the bottom of the hill close to the river. All of the buildings on King's Bench Walk were destroyed in the Great Fire of London in September 1666. Although there was some rebuilding, a further fire in October 1677 destroyed the houses here again, including the King's Bench Office which was never rebuilt.

The 13 buildings presently here give the impression of having been constructed together as one terrace which is not the case, as one may see from the stones over the lintels of each doorway. Numbers 9-11 appear to have been built at the same time, with 10 and 11 King's Bench Walk marked 1814. Number 11 contains the chambers of the former Lord Chancellor, Lord Irvine of Lairg, and were those of his pupil, the former prime minister, Tony Blair.

King's Bench Walk

The present buildings at 7-8 King's Bench Walk were constructed in 1782 and are mentioned in Dickens's *Mystery of Edwin Drood*. They stand on the south side of the gateway into Tudor Street on the site of Hampson's Buildings, which were constructed in 1671 together with Robinson's Buildings, which abutted the gate to the north. All were severely damaged by a fire in the summer of 1677.

What is now called Tudor Gate was from the earliest times known as Whitefriars Gate, leading as it did to the property of the Carmelites. Through it Charles Dickens caused to pass Rogue Riderhood in *Our Mutual Friend*, Pip in *Great Expectations* and Sydney Carton in *A Tale of Two Cities*.

Numbers 5 and 6 were rebuilt in 1684, both supposedly by Sir Christopher Wren. Number 5 became famous as the chambers of William Murray, afterwards Lord Mansfield, Solicitor-General 1742-54, Attorney-General 1754-6, and Chief Justice of the King's Bench 1756-88. He was a member of the government from 1742 until 1763 and continued to be active in politics until 1776. As such, rather than in his judicial office, he became the butt of satire. In *Venus and Horace* Alexander Pope wrote:

> *To Number Five direct your doves,*
> *There spread round Murray all your blooming loves.*

In one of his *Imitations of Horace*, written about 1737, Pope wrote of Murray:

> *Graced as thou art with all the power of words,*
> *So known, so honoured in the House of Lords.*

This was parodied by Colley Cibber as:

> *Persuasion tips his tongue whene'er he talks,*
> *And he has chambers in the King's Bench Walks.*

     Alexander Pope was not the only constant visitor to No. 5. Here Murray was also pestered with visits from Sarah, Duchess of Marlborough in 1738, after she sent him a general retainer of 1,000 guineas, of which he returned all but five. On one occasion she waited in vain for him until midnight. His clerk told Murray: 'I could not make out, sir, who she was, for she would not tell me her name; but she swore so dreadfully that I am sure she must be a lady of quality'.

     Nearly a century later these were also the chambers between 1818 and 1852 of Frederick Thesiger, who, as Lord Chelmsford, was Lord Chancellor 1858-9 and 1866-8. The address was afterwards associated with a significant number of Lords Justices of Appeal and Lords of Appeal in Ordinary, including in recent times Lord Havers, Lord Chancellor in 1986.

     Number 4 has four plaques over the doorway relating to the fire in the year 1677 and the rebuilding of the property in 1678 during the treasurership of Richard Powell. The first-floor room on the north side has a wonderful plaster ceiling which can be best seen from the steps leading up to No. 3.

At the corner of King's Bench Walk now occupied by No. 3 north stood the Alienation Office of the Court built in 1577 by Robert Dudley, Earl of Leicester, master of that office. His building was destroyed in the Great Fire of 1666. It was rebuilt by the Crown in 1668 and remained until 1835 when the office was abolished by Act of Parliament. In 1842 the building was bought from the Crown by Inner Temple. The brick front has been renewed but otherwise this is the building of 1668.

Behind the Alienation Office and between there and Serjeants' Inn was a garden, called Privy Garden, laid out in Dutch style after 1666. Here was constructed Niblett Hall and the Inn's arbitration room, erected under the provisions of the will of William Niblett, a barrister of Singapore who died in 1920. Niblett Hall became the main hall of the Inn after the destruction of Inner Temple Hall in 1941 and remained so until 1955. In March 1948 King George VI dined here as royal bencher of the society. Niblett Hall was demolished in 1996 and replaced by Littleton chambers.

6. Follow the building line around the corner to 2 King's Bench Walk.

1 King's Bench Walk contained the chambers of James Scarlett, called in 1791 and the greatest jury advocate of his day. Ennobled as Lord Abinger he was Chief Baron of the Exchequer 1834-44. A tablet inset by the door is surmounted by the royal cipher of George VI and states 'Be it remembered that on the 13th day of July 1949 His Majesty King George VI treasurer, opened this building as a temporary library until such time as a permanent library should be built'.

The area now bounded by 1 and 2 King's Bench Walk, Mitre Court Buildings, Francis Taylor Building and Inner Temple Library and Common Room was at one time known as Exchequer Court after the Exchequer Office which was on the site of the present 2 King's Bench Walk. Exchequer Court was itself built on the site of Old Fuller's Rents, which extended north to the site of Mitre Court Buildings, having been built by John Fuller, the treasurer in 1562 and extended in 1588.

Fuller's Rents contained the chambers of a number of famous men. In 1576 they were occupied by Francis Beaumont, a justice of the Court of Common Pleas whose son, also Francis,

3 King's Bench Walk.

was the Jacobean dramatist who wrote so successfully with John Fletcher between 1607 and 1616, their most famous works being *Philaster* and *A King and No King*.

Beaumont was in the chambers of Robert Dudley, Earl of Leicester, who also used 1 King's Bench Walk prior to the construction of the Alienation Office. Sir Edward Coke had chambers in Fuller's Rents from 1588 to 1634. The same chambers were taken by Sir Edward Lyttleton in 1634. He was a friend and contemporary of John Selden. Lyttleton became Chief Justice of the Common Pleas and Lord Keeper of the Great Seal in 1641. He joined King Charles I at York at the outbreak of the Civil War and was commissioned to raise a regiment of foot soldiers from the Inns of Court and Chancery. This he did and became its colonel. He died of a chill whilst training recruits at Oxford.

Mary and Charles Lamb lived here between 1800 and 1809 before moving to Inner Temple Lane, during which time they compiled the popular children's work *Tales from Shakespeare*, published in 1807.

Fuller's Rents were demolished in 1829 and Mitre Court Building erected the following year with its entrance on the exterior of the Inn. The poet Alfred Tennyson is known to have been a frequent visitor to 2 Mitre Court Buildings between 1842 and 1847 to see his friends Henry Lushington and George Venables.

Along the frontage of Mitre Court Building a plaque to the left of arch reads:

> *This inscription affixed by order of the masters of the Bench of the Inner Temple commemorates the reconstruction of this building after it had been destroyed by enemy action in 1941 and records with gratitude the name of C.J. Conway KC etc. Alfred Bucknill Treasurer 1951.*

A further permanent display of gratitude for particular assistance in the restoration of the war-ravaged site is to be found on Francis Taylor Building, erected in 1957 and named after Sir William Francis Kyffin Taylor, Lord Maenan, a master of the bench of Inner Temple for 46 years, 1905-51, 25 of those being after he had become treasurer in 1926. This is on the site of two ancient stairways known respectively as Packington's Rents, 1518, and, nearer the library, Babington's Rents, 1530, which had a wooden tower with cupola and bell, demolished in 1866.

7. Turn right under the archway formed by Inner Temple Library building into Church Court.

The passageway from King's Bench Walk has existed since medieval times and was originally between the library and a building known as Bradshaw's Rents after Henry Bradshaw, Chief Baron of the Exchequer in 1552. The building was occupied by Sir Laurence Tanfield, who was himself subsequently Chief Baron for 18 years.

On emerging into what is today called Church Court, the visitor is in an area that was once bordered by hall, Cloisters, Temple Church and Bradshaw's Rents and which was the burial ground of the Knights Templar.

In 1596 the church courtyard was cut in two by the erection of Caesar's Building, named for Sir Julius Caesar, then Master of the Rolls and treasurer, who was the son of Queen Elizabeth's Italian physician. The west portion became known as Cloister Court and the east, Tanfield Court.

Tanfield Court was the location of the robbery and murder of two women in February 1732, by Sarah Malcolm, a charwoman who strangled an old lady and cut the throat of her maid. She was executed in Mitre Court after her portrait had been painted by William Hogarth as Lady in Scarlet. Her corpse was exhibited for money at Snow Hill and subsequently buried in the churchyard of the Church of the Holy Sepulchre, the first executed criminal to be admitted to consecrated ground for 150 years. Afterwards she was disinterred and her skeleton placed on public view at the botanic gardens in Cambridge.

Tanfield Court, Temple c. 1880

Caesar's Building was popularly known as Lamb Building from the large wooden Agnus Dei mounted above the door. Although well within the bounds of Inner Temple, Caesar's Building was sold to Middle Temple to assist in financing the cost of reconstruction after the Great Fire in 1666. Its most well-known occupant was Judah Philip Benjamin, who practised on the ground floor here. Called to the Bar of New Orleans in 1832, he was an exceptionally able lawyer and advocate who became a Senator for Louisiana and Attorney-General for the Confederacy under President Jefferson Davis. He escaped to England towards the end of the American Civil War and was called to the English Bar in 1866. After taking pupillage with Mr Baron Pollock at 5 Child's Place, he settled here and had an exceptional practice until his retirement in 1883, when he was given a banquet in his honour by Inner Temple. His legacy to even the present generation of lawyers is *Benjamin's Sale of Goods*, a *magnum opus*.

An accurate picture of Temple life in the 1850s is conjured up by William Makepeace Thackeray in *Pendennis* which is chiefly set in Lamb Building. The Lamb Building of the 1850s was destroyed on the night of 11 May 1941 and has not been rebuilt. Middle Temple applied the name Lamb Building to a new building erected in 1955 abutting Middle Temple Lane with its entrance at the west end of Fig Tree Court.

On the left, adjoining the hall is the Inner Temple library and benchers' rooms, a prominent feature of which is the panelling and fireplace carvings in the Parliament Chamber attributed to Grinling Gibbons and dated 1705. Likewise over the stairwell of the benchers' entrance from Church Court is the carved Pegasus which was rescued from the burning hall in 1941.

The benchers' rooms contain two pictures of King's Bench Walk and Middle Temple Hall in 1734 by William Hogarth, and one of King's Bench Walk, Paper Buildings and Crown Office Row by Maurer.

Inner Temple had a library long before the reign of King Henry VII (1485-1508) on the site of the Knights Templar's strongroom, which once held jewellery and bullion to rival the Crown's treasury. At the east end of the original hall stood a little building constructed at some time between 1505 and 1530 as a library. This was blown up with gunpowder during the fire of 1679. It was rebuilt in 1680 and a notable contributor to the library fund was the then Serjeant Sir George Jeffreys, who gave £40.

Between 1866 and 1870 a new library was constructed at the same time as the hall was being rebuilt. In addition to new benchers' rooms, it consisted of ground and first-floor reading rooms, offices and a lecture room. When it opened, the Inn's holding was of 40,000 legal volumes and 25,000 non-legal items, acquired mainly by the donation by bequest of members' complete personal libraries. These included books on literature, the classics, archaeology, history, architecture, topography and fine arts, together with a substantial collection of manuscripts and a sizeable foreign-language collection. A north wing was added in 1882 on the site of Tanfield Court. The library building was completely destroyed in the Blitz with the loss of 35,000 volumes.

The present library was built on the site of its predecessor but is on the second and third storeys of the building. It has oak

Left: the stone Pegasus rescued from the bombing; Right: the carving over the fireplace in Parliament Chamber by Grinling Gibbons

fittings and tall windows, which makes it feel spacious and airy. The library staircase has a bas-relief of Gandhi, and portraits of Nehru and another favourite son of the Inn, Sir Alan (A.P.) Herbert (1890-1971).

Immediately on the right is the Master's House. This was formerly a substantial mansion, and at the time of the suppression of the Knights Templar in 1307 it was the residence of the master of the order in England, William de la More, together with 12 brethren, the preceptor, the treasurer, six chaplains, five clerks and their servants. When the Knights Hospitaller leased the Temple to the lawyers in the second decade of the 14th century they reserved for themselves the consecrated places under the responsibility of their own appointed 'custos' or 'magister' called Master of the New Temple. He was answerable for the maintenance of church

The Master's House

buildings and the upkeep of services. After the dissolution of the Order of St John in 1538, Master the Reverend William Ermsted and four stipendiary priests were left undisturbed in the Master's House. Under Queen Mary Tudor (1553-8) the house and church reverted to the prior of St John. In 1542 the house was leased by him to Sir John Baker, a bencher of Inner Temple and then the Speaker of the House of Commons. Under Queen Elizabeth I (1558-1603) for the first time both societies began to act jointly in the ecclesiastical affairs of the Temple, as a result of which new found cooperation the reversion of the house was purchased jointly in 1585 as the Master's residence. Under the patent of King James I of 1608 the two societies bound themselves to support and maintain the church and to provide the Master with a stipend and residence.

The Templars' mansion was rebuilt in 1664 for Dr Ball, but it was lost to the Great Fire only two years afterwards. It was replaced by a handsome building which itself was substantially altered in both 1700 and 1764. A brick wall was erected in the garden to divide off the property from Tanfield Court, but this was replaced with the iron gate and railings seen today. The Master's House was completely destroyed in the Blitz and the present building is not only a reproduction, it is also a façade of only one room in depth, handsome rooms though they may be.

8. Proceed across the courtyard towards Cloisters.

On the northern side of Cloister Court abutting the church was a row of shops with chambers above called Twisden's Buildings. There one could buy books, wigs and court dress. The buildings were removed in 1825 because of the potential danger to the church from fire.

The sundial in Pump Court

The original Cloisters was a covered passage linking the Temple Church with a smaller chapel immediately outside the north entrance to the hall. Chambers existed over the Cloisters before 1526, and by the reign of James I (1603-25) these extended to three storeys. Destroyed in the fire of 1679, the Cloisters was reconstructed with chambers by Sir Christopher Wren between 1679 and 1681. Next to the staircase at No. 1 stood a shop run by the well-known barber and wig maker Dick Danby, who was a friend of Lord Campbell, Chief Justice of the Queen's Bench 1850-9 and Lord Chancellor 1859-61. Destroyed in the bombing, the shop was rebuilt but was removed upon the reconstruction of the modern Cloisters in 1951-2.

On the south side of the courtyard a monument to the Knights Templar was erected in 2000 as part of the Inn's millennium celebrations. It takes the form of a single column surmounted by a recreation of one of the seals of the Knights, two serving brothers sharing a horse, a reflection of two of the precepts of the order, fraternity and poverty.

Monument to the Kinghts Templar

9. Pass under Cloisters into Pump Court.

Immediately on the left is the entrance to 1 Pump Court and Cloisters. The courtyard was laid out by Sir Christopher Wren in 1681, with the stairwells of Nos. 2 and 3 on the south side, Nos. 4 and 5 in the corners of the west side and No. 6, with a protruding staircase, to the north. The little courtyard is named for the pumps which stood here to draw water, to fight Temple fires, from a reservoir of 27 feet (8 m.) deep which is fed by an underground stream beneath the flagstones. Dickens called the place 'more quiet and more gloomy than the rest' in *Martin Chuzzlewit*, chapter 39.

Numbers 2-3 Pump Court are on the site of the Templars' Hall of the Military Knights, used by Middle Temple from some time between 1322 and 1326 until Middle Temple Hall was completed in 1575. The hall here was pulled down in 1627, although the site was not cleared for new building until 1639.

4 and 5 Pump Court

The fire of 26 January 1679 had a greater effect on the Temple than the Great Fire of London of 1666, and it started at Pump Court next to the lodgings of Elias Ashmole between Pump Court and Elm Court, one of the oldest courtyards in the Temple. The fire destroyed the whole of Pump Court, the greater part of Elm Court, Hare Court, Vine Court, Brick Court, Cloisters and part of Inner Temple Hall. A significant problem in operations to fight the fire was the fact that the Thames was frozen over so the chief means of dowsing the flames was to draw casks from the brewery at the west end of hall to feed the engines, and eventually buildings had to be blown up.

The Wren-designed buildings to the west and north of the courtyard are original. On the top floor of 6 Pump Court is a sundial with the inscription 'Oliver Montague Treasurer 1686: Shadows we are and like shadows depart'.

The whole of the south and east sides of Pump Court were destroyed on 15 October 1940. In its account of the bombing, Middle Temple Ordeal, produced by that Inn in 1947, the anonymous authors wrote:

> *Walking through the ruins by moonlight the sense of being in a doomed city was sometimes oppressive. The unspoken question in all minds was then most clear; were the troubles nearly over or was this a lull before another and perhaps even more terrible storm? The sundials were easier to read now that so many buildings were down; 'Shadows we are and like shadows depart', on the north side of Pump*

Court, from which you could see river craft on the Thames without interruption of view.

The buildings at Cloisters and 1-3 Pump Court which stand today were designed by Sir Edward Maufe and completed in 1952.

Lord Alverstone, the Attorney-General in Gladstone's last and both of Lord Rosebery's ministries, was Lord Chief Justice 1900-15. His chambers were on the ground floor left at 2 Pump Court.

The ground floor left pair at No. 3 was occupied by Sir William Blackstone 1766-70 at a time when he was compiling his *Commentaries on the Laws of England*. It is said that he moved here from 2 Brick Court to escape the rowdy parties given by Oliver Goldsmith on the floor above.

The more famous occupants of Pump Court included Henry Fielding (1707-54), author of the social comedies *Joseph Andrews* (1742), *Tom Jones* (1749) and *Amelia* (1752), who had chambers at No. 4 from 1737 to 1748. The poet William Cowper (1731-1800) was here in 1759, and W.S. Gilbert (1836-1911) undertook his pupillage with Sir Charles Watkin-Wilkins in the same chambers in 1863.

10. Pass through Pump Court emerging back into Middle Temple Lane and turn right.

The frontage of Middle Temple Lane is here occupied by the recently refurbished 1 and 2 Hare Court. Sir Nicholas Hare, the elder, was a remarkably gifted advocate who was retained in his defence by Cardinal Wolsey in 1530. In 1540 he was elected Speaker of the House of Commons and is said to have submitted passively to his Sovereign's suppression of the monasteries and divorce from Anne of Cleves. He became Master of the Rolls under Mary Tudor, and his elaborate tomb is to be found in the Temple Church. His son, also Nicholas, was admitted in 1567 to the chambers of a bencher of Inner Temple, James Ryvett, on condition that he rebuilt Hare Court, the triangular courtyard which abuts the Lane to the west. These chambers were rebuilt in 1679 following the fire.

On the second floor of what was then 3 Hare Court, on the site occupied by the present No. 2, were the chambers of Judge Jeffreys. They remained almost untouched from his death in the Tower of London (where he was lodged to protect him from an angry populace) in 1689 until the entire building was demolished in 1893 and replaced by the block which remains today.

At the top of the Lane stand the 17th-century buildings of 1, 2, and 3 Middle Temple Lane. Two quaint staircases give access to the sets of chambers on their upper floors. Although the present buildings look very much as if they predate the Great Fire of London 1666, the original buildings on the site dated from 1570 and were destroyed in the fire of 1679. Numbers 2 and 3 were rebuilt then, and No. 1 in 1693. With their projecting upper storeys they are a startling illustration of how fires in medieval and pre-Great Fire London were capable of spreading with such rapidity, and also how, in the absence of any public health, epidemic disease could also be spread. The 1679 rebuilding in this fashion was only allowed when express permission was sought by and granted to the builders to construct jetties (projecting upper storeys).

For the history of Middle Temple gatehouse and Child's Place see chapter 5.

The gatehouse of Middle Temple was erected by Sir Christopher Wren in 1684, built on the site of an earlier one of 1570. In Barnaby Rudge, chapter 40, Hugh crossed Fleet Street by Temple Bar for the purpose of visiting Sir John Chester, and plied the knocker of the Middle Temple Gate, only to be regarded suspiciously and told 'We don't sell beer here'. From 1733 until 1840 there were two shops inside the gatehouse, a stationer's and a shoemaker's.

11. Return down Middle Temple Lane into Brick Court.

Only 1 and 4 Brick Court remain of the block lost in the Second World War which formed a self-contained courtyard between Essex Court and Hare Court, where the upper car park of Middle Temple is to be found today. Brick Court was so named as supposedly the first brick-built structure in the Temple, erected about 1570. It contained a garden and was rebuilt after fire damage in 1679, 1704, 1883 and 1908. Oliver Goldsmith lived for the last nine years of his life at No. 2 'up two pair right', and here he died on 4 April 1774, a year after completing his most lasting work, *She Stoops to Conquer*. His apartment was extravagantly furnished with blue velvet, showy carpets and gilt mirrors and he gave celebrated and somewhat rowdy literary dinners to Dr Samuel Johnson (1709-86) and the composer Dr Thomas Arne (1710-78), among others, to the apparent disturbance of Sir William Blackstone who was working on his Commentaries on the floor immediately below. 'Apparent' disturbance is correct for curiously, while his biographer, Sir James Prior, claims that Blackstone resided immediately below Goldsmith from 1746 to 1766, the Inn's records do not show Blackstone at 2 Brick Court.

Also here between 1853 and 1859 were the chambers of William Makepeace Thackeray. At No.1 John Duke, prosecutor of the Tichborne claimant, was in chambers prior to his elevation as Lord Coleridge and appointment as Chief Justice of the Common Pleas 1873-80 and Lord Chief Justice of England 1880-94. His immediate successor as Lord Chief from 1894 to 1899 was Lord Russell of Killowen, who between 1866 and 1885 had chambers at No. 3 Brick Court.

The projecting upper storeys of 1-3 Middle Temple Lane

The Temple

A sundial mounted on Brick Court and lost with the war read 'Time and tide tarry for no man'. This replaced a 17th century one which stated 'Begone about your business'. This was said to have been addressed by an absent-minded treasurer of the day to the dial-maker's boy calling for an appropriate inscription. It is a nice tale but, in fact, a common inscription, and a similar example still appears at the church of St James at Bury St Edmunds.

Essex Court, like Essex Street, is named for its long association with Essex House, the palace of Bishop Stapleton of Exeter in the reign of King Edward II. In 1326 the palace was stormed by a mob and the unlucky prelate was seized, carried off and beheaded. That able historian, Sir Walter Besant (1836-1901), in his *Fascination of London* (London, 1902-8) believed that the house was cursed since nearly all of its owners shared an unhappy fate. Lord Paget obtained the palace after the Reformation, but lost the favour of King Henry VIII and very nearly his head; Thomas Howard, who succeeded to it, died in the Tower after many years' imprisonment. The House passed from Robert Dudley, Earl of Leicester by bequest to his son-in-law, Robert Devereux, Earl of Essex, who plotted here against Queen Elizabeth I and was taken after artillery was mounted against the mansion, and executed in 1601. By 1640 the mansion had been divided up into tenements, as was recorded in the diary of John Evelyn of that year. Evelyn was himself a member of Middle Temple and was master of Revels for 1642 although never called to the Bar.

The Victorian arcade leading from 'Outer Temple' to Essex Court

These tenements included a group of buildings called Old Essex Court, one of which was known as Palgrave Buildings, and this was partly destroyed in the fire of 1679. It was linked to the Strand by a passageway from a tavern called the Palgrave's Head.

The original buildings of Essex Court were replaced by tall, gabled, red brick buildings on the east side in 1656 and the west side in 1677. At 4A Essex Court was a converted shop which for over a century contained the wig makers, Allin's, afterwards becoming a barber's. In 1882-3 most of Essex Court, except for Nos. 2 and 3, was demolished and reconstructed.

12. Proceed under archway between 2 and 3 Essex Court into New Court.

New Court is a handsome Wren-designed town house built in 1676 (not 1667 as dated on the lintel) together with the Judge's Gate leading out into Devereux Court. It stood on ground formerly part of Essex House garden. By the second half of the 17th century the land belonged to Thomas Thynn, Viscount Sidmouth. Essex House was sold to a Dr Nicholas Barbon who in 1676 sold a parcel of land to Middle Temple where now stands Garden Court, New Court and part of Essex Court. Barbon built Essex Street in 1680 and also the water gate of Essex House, which remained standing until 1777.

13. Bear right, through Judge's Gate.

Devereux Court and Devereux Chambers are outside the precincts of Middle Temple. They are named after one of a number of men each called Robert Devereux, Earl of Essex. It is likely that they would not have memorialised the second earl of Essex, a convicted traitor, but the famous Parliamentary general of some 60 years later. Devereux Court was the location of two famous 18th-century coffee houses, 'Tom's', familiar to Alexander Pope, and 'The Grecian', known to be standing in 1665 and one of the earliest in London, run by a Greek called Constantine and the meeting place for classical scholars. It was frequented by writers, poets and dramatists, including Sir Richard Steele (1672-1729), founder of *The Tatler*, and Joseph Addison (1672-1719), and from here they founded *The Spectator* magazine.

14. Return from Devereux Court into the precincts of Middle Temple and proceed down the steps to Fountain Court.

The single fountain that plays in the centre of a circular pool has been a feature of this courtyard since the original was placed here about 1681. The present fountain was part of Middle Temple's Millennium 2000 project of reflagging and planting Fountain Court. The fountain itself is said to be precisely on the boundary of the cities of London and Westminster. The pond was originally part of the Middle Temple benchers' garden between hall and Brick Court, once called Hall Court. This shaded, tranquil spot was where Dickens had his lovers John Westlock and Ruth Pinch meet in *Martin Chuzzlewit*: 'Merrily the tiny fountain played, and merrily the dimples sparkled on its sunny face'. This must have been a happy place for the young Charles Dickens to saunter in, both as an attorney's clerk and a court reporter, for it also achieves a mention in *Barnaby Rudge* and *Great Expectations*.

The fountain features in Walter Thornbury's *Two Centuries of Song*:

> *And when others fled from town to lake and moor and mountain –*
> *I have laid my trouble beside the Temple fountain.*

Fountain Court with New Court and Judge's Gate to the rear

From the 1730s the pond was caged with railings matching the ironwork of the two huge gas carriage lamps, suspended on iron brackets, which remain, sentinel-like at the top of the steps.

Immediately on the right of the fountain is Fountain Court Chambers, built in 1884. It was here in 1885 in the chambers of Sir Forrest Fulton that Edward Marshall Hall took his first seat in chambers, the first of four sets with which he was to become associated during his illustrious career. Today it is the Temple's leading banking and commercial chambers.

15. Pass down the steps to Garden Court on the right, Middle Temple Gardens and hall on the left.

The Middle Temple Gardens are neither as old nor as extensive as the famous lawns and walks of Inner Temple. Mainly laid out between 1770 and 1865, an avenue of elms with rookeries led between Plowden Buildings and the original Garden Court, which lay to the south and abutted Middle Temple Lane. The upper terrace was laid on land that had been derelict up to 1649, its pedestal sundial placed there in 1719. A garden gate was erected under the library stairs, and though the library was bombed flat in the Second World War the gate and stairs remain.

The chambers at present named Garden Court, like New Court, were built on the site of a terraced garden running along the west boundary of the Temple down to the river. The land was part of that purchased from Dr Barbon in 1676 though the chambers built here were replaced in 1830 and again, with those now standing, in 1883. At No. 2, second floor left, were the chambers of Rufus Isaacs QC, later the first Marquess of Reading (1860-1935), whose distinguished career included the posts of both Solicitor and Attorney-General, Britain's ambassador to the United States, Viceroy of India, Lord Chief Justice and Foreign Secretary. On the top floor of the far entrance Dickens placed Pip in chapter 39 of *Great Expectations*:

> *Alterations have been made in that part of the Temple since that time, and it has not now so lonely a character as it had then, nor is it so exposed to the river. We lived at the top of the last house, and the wind rushing up the river shook the house that night.*

16. Proceed along the terrace to the end.

The steps that lead to nowhere but a forlorn bench are all that remain of the entrance to the Gothic building that was Middle Temple Library, opened by Edward, Prince of Wales in October 1861 to a design by the celebrated architect H.R. Abraham. In December 1940 the building was completed destroyed by incendiary bombs, but the 70,000 volumes it contained were saved. In its place Queen Elizabeth Building was constructed and was, for many years, well known as a centre for large and successful criminal chambers. On the right is Blackstone House, which houses Blackstone Chambers, the formidable public law and human rights set.

17. Return to Fountain Court and turn right.

Mounted on the southern side of 1 Essex Court, marking the treasurership of William Thursby in 1685, is a sundial. The motto, *Discite justitiam moniti*, commands 'Learn ye justice, ye who are now being instructed'. To the right are set the triple coats of arms of three eminent treasurers of the Middle Temple, Mr Justice Phillimore (1908) (later Lord Phillimore), John Digby (1909) and Lord Justice Fletcher Moulton (1910) (later Lord Moulton of Bank).

Sundial at 1 Essex Court

Directly opposite is Midle Temple Hall, that pearl of late Tudor architecture. This fine hall is unique amongst the Inns as being mainly original, save that in 1757 an exterior casing of stone was added as an 'improvement' which hid much of its red-brick façade. The fact that so much of it survived the Blitz was due to a mixture of miracle and diligent fire watching. It remains a focal point for the history of the Inn from the mid 16th century, though the Middle Templars had much earlier roots, and indeed an earlier hall. It is thought that lawyers and their students who became the founders of the Honourable Society of the Middle Temple first migrated from St George's Inn, near Newgate, a little after the turn of the 14th century and occupied buildings that had formerly belonged to the Knights Templar in the vicinity of the modern Goldsmith Building between 1322 and 1326. They took for their use the Templars' Hall of the Military Knights which was then located where Pump and Elm courts now stand. They were governed by elected masters of the bench, formerly known as masters of the hostels, and students were introduced for instruction and learning. They resided in commons, meaning that they attended hall to dine twice daily, sitting with their brethren in order of seniority as students, clerks, fellows or socii and then masters in commons. This former hall remained in use until it was demolished in 1639.

Although the society's own records date back only to 1501, the expression Middle Temple is known to have been used in a will of 1404. It is fair, therefore, to assume that the name was probably known before 1400. Certainly Wat Tyler's peasants in the revolt of 1381 had as one of its more successful aims the sacking of the Temple and throwing out of the lawyers. Moreover Chaucer's Manciple in the *Canterbury Tales* of c. 1388 is engaged as a chief cook in the Middle Temple. The Black Book of Lincoln's Inn for 1422 mentions the Middle Temple and in 1429 one of the new serjeants-at-law was elected from Middle Temple.

What of its famous symbol, the Agnus Dei or 'lamb and flag'? This badge was in use as early as 1241 and was taken by the Knights Templars as their second seal in 1273. Technically it is the Agnus Dei with cruciform nimbus and banner surrounded by the legend *sigillum templi* (seal of the Temple) with beaded border. It was adopted as the emblem of the Honourable Society of the Middle Temple in 1615, although the lamb was turned to the left and placed at the centre of a red cross on a silver ground.

Emblem of Middle Temple

The Temple

Edmund Plowden (1518-85), in whose memory Plowden Buildings are named and whose bust by Martin Edwards is to be found in hall, was treasurer from 1561 to 1567 and chairman of the committee established to manage the building of this new hall. An eminent jurist, he was offered the Woolsack by Queen Elizabeth I if he would renounce his Catholicism, but declined. Work commenced in 1562 and lasted until 1571 and Plowden was continued in office for as long as it took him to supervise. He was not popular with the entire membership: as procurator, Plowden imposed compulsory levies on all members of Middle Temple to cover the not inconsiderable cost of the building works.

The entrance tower with a fine clock was added in 1667 and replaced in 1832 by the architect James Savage (1779-1852). On the night of 15 October 1940 the Hall was damaged by incendiary bombs, the clock tower and eastern gable wall were demolished, and the minstrel gallery and screen destroyed. The east end of hall and its tower were rebuilt between 1946 and 1948. Hence on the exterior of the tower the plaques now marking the treasurerships of W. Craig Henderson, James Cassels and E. Tyndal-Atkinson are for each of those years respectively.

Middle Temple Hall

At over 100 feet (30 m.) in length, 40 feet (12 m.) in breadth and, with the louvre window 59 feet (18 m.) high, Middle Temple Hall contains the finest remaining Elizabethan double hammerbeam roof, consisting of eight roof trusses. The joists are each 44 feet (13.4 m.) in length made from single oaks, estimated to be nearly 900 years old. The famous intricate oak screen, shattered by bombing, but restored by hand with the assistance of funds from the American and Canadian Bar Associations after the war, was erected in 1574. The screen doors were added much later, in 1671, and are mentioned in Thackeray's *Pendennis*.

The furnishings and decor of Middle Temple Hall have also become well known. The walls are wainscotted up to the windowsills and bear the names and arms of readers and treasurers from 1597. Below the windows originally stood bronze busts of 12 Caesars, but these were replaced in the 20th century by sets of 17th- century body armour and weapons from military companies raised from the Inn for the Parliamentary cause in the Civil War. It is ironic that the painting dominating the west end of hall above the bench table is the magnificent equestrian portrait of King Charles I, a copy of the Van Dyke at Windsor either by the master himself or by one of his students, Henry Stone.

Other portraits hanging are of King Charles II by Sir Godfrey Kneller, of James, Duke of York, afterwards King James II by John Riley, and King William III, Queen Anne, Queen Elizabeth I, King George I and King George II.

Hall was refloored in 1730 when the present benches and tables were provided. An ancient louvre was opened in the centre of the roof to give vent to smoke from an open charcoal fire beneath. This was replaced by a cupola and vane in 1732. The fire was extinguished in 1830 and hall was lit by candles, subsequently gas. Electric lights were introduced from 1894 and the Inn was completely wired for electricity in 1902.

The glass in the bay windows display the armorial devices of the Middle Temple Lord Chancellors: Cowper, Somers, Hardwicke, Eldon, and Stowell, together with those of Lord Chief Justice Kenyon. The arms of King Edward VIII are depicted in the middle window south, adjoining those of the Duke of Clarence, his uncle, since both were royal benchers. Plowden's arms are in the middle of the top lights together with the legend 1573 and an

The Temple

inscription in Latin commemorating the opening of hall under his auspices which may be translated as *'This man completed this work for those who cultivate the laws: to them be honour through all time'*.

Among the curios of this hall three stand out for mention: a brass lantern suspended from the minstrel gallery has glass lights bearing the arms of Queen Elizabeth I, Sir Walter Raleigh, Sir Francis Drake, and the two crests of the Knights Templar. In the south bay is a leaden coffer, its lid made from timber of the original Temple Stairs, erected by the Knights. And, perhaps most famous of all, is a small, nondescript serving table, said to be made from a hatch cover of Drake's ship which circumnavigated the globe in 1580, *The Golden Hind*.

The benchers' table, traversing hall upon a raised dais, is 29 feet (8.8 m.) long and made of a single oak, the gift of Queen Elizabeth I floated from Windsor down the Thames. From here the self-elected body which governs the Inn looks down on those lesser mortals who in more ancient times scrambled up the ladder of seniority which was established by the mid 16th century. Passage to the Bar of England and Wales took some seven or eight years, the first two of which were spent as students at a satellite Inn of Chancery. Then, for two years, students would dine here at tables known as clerks commons. They passed on to the table known as masters commons, and sat in order of seniority as 'mootmen' for a further five years after which they were called to the outer or 'utter' Bar. Having achieved some degree of seniority these would in turn be chosen as readers, providing legal education in hall after the meal during the law terms, giving lectures and contesting moots and bolts, legal argument in Norman (law) French, and, at last, elected as benchers. Those, however, not chosen to be readers became known as 'ancients' and occupied their own table at the north side of the hall. Although this practice fell into disuse after public readings ended in 1608, the table itself was restored for the use of senior practitioners in 1876 and occupies the centre of hall.

The term 'commons' was adopted from its medieval sense to refer to the attendance of students at the moots and exercises in hall heard before benchers during term. During vacation a senior barrister presided, when attendance was compulsory at moots in hall for up to three years after call; young barristers were penalised financially by the Inn for their absence. Those attending became known as 'vacationers'. Of the lecturers there were four known as the 'cupboardmen' who argued cases with the reader. The 'cupboard' or square table at which they sat is also said to have been presented by the Virgin Queen. The Inn's very substantial collection of silver plate is today displayed on the cupboard on Grand Nights.

The attendance of royalty has long been a feature of Middle Temple Hall since Queen Elizabeth I came to open it formally in 1576. In those days it was as much a social gathering place for the gentry as a university for the study of law, and was particularly in season between All Hallows (1 November) and Candlemas (2 February) when readers' entertainments were given at enormous expense. The grandest was a masque given in 1633 to King Charles I which cost £21,000. These feasts, together with Christmas revels, attracted the lighter work of the great dramatists of the age and encouraged the talent of the more literary lawyers. The performance of greatest renown occurred after the revels of Christmas 1601. On 2 February 1602 *Twelfth Night or, What You Will* was presented here by Shakespeare. It is impossible to believe that the playwright was not present in person, for his audience in hall that night included the Queen, the Lord Chancellor, Sir Christopher Hatton, the Chancellor of Oxford University, Thomas Sackville, the Lord High Admiral, William Howard, the Duke of Effingham, Lord Burghley, Sir Robert Cecil, Sir Walter Raleigh, Sir Francis Drake and Sir Philip Sidney. It is popularly believed that the premiere of the play was given that night, but a first-hand account casts some doubt on that fact.

In 1828 a diary was discovered at the British Museum belonging to a member of Middle Temple, John Manningham, who was present for the occasion. His entry for 2 February 1602 was as follows:

> *at our feast wee had a play called Twelue night or what you will much like the commedy of errors, or Menechmi in plautus, but most like and neere to that in Italian called Inganni.*

Manningham went on to describe the plot, but makes no mention either of the presence of the Queen, or that the piece was being given its first performance. Of course it is always open to conjecture that the barrister's recollection may have been impeded by the Inn's hospitality on such an occasion.

The Temple

On 1 and 2 February 1951 Donald Wolfit presented *Twelfth Night* supposedly as its 350th anniversary performance: unfortunately he had been caught by a mistake of one of the Temple historians, and it was only the 349th anniversary.

The Middle Temple has a long tradition of electing honorary Royal Benchers, dated back to King Edward VII, then Prince of Wales, in 1861. In July 2009 HRH Prince William of Wales became the sixth member of the Royal Family to be elected to the Bench of the Inn, following the footsteps of the late Queen Mother, called in 1944, and his own mother Diana, Princess of Wales, called in 1988. The post-war restoration of the hall was completed in 1949, the year of the honorary treasurership of the Queen Mother, and it was formally reopened by her. To mark the occasion a new east window was inserted above which a panel in stone is inscribed: 'E. T R. Treasurer Elizabeth *Regina Denud surrexit domus. AD MCMXLIX, Vivat crescat floreat*'. The house which was destroyed is raised up AD 1949. May it live, thrive and flourish.

The benchers' rooms are reached by a corridor from Middle Temple Hall to the Parliament Chamber via a pair of ancient carved doors, said to be relics of Old Hall in Pump Court. The chamber boasts portraits of Sir Walter Raleigh, and the following Lord Chancellors: Edward Hyde, Earl of Clarendon (who was Lord Chancellor 1658-67), Francis North, Lord Guildford (Lord Keeper 1682-5), Sir John Somers, Lord Somers (Lord Keeper 1693-7, Lord Chancellor 1697-1700), William Cowper, Lord Cowper (Lord Keeper 1705-7, Lord Chancellor 1707-8 and 1714-18), Lord Hardwicke (Lord Chancellor 1737-56), Lord Eldon (1801-6 and 1807-27) and Lord Westbury (1861-5). There is also a suit of ancient armour and weapons. The Parliament Chamber is dominated by a striking full length portrait of King Edward VII by Frans Hal. The room housed a magnificent pair of globes dated 1592 and purchased by William Sanderson, Raleigh's financier. These have since been placed in the gallery of the library.

The roll of eminent Middle Templars is impressive and extends well beyond those purely engaged in the law. Of course the Inn has its fair share of the great jurists: Lord Chancellors Lord Clarendon, Lord Hardwicke, Lord Eldon and, of course, Sir William Blackstone, the great commentator on the law.

In the field of literature the Middle Temple ranks include Henry Fielding, who was admitted as a student in November 1737 and called to the Bar on 20 June 1740; John Evelyn, admitted 13 February 1637 but never called, although he took a seat in chambers for three years; William Congreve, admitted on 17 March 1691 but, like Evelyn, never called; William Cowper, admitted in April 1748 and called on 14 June 1754; Edmund Burke, called 1747; William Makepeace Thackeray, admitted 3 June 1831 and called, at long last, on 26 May 1848; Thomas de Quincy, called 1808; Richard Brinsley Sheridan, called 1773; and Charles Dickens, admitted as a student on 6 December 1839 but never called.

Other walks of life have been represented in the Middle Temple. For example, Inigo Jones was called *honoris causa* in 1613. And, as has already been noted, the social gatherings at the Inn would not have been complete without the attendance of Queen Elizabeth I's famous sea captains.

18. Cross Middle Temple Lane beneath archway into Elm Court.

Immediately opposite Fountain Court is an archway leading into Elm Court between the post-war Lamb Building of 1953 and 4 Pump Court, surmounted by a crest dated 1952. Elm Court is first mentioned in the records of Middle Temple for 1620, and was named for the elm trees it contained. Long before it was the site of the Hall of the Military Knights of the Templars but by 1632 it contained two buildings. These escaped the fire of 1679 and contained two sets of chambers and two shops. The structures

Elm Court and ancient buttery

were so dilapidated that by 1879 they were considered dangerous and were demolished. The space which Elm Court now occupies was at one time divided by the chambers which were removed. In their place is now a delightful but small ornamental garden.

An even smaller courtyard existed between Elm Court and Inner Temple Hall called Fig Tree Court. The ancient buttery abutting on to hall bears a plaque which states 'Fig Tree Court adjoined this ancient buttery 1515-1666. It was destroyed in the Great Fire of London, rebuilt in 1679 and again destroyed by enemy action 1940.'

Fig Tree Court contained one of the oldest sets of chambers in the Temple, mentioned in 1515 as 'the chambers next to the fig tree'. A back door led into Elm Court, and it was occupied by many well-known parliamentarians between 1580 and 1640. Edward Thurlow, who was Lord Chancellor 1778-92, lived here. Called together with his fellow pupil, William Cowper, the poet, in 1734, he died in 1806 and was buried with great pomp in the south aisle of the Temple Church. Thurlow's portrait hangs in the Parliament Chamber of Inner Temple.

The Temple Church from Church Court

19. Bear left past the buttery up the steps to Cloisters and across to Temple Church.

The story of this place of worship is bound up with the history of the Knights Templar, the order formed as a result of the enthusiasm of the ecclesiastical authorities for, and the military successes of, the First Crusade of 1099.

On 15 July 1099, a Christian army under Godefroi de Bouillon captured Jerusalem from the Saracens. Within a year Godefroi's brother, Baudouin de Boulogne succeeded him as leader of the multinational force and crowned himself King of Jerusalem. He was followed by his cousin, Baudoin du Bourg (1118-31), who in 1119 founded the Knights Red Cross of the Order of St Augustine. Two French knights of this order, Hugo de Paganis (Hugues de Payens) and Godefridus de Sancto Andomaro (Godefroi de Champagne), who had been companions of Godefroi de Bouillon, bound themselves by solemn oaths to defend pilgrims coming to Jerusalem from the Turks. Their objective was to combine the obligations of a soldier and monk, and to do so they set out elaborate rules for the formation of a new order which required military service, poverty, chastity and obedience. They were given quarters by Baudouin du Bourg in his palace near the site of the Temple of Solomon, and they called their new order, the Brethren of the Militia of Christ and of the Temple of Solomon (*pauperes commilitones christi templique salomonici*).

In 1128 Hugues de Payens, as grand master (designate) persuaded the Council of Troyes, with the support of the Cistercians, formally to establish the order, which was then granted a white habit by Pope Honorius II (1124-30). His successor, Pope Eugenius III (1145-53) added permission to wear a red cross made of leather and initially sewn on the left sleeve of the mantle. Those below the rank of knight, esquires and serving brothers wore black or grey. Then a development advanced the well-being of the order immeasurably. In 1172 Pope Alexander III issued the bull '*Omne datum optimum*' which sanctioned the admission of clergy to the order. This introduced a substantial body of recruits, priests who wanted to be associated with a very popular military but ascetic aristocracy. This caused the order to spread throughout the then Christian world, extending to the three eastern provinces of Palestine, Antioch, Edessa and Tripoli, and the nine western:

Apulia and Sicily, Northern and Central Italy, Portugal, Castile and León, Aragon, Germany and Hungary, Greece, France and the low countries, and England. More than that, the chaplains were placed under the general obligations of the order and the jurisdiction of the secular grand master, whose only ecclesiastical superior was the pope himself. This effectively meant that the Knights Templar could operate outside both the ecclesiastical and feudal regimes in their host States, and were under neither fiscal obligations nor those of fealty. Their privileges included sanctuary, exemption from interest, tithes and taxes, and independence from episcopal rule; and, of course, they bore arms outside the control of the local civil authority and had significant military training.

The entire order was under the actual and effective control of the grand master in Jerusalem until the capture of the city by Saladin in 1187, when the headquarters of the Templars moved to Acre. In order to strengthen further its position Pope Innocent III (1198-1216) was admitted as a member of the order and bound by the same vows and obligations which governed the whole body. It became a crime to hinder or wound a Knight Templar, punishable with excommunication. Therefore the Templars' property was under both sanctuary and military guard.

The original establishments of the Templars took the form of priories under a governing prior. It is not known precisely when the English branch of the order was founded, although it can reasonably be assumed to be in the second or third decade of the 12th century. The first English preceptor was Richard of Hastings in the 1160s, a friend of Thomas à Becket, the ill-fated archbishop of Canterbury, and who tried but failed to keep him from conflict with King Henry II. After 1180 the administrative unit of the Templars was more usually a commandery governed by a preceptor. The privileges of 1172 were confirmed and extended by popes and recognised by kings throughout the 13th century.

The first known seal of the English Templars is dated 1202, and was affixed to a charter cast in sulphur and is in the possession of the British Museum. This depicts two knights in armour, with hemispherical helmets and long pointed shields, sharing one horse with the legend '*Sigillum Militum crsisti*'. The depiction represents poverty, fraternity and military prowess. Later devices show the horse as a piebald and two brethren without armour. The pedestal in Church Court, which was commissioned as a Millennium 2000 project, is surmounted by a representation of the Templars' seal. It is said that early attempts to print the seal of the Templars smudged the two riders and their shields together so that the image became one of a horse with wings, from which is derived Pegasus, the cipher of the Honourable Society of the Inner Temple.

As is not difficult to imagine, the order became a dangerous rival to the civil powers in the land, and even to those who had rendered it independent of all authority – the papal authorities themselves. The order attracted great wealth, becoming a repository for the valuables of others, notably jewellery and revenues of the aristocracy, since its treasuries were protected by experienced soldiery, and in the two centuries or so after its foundation the Templars were not motivated by the high monastic principles of its founder. For example, in 1232 Hubert de Burgh, Earl of Kent, was sent to the Tower of London by King Henry III and his property, which was secured in the treasury of the Knights Templar, was escheated to the Crown. The Templars declined to give it up to the king, and no amount of pressure could force them to do so.

At the height of its fortune the order is said to have possessed 9,000 properties in Europe to house its 20,000 brethren. However, its downfall, when it came, was swift, and due principally to its rivalry with the Order of the Knights Hospitaller of St John of Jerusalem in the east, an open quarrel since 1178, in which the Hospitallers had been encouraged by the avarice of the episcopal establishment. During the last Crusade, which ended with the surrender of Acre in 1291, the order's eastern knights were virtually wiped out by the Saracens. It was a blow to the military power of the order from which it never recovered. In name as well the order had lost its raison d'être. It no longer had the power to secure the passage of pilgrims to the Holy Land.

Such was the power of the Knights that King John used their protection for the repository of state regalia and treasure in the Temple, and much of the convoluted negotiations leading to the signing of Magna Carta in June 2015 at Runnymede took place in the Church. An exhibition charting the development of Magna Carta together with facsimiles of the charter and subsequent documents is on display in the Round. It draws visitors from around the world as perhaps the birthplace of modern bills of rights.

The Knights Hospitaller over the following decade were encouraged in their desire to become the predominant secular order of knights in Christendom at the expense of their now weakened rival. A scheme was hatched by King Philippe IV of France, known as 'the Fair', a man of considerable evil by all repute, and Pope Clement V, both of whom were keen to break the power of the Knights Templar and seize their wealth. Indeed they wished to destroy the Hospitallers at the same time.

In the summer of 1306 the grand masters of the Knights Templar and Knights Hospitaller were invited jointly by Philippe IV and the Pope to meet in Paris to discuss plans for retaking the Holy Land. The grand master of the Hospitallers sensibly excused himself. Jacques de Molay, grand master of the Order of the Knights Templar arrived in Paris with 60 knights and was asked to remain whilst plans were formulated.

On 13 October 1307 the grand master and 140 Templars were seized at the Temple in Paris, and simultaneously every known Templar in France was taken and imprisoned. They were held without trial until 1311 and charged with heretical practices, Christ denial, indecent reception ceremonies and idol worship.

There were about 280 Templars at that time in London, and they were considered to be a reasonably formidable force to overcome in the absence of a standing army. King Edward II became Philippe's son-in-law in 1308 but was very nervous of the French king's action. He wrote to Paris on 30 October 1307 saying that Philippe's charges against the Templars were incredible and his Council would not act upon them. As a result Pope Clement issued a bull from Poitiers on 22 November 1307 exhorting Edward to follow the example of France and seize all the Templars in one day and hold them and their property for an inquisitorial investigation. Edward still held out. On 4 December he wrote to the Kings of Aragon, Castile, Portugal and Sicily saying that he was not convinced and urging them not to listen too readily to charges being brought against the order. However on 20 December 1307 the Papal legate in London issued writs directed at the sheriffs of London and the counties to effect the arrest of the Templars and 229 were seized in London. Edward need not have worried about the knights' fighting prowess, since the records of the seizure disclose that only three swords and two ballistae were found in the Temple precinct, of which one was broken.

Meanwhile the Knights Hospitaller had secured and strongly fortified the island of Rhodes and had made preparations to resist. Philippe decided that he did not need to fight.

At the General Council of Vienne, near Lyon, in October 1311 the charges were laid formally against the Templars. Despite no defence being permitted a majority of the judges refused to deliver a verdict. On 22 March 1312 Philippe persuaded Clement to issue the bull 'Vox in excelso' which suppressed the order. Some six weeks later on 2 May 1312 a further bull *'Ad providam'* was issued. This transferred all of the Templars' property to the Hospitallers, less a substantial portion for Philippe's expenses.

The grand master of the order was burned at the stake on the Île de la Cité on 19 March 1314 together with the master for Normandy, Geoffroi de Charney, they having recanted of their 'confessions' extracted under torture. At his death de Molay called for the Pope and the king of France to meet him before the judgment seat of Almighty God within 12 months. Pope Clement died a month later, and Philippe IV the following October.

The first establishment of the Knights Templar in London is now the site of Southampton Buildings, off Chancery Lane. Early in the reign of Henry II (1154- 89) land was aquired for the erection of a 'new Temple' (*novi templii*) as the order expanded. The site was bounded by Strand, the River Thames, the Monastery of the Carmelites (White Friars), Essex House, and a tilting ground called Fickett's Croft or Field (the location of the present Law Courts, New Square and part of Lincoln's Inn Fields). A round church, modelled as all Templars' churches were, on the round 4th century Church of the Holy Sepulchre in Jerusalem, a large house, offices, stabling, a garden and a burial ground were all laid out.

The church was consecrated on 10 February 1185 by Heraclius, Patriach of Jerusalem, then on a mission to King Henry II, in the presence of the King, Queen Eleanor and his court, and dedicated to the Virgin Mary. An inscription to that effect was placed in the tympanum of the doorway (west door), which was damaged in 1695, and reproduced on the inner side wall above the door, where it is today.

A rectangular choir 82 feet (25 m.) long by 53 feet (16 m.) broad and 37 feet (11 m.) high was added to the circular nave, and this was consecrated on Ascension Day 1240 in the presence of King Henry III. The rose window above the great west door dates from that time.

The property of the Templars in England was not seized until 11 January 1308 and the master, Walter de la More, was notionally imprisoned at Canterbury but given his personal freedom, vestments of office and a pension. However, in November 1308, in response to papal pressure, he was arrested once more and held for the arrival of the Papal Inquisition who came in September 1309. Torture was outlawed in England, and King Edward II was most reluctant to permit the work of the inquisitors. After severe pressure from the Church he directed the use of torture against the Templars in February 1310, and by August some 59 former knights had made confessions, abjured their errors, and were received back into other ecclesiastical orders. De la More died in the Tower of London in December 1312.

After 1314 all the property of the Templars became vested in the Crown pending arrangements for its redistribution under papal direction. Edward II refused to hand the property over to the Hospitallers without the sanction of Parliament or its original donors. Not until 1324 did Parliament, in compliance with the Pope's instructions pass the Act (17 Edw.2 stat. 2) which gave the Temple, less the Outer Temple, to the Hospitallers. By that time the Hospitallers had no need for extra space and were content to lease the area out to lawyers. In 1340, in consideration for a donation of £100 by the Knights Hospitaller towards an expedition to France, King Edward III endowed the church with lands and 1,000 faggots a year from Lillerton Wood (Lisson Grove) to keep up the church fires.

Temple Church from Church Court

Choir of Temple Church

Originally the church was built of Caen stone. The west doorway is original but not its oaken door. The small figures under the canopy of the porch, erected in 1195, weathered and marred over eight centuries, crumbling in spite of recent attempts at preservation, are supposed to represent on the north side King

Henry II with three Templars to whom he presented the charter of foundation. On the south side is Patriarch Heraclius with three attendant clergy and Queen Eleanor. The porch itself was saved from weathering when in the 18th century a building was constructed over it.

The Round in the church, in fact an irregular polygon of four storeys, 58 feet (17.7 m.) across, is divided concentrically by six clustered columns of Purbeck marble. The central space on the floor is occupied by eight recumbent effigies, which are said to be certain members of the order, but with what justification, who can say? They were defaced, almost beyond recognition, during the Reformation in 1537. Around the wall of the ambulatory is a low stone bench with shallow arcading surmounted by billet moulding. The spandrels contain 64 sculpted heads. It is said that the expression 'being sent to the wall' derives from here, referring to members of the order unable to partake of divine service while standing in the ambulatory.

From the Round one can see on the stairway to the triforium a penitential cell for the confinement of disobedient members 4 feet 6 inches (1.37 m.) by 2 feet 9 inches (0.84 m.) wide. It is a cell of little ease, where one can neither lie nor stand, and by reputation the place in which a knight named Walter le Bacheler, grand preceptor of Ireland, was confined to his death and afterwards buried in the churchyard.

Two storeys above the Round is the triforium, a passage about 10 feet (3 m.) broad encircling the Round, originally open to the air but now roofed in. This was a meeting and walking place for the lawyers in inclement weather when they could not otherwise use Inner Temple gardens. Even the Round below was used as a meeting place for lounging or conversation, a place for the payment of rent, discharge of mortgages and negotiation of contracts. The Round is appointed as a meeting place for business in Ben Jonson's *The Alchemist* and Samuel Butler, in *Hudibras*, says: Retain all sorts of witnesses

> *That ply i' the Temple, under trees,*
> *Or walk the Round with Knights o' the Posts,*
> *About the cross-legg'd Knights their hosts;*
> *Or wait for customers between*
> *The pillar rows in Lincoln's Inn.*

Temple Church became neglected when the resources of the Inns had to be diverted to reconstructing the houses destroyed in the major fires of 1666, 1668, 1677 and 1679. However, in 1681 a major restoration for 18 months started under the direction of Sir Christopher Wren. A new altar with carved background by Grinling Gibbons was installed together with a new pulpit. The church was re-dedicated on 11 February 1683 by the bishop of Rochester.

In 1691 the exterior of the choir was rebuilt with new stone and 10 years or so later the whole church was whitewashed. In 1819 the houses and shops which had been built in Cloister Court leaning against the church were removed, and in 1840 a conical roof was added to the Round, restoring the appearance of the church to its original form. An organ loft was added in 1842 and a vestry in 1886.

The church has been in the joint maintenance of the Honourable Societies of the Middle and Inner Temple since 1542. In 1601 the then Master, a Reverend Dr Masters, caused offence by giving Inner Temple members communion before those of Middle Temple. The matter was referred to a joint committee of the Inns which decided there should be no distinction between the societies. The bread and wine should be administered alternately on alternate Sundays to members of the respective societies. Having said that, the choir is divided between the societies with the south side allotted to Inner Temple and the north to Middle Temple.

Of the many memorials in the church perhaps three only are of note. The memorial to the legal historian John Selden (1584-1654) is a tablet proximate to the grave which can be seen in a vault at the end of the choir near to the Round. A prominent colourful monument in the figure of a man kneeling is of Richard Martin, the recorder of London, who died in 1615; and the recumbent effigy from the triforium of a man lying on his back with his hands clasped over his breast is Edmund Plowden (1518-1585). Many other memorials were contained in the triforium and brought down over the centuries to decorate the church but many, too, were lost in the bombing.

The choir stalls are made of oak and face each other inwards. There has been an organ in this church since 1307. In 1686 a famous competition took place for a replacement organ between two organ makers, Bernard Schmidt, known as 'Father Smith', and one Harris. The competition lasted some 12 months and Judge Jeffreys, then Chief Justice of the King's Bench and an accomplished musician, was appointed the arbiter. All manner of allegations of foul play and sabotage were raised. Henry Purcell was engaged to demonstrate the Schmidt organ, while the French organist to the court of the dowager Queen Katherine played the Harris. The stakes were high, since the winner would not only provide the Temple Church with an organ but also receive the contract for one to be installed at the new St Paul's Cathedral. The loser would have his placed at St Andrew's Church, Holborn. Jeffreys opted for the Schmidt organ, and a contract was issued dated 21 June 1688 for £1,500.

Alterations to the Temple organ were made in 1729 by Christopher Schreider, in 1741 by John Byfield, by T.J.F. Robson in 1856, and it was reconstructed by Forster and Andrews of Hull in 1878. Tragically, on the night of 10/11 May 1941 the Temple Church was burned out by incendiary bombs, leaving the empty shell of a building open to the sky. All the interior fittings were destroyed, including the organ. It took more than 10 years to restore, and when it reopened in 1954 the interior was that of an entirely new church, stripped of its 19th-century Gothic decoration. The conical roof made way to a crenellated tower.

The devastation of the church in the Blitz and its restoration work are commemorated in the stained glass above the altar. Here can be seen the original church in flames, the emblems of the societies, and the coats of arms of the livery companies of the City which donated funds for its restoration. Much work in recreating the spirit of the congregation, this being a functioning church, open for services every Sunday at 11.15 a.m., was undertaken by the choirmaster and famous organist Dr George Thalben-Ball (1896-1987).

The Temple Church is a chapel royal to the Sovereign, whose coat of arms is mounted on the organ loft. The church continues to serve the members of the two Inns but is also open for divine service to anyone, and on most days is open between 10 a.m. and 4.00 p.m. for visitors and for personal contemplation. It has an atmosphere of quietude worth experiencing.

To the south side of the church a small chapel dedicated to St Anne was constructed at about the same time as the choir of the main church, between 1220 and 1240. A connecting door and staircase led to the triforium. In this chapel novices were inducted into the order

Call Ceremony in the Temple Church

by the master, but the building fell into disuse in the 15th century and was destroyed by gunpowder in 1678 in an effort to stop the spread of the serious fire of that year. Its remains were cleared in 1825.

The chapel of St Anne led by the Cloisters to a further small chapel of St Thomas, named for the patron saint of the serjeants, next to the door of hall. This was lost in the fire of 1679.

20. From the church turn right, bearing round to the west door and canopy.

There is an arcaded walk beneath the pavement in the present churchyard but this allows no space for burial. It contains six raised ancient stone coffins which were discovered and opened in 1861 when the chambers and vestry that had stood against the north-west wall of the church were removed. They were empty. In the restoration works on the church in 1823-5 the graveyard of the Templars was cleared and paved.

Opposite, between Dr Johnson's Buildings and Farrar's Building is the interior of Hare Court of which Nos. 1-3 have entrances on this side. Between Nos. 2 and 3 is a substantial plaque in colour with the full coats of arms of Alfred George Martin, treasurer of Inner Temple in 1893, and Arthur Cohen, the same for 1894. This replicates a plaque facing Middle Temple Lane.

The Temple

The courtyard was named after Nicholas Hare, a treasurer and nephew of his more famous uncle Sir Nicholas Hare, Privy Councillor to King Henry VIII and Master of the Rolls to Mary Tudor, who was counsel to Cardinal Wolsey in 1530 and Speaker of the Commons in 1540. His nephew was admitted to Inner Temple in 1547 and subsequently several generations of the Hare family lived here.

When lawyers first occupied the site of the Knights Templar the prior of the Hospitallers of St John retained Hare Court. In 1368 it was rented to the second migration of lawyers coming down from Clifford's Inn and it became known as the Bishop of Ely's Chambers, which occupied this site and that of present day Farrar's Building. Close by was the site of the original Exchequer Office, afterwards known as Fine Office Court. In 1590 John Hare pulled down Fine Office Court and built offices and chambers which became attached to the present Hare Court but which were lost in the fire of 1679. In 1800 Charles Lamb lived in Dr Johnson's Buildings and overlooked Hare Court from his window. He described it as a gloomy, churchyard-like court with three trees and a pump in it. In 2007 a new contemporary garden was planted, which is now flourishing.

Over the entrance to Farrar's Building is a double coat of arms featuring those of Frederick Liddell, treasurer in 1875 and of George Boden, treasurer in 1876 when the building was constructed. In 1338 the bishop of Ely had a town house here at a time when he was Chancellor of the Exchequer to King Edward III. For his convenience the Exchequer Office of the King's Bench was here. By the 17th century the building then on this site formed part of a quadrangle with Cloisters, the church porch, and the houses then abutting on to the church, which became known as Temple Court. Here were later the chambers of Dr Johnson's biographer, James Boswell, who was called to the Bar of Inner Temple in 1786.

Aerial view of the Temple

21. Proceed up Inner Temple Lane by 3 Dr Johnson's Buildings, then Nos. 2 and 1.

From the earliest times an alleyway led from Inner Temple gate to the Temple Church with houses on either side. In 1657 the timber and roughcast buildings were replaced by brick under the treasurership of Edmund Prideux, and these became Nos. 1-5 Inner Temple Lane. The present Dr Johnson's Buildings were built in 1857-8 and replaced the block of five houses. Dr Samuel Johnson (1709-84) lived at 1 Inner Temple Lane from 1760 to 1765. James Boswell (1740-95), who first came here on 24 May 1763 after meeting Johnson for the first time on 7 May that year in Covent Garden, described Johnson's rooms as very airy, and commanding a view of St Paul's and many a brick roof.

Johnson's library was contained in two garrets over his chambers. Whilst here he formed his famous literary club, which met weekly from 1763 until 1772, after which meetings were fortnightly. Its members included the painter Sir Joshua Reynolds (1723-92), who is thought to have proposed setting up the club, the writer Oliver Goldsmith (1730-74), the statesmen Edmund Burke (1729-97) and Charles James Fox (1749-1806), the physician Dr Nugent, who was Burke's father-in-law, the historian Edward Gibbon (1737-94), the economist Adam Smith (1723-90), the lawyer Lord Stowell (1745-1836), the orientalist Sir William Jones (1746-94), the poet Thomas Warton (1728-90), the musicologist Charles Burney (1726-1814), and from the theatre, George Colman (1732-94), David Garrick (1717-79), and Richard Brinsley Sheridan (1751-1816).

Another literary salon took place each Wednesday evening four doors away, though 40 or so years later. In 1800 the essayist Charles Lamb (1775-1834) and his sister Mary (1764-1847) moved from Mitre Court Buildings to 4 Inner Temple Lane, and took two rooms on the 3rd floor and five above. The Lambs' circle of artists, writers, poets and painters included the poets William Wordsworth (1770-1850) , Samuel Taylor Coleridge (1772-1834) and Thomas Hood (1799-1845), the writer William Hazlitt (1778-1830), and the painter Benjamin Robert Haydon (1786-1846). Theatre folk such as Fanny Kelly (a soubrette of the day) and Charles Kemble (1775-1854) would look in. In the same building were the chambers of the last serjeant, Serjeant Ballantyne.

In 2008 Her Majesty Queen Elizabeth II marked the 400th anniversary of the charter by which King James I granted the land on which Middle and Inner Temple are situated to the societies in perpetuity by sealing new letters patent confirming the earlier document. This new charter is held in the benchers' rooms at Inner Temple, but a new stained glass window commemorating the event was placed in the south transept of the Church.

The new Dr Johnson's Buildings contained, at No. 3, the chambers of Edward Carson, later Lord Carson of Duncairn, a Lord of Appeal in Ordinary 1921-9 but far better known as one of the greatest of late Victorian advocates, and as leader of the Irish Unionists in Parliament 1910-18. He served as Solicitor-General in Ireland (1892) and England (1905-1910), Attorney-General (1915) and as First Lord of the Admiralty (1917-18) in the War Cabinet of David Lloyd George.

On the right-hand side above the churchyard is Goldsmith Building, erected in 1861, the large stone engraved crest at its corner being the arms of Jacob Anderson, treasurer for Middle Temple in that year. The large Agnus Dei over the entrance canopy confirms that this property does indeed belong to Middle rather than Inner Temple.

Between 1322 and 1326 the first lawyers came to the precincts of the Temple from St George's Inn, a hospitium near the Old Bailey. These *apprenticii di banco* purchased 13 houses built by Roger Blom, a nuncius, or messenger, to the Knights Templars, on the site of the present Goldsmith Building and since that time it has been settled for Middle Temple.

Those ancient houses were pulled down in 1567 and replaced by a row of tenements in 1608. It was these, referred to by Dickens in *Our Mutual Friend*, which remained on the site until between 1850 and 1860 when they were gradually demolished. The building of 1861 has no connection whatever with Oliver Goldsmith other than its proximity to his grave, which is in the elevated part of the churchyard, and called Churchyard Court when he was buried there in 1774. The neighbouring pavement is made up of other headstones removed from the church during the Reformation. His is not the ostentatious reclining figure on the ornate tomb of an 18th-century merchant nearby, but a greening, slightly raised stone sarcophagus bearing the simple inscription 'Here lies Oliver Goldsmith' and on the opposite side 'Born 10th November 1728. Died 4th April 1774.'

Inner Temple Lane at dusk

22. Proceed to the head of Inner Temple Lane.

At No. 1 Dr Johnson's Buildings were the chambers of John Mortimer QC, the writer and dramatist, and the creator of *Rumpole of the Bailey*. Aficionados of the television series may see that 1 Equity Court is in reality 3 Dr Johnson's Buildings. The name board follows the tradition of the Bar that Queen's Counsel do not have their designation shown on the board advertising their presence.

Just inside Inner Temple gatehouse was the Pope's Head, a shop owned by the publisher Jacob Robinson. Above, the great orator Edmund Burke took two-pair of chambers in 1756, having entered as a student of Middle Temple in 1747. Whilst he kept terms to 1750, he was never called.

In 1780 the Gordon Rioters assaulted the Temple at this point and all gates were closed to them. This was a serious attempt to sack the buildings and attack the lawyers, and shouts of 'Kill the lawyers' (a popular cry over the years) could be heard by the occupants. One such was a Judge Burrough, who used later to relate that when the rioters besieged the Temple he and a strong body of barristers, headed by a sergeant of the Guards, were stationed in Inner Temple Lane, and that, having complete confidence in the strength of their massive gate, they spoke bravely of their desire to be fighting on the other side of it. At length the gate was being forced. The lawyers fell into confusion and were about to beat a retreat, when the sergeant, a man of infinite humour, cried out in a magnificent voice, 'Take care no gentleman fires from behind'. The words struck awe into the assailants and caused the barristers to laugh. The mob, who had expected neither laughter, nor armed resistance, took flight, telling all whom they met that the bloodyminded lawyers were armed to the teeth and enjoying themselves.

May it always be so.

Oliver Goldsmith's plain tomb by the staircase leading to Falcon Chambers

The world famous statue of Justice by Pomeroy on top of the Central Criminal Court

5. From Fleet Street to Old Bailey

And now Sir, we will take a walk down Fleet Street.
Motto of the Temple Bar magazine,

George Augustus Sala.

Fleet Street to Old Bailey

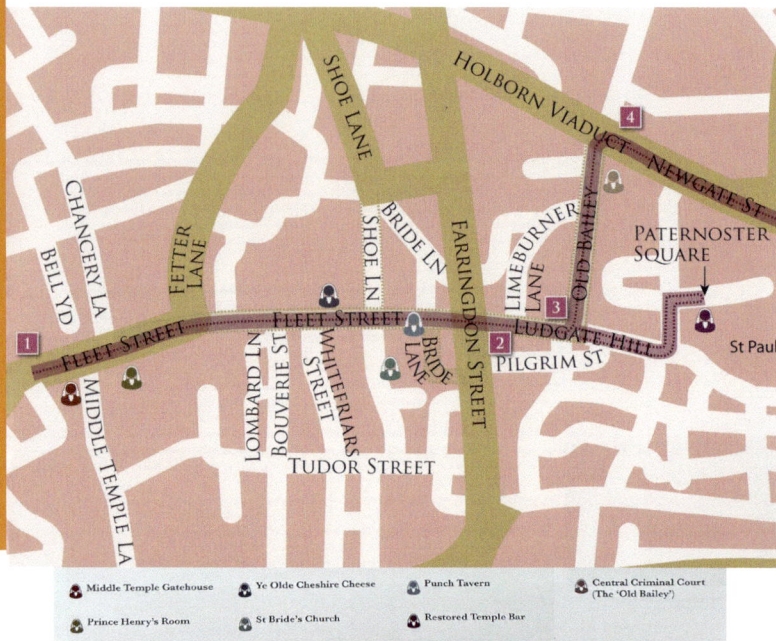

1. Walk commences at the junction of Strand and Fleet Street by the monument to Temple Bar by the clock tower of the Royal Courts of Justice.

2. Cross Ludgate Circus and proceed up Ludgate Hill to the second turning on the left, the Old Bailey. (For those wishing to see the restored Temple Bar – see p.41 – continue up Ludgate Hill and bear left at St Paul's Cathedral into the precinct of Paternoster Square. The gates of Temple Bar are open and the structure is on your left. Return the way you came.)

3. Proceed along Old Bailey to the Central Criminal Court, the public gallery of which is open from 10.30 a.m. to 4.00 p.m. on court sitting days.

4. Proceed from Old Bailey turning right into Newgate Street. St Paul's Underground station is 300 yards (275 m.) ahead.

1. Walk commences at the junction of Strand and Fleet Street by the monument to Temple Bar by the clock tower of the Royal Courts of Justice.

The existence of a thoroughfare running along the north bank of the Thames from the City to Westminster dates back to the reign of Edward the Confessor (1042-66), although the plea rolls indicate that it was not in fact one continuous street until about 1311. Before that time Fleet Street is likely to have consisted of a broad, winding path studded with bushes and thickets. Although the roadway was paved during the reign of Edward II (1307-26), no side pavements were laid until 1766. In that year Dr Johnson recorded in his journal the famous race between two English and four Scots workmen vying to complete their side of the road first. The Englishmen won the wager.

In this street, during the Peasant's Revolt led by Wat Tyler in 1381, the two forges built on either side of St Dunstan's church by the Knights Templar were sacked. Here Geoffrey Chaucer (1345?-1400) had a fight with a Franciscan friar and was fined 2 shillings by the benchers of Inner Temple. In 1458 widespread rioting took place in Fleet Street, organised by the students of the Inns of Chancery. The riot was so serious that the governors of Barnard's, Clifford's and Furnival's Inns were all committed to imprisonment at Hertford Castle by King Henry VI for failing to control their charges. And in 1627 an armed fight broke out between the Temple revellers and the Lord Mayor of London's watch.

This then, was the flavour of medieval Fleet Street. Many of the buildings were gable-ended houses, highly decorated and painted in gaudy colours. Until the 18th century the street was renowned for taverns, drinking clubs, exhibitions and shows and, of course, the booksellers. For some two centuries afterwards it was the home of the third estate, the nation's press, with which it became particularly associated after 1825 when the *Morning Advertiser* moved here from Strand.

Fleet Street today starts at the memorial to Temple Bar (see chapter 2), and not, as is often supposed, at its junction with the southern end of Chancery Lane. Thus proceeding easterly, the first turning to the north is Bell Yard which runs along the side of the East Block of the Royal Courts of Justice. On the corner of that lane is a granite-faced building whose highly decorative ground-floor ceiling reveals that this large room was once the Law Courts branch of the Bank of England and now houses a pub of that name. The building in which it is contained stands on the site of Rackstrow's Museum of Natural Curiosities and Anatomical Figures, a popular late 18th century pastime.

A gateway into the Temple has stood at the top of Middle Temple Lane since at least 1330. In that year King Edward III ordered the Lord Mayor of the City of London to keep it open to allow the King's justices, clerks and the lawyers free access down Middle Temple Lane to Temple Stairs for a river passage to Westminster. The 'Great Gate' which formerly stood at this spot was built in 1620-1 with funds provided by Sir Amyas Paulet, Treasurer of Middle Temple during those years, and the gateway bore his arms. It is reputed that Cardinal Wolsey (1475-1530) was held a prisoner for six years in the gatehouse. Equally the story goes that after the his rise to power, the exterior of Middle Temple gatehouse was decorated with a mitre and arms, and a cardinal's cognisance, badges and devices in order to appease him. After his elevation he would ride in state from a house at the top of Chancery Lane, passing through the gateway and down to the river.

Statue of Mary, Queen of Scots, 143/4 Fleet Street, detail

On the roadway in front of the gatehouse a pillory was set up during the reign of King Charles II (1660-85). In 1670 Titus Oates (see chapter 1) was confined in it. Just inside the archway, on its eastern side was the bookshop of Benjamin Motte, the first publisher of Swift's *Gulliver's Travels* in 1726. Here, too, was produced Nicholas Rowe's 1709 edition of Shakespeare's plays, the first to divide them into acts and scenes. Later the same premises became the office of the Queen's Printer and, after the introduction of the penny post in 1840, one of the first modern post offices in Britain. Two quaint staircases give rise to chambers in the upper floors of the current gatehouse, which was designed by Sir Christopher Wren in 1684.

The premises at 15/16 Fleet Street have changed little since their construction during the early part of the 17th century.

Middle Temple gatehouse

They contained for many years Simmonds, the booksellers, who set a history of the building on a tablet in the door post showing its occupancy as a bookshop for at least 200 years. In 1999 Wildy's continued this unbroken tradition, now sadly ended.

On the ground floor west of 15 Fleet Street, Nando's, only the second coffee house to be opened in London, was founded in 1667. It has no connection with the adjacent sandwich bar. Nando's was renamed the Rainbow Tavern in the 20th century. From 1637 to 1682 the upper floors contained the Phoenix Fire Office, a well-known firm of fire insurers. Number 16 was the house of Bernard Lintot (or Lintott) (1675-1736), publisher of many of the works of Alexander Pope, John Gay and Sir Richard Steele's *The Statesman*. Edmund Burke, when a Temple student, lodged here in 1750.

17 Fleet Street has contained a gateway into the Inner Temple since at least 1563. A later gate and the house above which still stands were built around 1610 by one Bennett, a king's sergeant-at-arms, though the design is attributed to Inigo Jones, who was Prince Henry of Wales's surveyor-general in that year. Henry was the eldest son of King James I, and was invested as Prince of Wales and Duke of Cornwall in 1610, though he died a mere two years later. A room on the first floor of this building was used as the office of the Duchy of Cornwall, possibly its council chamber, and contains an elaborately decorated gilt and painted ceiling with ribs, ornaments and panels depicting foliage and armorial bearings carved in relief. These show the Prince of Wales' feathers and the motto 'Ich Dien' (I serve). The office of the Duchy continued to use this room, now called Prince Henry's Room, between 1618 and 1641, after which it was closed during the Civil War. Charles I came here as Duke of Cornwall in 1635. It is known that by 1693 the room was in use as the Fountain Tavern. Between 1709 and 1739 the Society of Antiquaries met here, and a permanent exhibition of waxworks was opened here from 1795 to 1812. The house was purchased by the London County Council after the Second World War and restored to its original state. It then contained the museum of the Samuel Pepys Society.

The Samuel Pepys Society Museum in Prince Henry's Room

*Still from The Da Vinci Code. Tom Hanks and Audrey Tatou run past Wildy's bookshop in Fleet Street.
Picture by courtesy of the Corporation of London*

The second floor front office now houses the International Office of Catalonia in London, and the building flies the Catalan flag. At 18 Fleet Street is Goslings Bank, now absorbed into Barclays. Goslings was founded in 1650 by Henry Pinckney, a goldsmith trading 'at the sign of the three squirrels'. It operated the funds for King Charles II's secret service. At an office in this building the Automobile Association held its first meeting in 1905. Ye Olde Cock Tavern next door is the namesake of the more famous Cock Tavern, situated formerly on the opposite side of the road back towards Temple Bar. This haunt of Pepys, later immortalised by Tennyson in 'Will Waterproof's Lyrical Monologue', was originally the Cock and Bottle, and occupied the site from 1655 until 1887 when it was demolished to make room for road widening.

On the north side of Fleet Street is the passage running up to Clifford's Inn gatehouse. Although Clifford's Inn was the oldest of the Inns of Chancery, the gatehouse, which abuts the rear of St Dunstan's Church, is modern in the sense that it dates only from the 1840s. It bears the arms of the Barons Clifford and survived the general demolition of 1935 which swept away the Inn. The passage formerly led through to Rolls Gardens, which were on the site of the Public Record Office building, and now emerges on to Chancery Lane.

The focal point of the nation's printing and publishing industry was for centuries in close proximity to the church of St Dunstan's-in-the-West. The present edifice was constructed in 1831 but there has been a church on this site since prior to 1237. Here John Donne held a stipend whilst the publisher of his sermons traded outside, for the churchyard of St Dunstan's was a famous meeting place for publishers and booksellers from the middle ages right up to the Victorian era. John Smethwicke (or Smethwick), who traded 'under the dial of St. Dunstan's clock' published early quarto editions of Shakespeare's plays, including *Romeo and Juliet* (1609) and *Hamlet* (1611). Among other generations of churchyard publishers were Richard Marriot who published Donne's sermons (1640), Isaak Walton's *Compleat Angler* (1653) and the first part of Samuel Butler's *Hudibras* (1663); and Matthias Walker, who published Milton's *Paradise Lost* (1667).

Under the clock of St Dunstans-in-the-West

Pepys recalls in 1671 that the clock of St Dunstan's was one of the sights of London, and fortuitously so, since the Great Fire burned itself out only three doors away, five years earlier. The clock is still surmounted by figures which appear to strike the chimes.

When the gates to the City of London were destroyed in 1786, the figure of Queen Elizabeth I which had been mounted on Ludgate was brought to the church and placed in a niche at its eastern end where it stands today. Set below is a bust of Lord Northcliffe, a further reminder of the relationship between this church and the printing industry, although this was in recognition for his support for the church's parochial school.

Printing in Fleet Street began in a house called the George, which stood next to St Dunstan's. Here Richard Pynson, who had very likely worked with William Caxton, produced some 400 books from 1492 to 1530. In 1508 Pynson was appointed printer to King Henry VII and about one third of his publications were law books, including editions of statutes and year books (law reports).

Returning to the south side of Fleet Street, at No. 32 was the bookshop of John Murray, Lord Byron's publisher. *Childe Harold's Pilgrimage* was published here in 1812. Murray also founded The

Clifford' Inn gatehouse

Quarterly Review in 1809. Hoare's Bank at No. 37 was founded in 1672 by James Hoare, a cooper who kept running cash at 'the sign of the Golden Bottle' in Cheapside. It removed here in about 1687 and, like its neighbour down the road, also kept a secret service account, this time for King James II.

Next to Hoare's stood the Mitre Tavern, a haunt of Shakespeare, but more well known for meetings between Dr Johnson (1709-84) and his biographer James Boswell (1740-95). From 1728 to 1753 it was the home of the Society of Antiquaries, but was pulled down in 1829 when the bank wished to expand. Samuel Pepys's diary mentions two visits made during 1660. In a passageway behind the tavern stood the original Mitre Court Chambers where the essayist Charles Lamb (1775-1834) resided at No. 16 from 1800 until 1809. Here his famous literary salon met regularly on a Wednesday evening, when his gatherings included the presence of the essayist William Hazlitt (1778-1830) and the poet Samuel Taylor Coleridge (1772-1834).

Statue of Queen Elizabeth I at St Dunstans which formerly occupied a niche on Ludgate

Immediately beyond the site of the Mitre Tavern is the modern entrance to Mitre Court, a pathway leading down through the courtyard of the post-war Serjeants' Inn to Mitre Court Buildings, Inner Temple.

The pub which in its most recent incarnation was called 'Serjeants' at Hare Place, Old Mitre Court, was founded in 1749 as Joe's Coffee House. When the Mitre was demolished in 1829 this hostelry took the name and used it until sometime after 1865 when it became the Clachan. It was long a haunt of Temple clerks – less so their guv'nors for whom the rear entrance of El Vino's is in close proximity.

Opposite the entrance to Mitre Court is Fetter Lane, the existence of which is recorded as early as 1292. Then, and until the reign of James I, it was known as Fewtor Lane, derived from the law-French for 'loafer or idler'. The name may be the same word as 'faitour' meaning vagabond. It was the location of the

'Waller conspiracy' of 1643, which resulted in two Cavaliers, Tomkins and Chaloner, being publicly executed at this spot. In it was also situated the home of the fanatical puritan preacher 'Praise-God Barebone' Cunningham (1596?-1679), after whom Cromwell's provisional council, of which he was a member, was called Barebone's Parliament. Charles Lamb is known to have spent his boyhood around Fetter Lane, and the poet John Dryden (1631-1700) owned a house here.

On the south side of Fleet Street at the foot of Fetter Lane is the wine merchant El Vino, which has been famous as a haunt of counsel for over a century and the subject of a sex discrimination case because of the refusal of the management to serve unaccompanied women at its bar.

Serjeants' Inn on Fleet Street was once known as Fleet Street Inn. It was home to the Order of the Coif, named after the headgear of its members, servants of the Crown since before 1250, whose symbol was an intertwined dove and serpent. The serjeants were advocates of the highest rank, who claimed exclusive rights of audience in the Court of Common Pleas when sitting in banc (on appeal). From the 14th century only serjeants could be appointed judges of the common law courts of King's Bench and Common Pleas. From the 16th century such a monopoly of appointments was extended to the barons of the Exchequer, save only the Chief Baron. Elevation to the rank of serjeant was made by the Crown on the advice of the Lord Chancellor and Chief Justice of the Common Pleas. On his appointment a serjeant would leave his own Inn with the status of bencher to join Serjeants' Inn.

Serjeants' Inn was owned by the Dean and Chapter of York Minster, who had been granted the freehold by King Henry IV in 1409. Its buildings surrounded an L-shaped courtyard which contained drinking houses and shops. It was first settled by the serjeants at some point between 1424 and 1442 and was connected by a passage to Inner Temple. In 1459 most of its occupants moved to premises near the foot of Chancery Lane and established a new Serjeants' Inn there. For a short period after 1496 the serjeants remaining in Fleet Street moved to Scrope's Inn, but returned at some time before 1516. After that the two Serjeants' Inns were run as one institution with the different locations vying with each other for predominance over the succeeding centuries. In truth it mattered little since the number of serjeants rarely exceeded 45 at any one time, and for much of the 15th century was about half of that.

In King Henry VIII's reorganisation of Church affairs, ownership of this precinct passed from the see of York to the Crown. In 1627 King Charles I granted a lease to nine judges and 15 serjeants, who administered the affairs of the Inn. From that time on, of the two Serjeants' Inns, this gained the ascendancy. Although burned down in the Great Fire of September 1666, within three years it had been rebuilt. It was lost to the serjeants not by fire or natural disaster but pure commercialism: in 1733 the residents failed to get the lease renewed, and in April and May of that year the remaining occupants removed to join their brethren in Chancery Lane at a cost of £10 per head. The Inn was leased as residential accommodation for the next 40 years and afterwards demolished.

In 1837 19 houses were built on the site, the freehold of which was purchased in 1865 by the Economic Assurance Society, one of the original constituents of the Norwich Union, which owns the property today. By the end of the 19th century the buildings, by then known simply as 49 Fleet Street, were back in mixed use and by 1922 were wholly professional. The houses were severely damaged in the Blitz, and afterwards Norwich Union rebuilt the spacious L-shaped courtyard and restored the ancient name to what are modern offices and a bijou hotel.

Bouverie Street was the home of the *Daily News* from January 1846. At first it was something of a family affair: its editor was the novelist Charles Dickens, its manager was his father, and the music critic, his father-in-law; but Dickens resigned as editor after only 17 issues. For much of the 20th century Bouverie Street was more famous as the home of the *News of the World* and, for a shorter time, the *Sun*. Round the corner in Tudor Street was Northcliffe House containing the editorial offices of the *Daily Mail*. At the foot of Bouverie Street stood the Old Boar's Head, named after a tavern granted to the Carmelites in 1443.

On the north side of Fleet Street a series of alleyways with ancient names, Johnson's, Hind, Bolt and Wine Office Court lead to small, hidden courtyards, now occupied mainly by modern office blocks. Of these Johnson's Court is not named for its later and more famous resident, Dr Samuel Johnson, but after Thomas Johnson, an Elizabethan worthy of 1598-1626. The scurrilous paper *John Bull* was published here from 1820. The illustrious Samuel Johnson lived at 7 Johnson's Court from 1765, but he also lived at 8 Bolt Court from March 1776 until his death in December 1784, entertaining the painter Sir Joshua Reynolds, the historian Edward Gibbon, the actor David Garrick, Bishop Thomas Percy and the scholar and soldier Bennet Langton among others and writing there his *Lives of the Poets* (1779-1781). Also from Bolt Court William Cobbett's *Political Register* (1802-35) was produced, since Cobbett could not find a Fleet Street publisher willing to risk taking it during an era of surprisingly repressive control of the press. Another local printer who took to self-help was Samuel Richardson, who had premises at 76 Fleet Street. He wrote and published his novel *Pamela* (1740-2) to great acclaim.

At the corner of Whitefriars Street are two blue plaques on the same building. The first commemorates the meeting place of the Anti-Corn Law League of Richard Cobden (1804-65) and John Bright (1811-89), perhaps the most successful pressure group of the 19th century; the second marks the workshop of perhaps the finest of English clockmakers, Graham and Tompion, who traded here from 1639 to 1713. Whitefriars Street leads down to the precincts of the medieval monastery and gardens belonging to the White Friars or Carmelites, or, to give them their full title, the Brotherhood of the Virgin of Mount Carmel, founded in 1241.

Wine Office Court, so named as the location of the Excise Office in 1665, was home to the *Dispatch*, founded in 1801, and for a considerable period the principal rival to *The Times*. Oliver Goldsmith (1730-74) lived at No.6 from 1760 to 1762 and worked there on his novel *The Vicar of Wakefield*; next door was occupied by Dr Johnson writing his *Dictionary* five years earlier. Goldsmith and Johnson had their own seats at the table in the north-east corner of one of the most famous drinking houses in London, Ye Olde Cheshire Cheese, where they met and dined with their circle, which included Sir Joshua Reynolds, the musicologist Dr Charles Burney, Edward Gibbon, David Garrick and James Boswell. This inn, rebuilt after the Great Fire of September 1666, and much the same since, has entertained such circles of literati in every age. The French writer Voltaire (1694-1778), during his English exile of 1726-9, the dramatist William Congreve (1670-1729) and poet Alexander Pope (1688-1744) were other 18th-century visitors. In the 19th century the Cheshire Cheese entertained the two famous historians and men of letters Thomas Carlyle (1795-1881), Lord Macaulay (1800-59), the poet laureate Alfred Tennyson (1809-

92), the poet Thomas Hood (1799-1845), the novelists William Makepeace Thackeray (1811-63) and Wilkie Collins (1824- 89), the graphic artists George Cruikshank (1792-1878) and John Leech (1817-64); and Dickens's friend and biographer John Forster (1812-76); and into the first decades of the 20th century, Sir Arthur Conan Doyle (1859-1930), the inventor of Sherlock Holmes, the writers and wits Sir Max Beerbohm (1872-1956), G. K. Chesterton (1874-1936) and Mark Twain (1835-1910), United States President Theodore Roosevelt (1858-1919), and poets W.B. Yeats (1865-1939) and Ernest Dowson (1867-1900).

Wine Office Court leads to Gough Square, No. 17 being the home of the bookseller Wilcocks whose patronage of Garrick and Johnson enabled them to reach the heights of their respective professions. Dr Johnson eventually lived here from 1748 to 1758, compiling much of his *Dictionary*, and it is here that a museum is dedicated to his life and work.

Next door to the Cheese at 143/4 Fleet Street, an ornate Gothic frontage rises above a restaurant. In a niche above the first floor is set a full-size statue of Mary, Queen of Scots (1542-87), unnoticed by the throng passing busily below.

Outside 72/8 Fleet Street, Chronicle House, a bust and plaque dedicated to the great journalist T.P. O'Connor is a reminder of how fleeting is the passage of time. Gone is the world-famous news agency Reuters from No. 85, together with the Press Association; gone from the opposite side of the street are *The Daily Telegraph*, published in Fleet Street from June 1855 to 1988, and the *Daily Express*, published from it famous black art deco building from 1932 to 1989. Gone also from its premises in Shoe Lane, an ancient track featuring in records of 1272, and named from Sholing, the palace of the bishops of Bangor 1378-1828, is the *London Evening Standard*, first published in 1827. With the removal of the print from Fleet Street much of its character has gone. It is astonishing to think that it is already more than three decades since the last newspaper in Fleet Street rolled off the press, the *Sunday Express* of 9 April 1989. Though still synonymous with the nation's newspapers, the term 'Fleet Street' has already lost its meaning to the coming generation.

Proceeding down towards Ludgate Circus there are three more buildings worthy of mention. Set back from the roadway is the printers' church, St Bride's, with its wedding-cake spire, the

Ye Olde Cheshire Cheese

tallest ever built by Sir Christopher Wren. This building is the eighth church to occupy this site, the earliest dating back to the sixth century, although Roman remains have been uncovered in its burial ground. Indeed the crypt contains a fascinating exhibition of life in the parish over the course of 2,000 years and a Roman pavement and medieval chapel can be seen, together with artefacts and printed works from each age. The present edifice was constructed in 1952 after the bombing destroyed all but Wren's tower, spire and outer walls. His church was itself constructed out of the ruins of that which fell victim to the conflagration of 1666. Here the Curia Regis of King John met on many occasions; here Pepys was baptised; and here was celebrated the marriage of the parents of Virginia Dare, the first European child to be born in colonial America in 1587. Milton lived in the churchyard of St Bride's, opposite which and emerging back on to Fleet Street is the Old Bell, a public house built by Wren in 1670 as a hostel for his workers occupied in the construction of the church.

The Punch Tavern, with its elaborately tiled entrance and hanging sign depicting Mr Punch occupies 99 Fleet Street. The famous satirical magazine was founded in July 1841 by Henry Mayhew (1812-87) but quickly came to be associated with Mark Lemon (1809-70), who remained its editor from 1841 to 1870. Lemon commissioned the finest wits, illustrators and cartoonists of the day, including Sir John Tenniel (1820-1914), George Du Maurier (1834-96), Charles Keene (1823-1891) and John Leech (1817-64). Lemon held weekly editorial lunches in a first floor room here, and this became a tradition lasting well over 100 years until the demise of the original magazine in the 1980s. It was briefly revived by Mohamed Al Fayed, closing finally in 2002.

Ludgate Circus is on the site of the Fleet Bridge, a stone bridge with coping on either side which was built to cross the Fleet River in 1431 and reconstructed in 1699. The course of the river, which rises at Hampstead and Highgate ponds, runs approximately along the line of Farringdon Road and emerges into the River Thames a little west of Blackfriars Bridge. In use from medieval times, it was navigable from the Thames to Holborn Viaduct, having been canalised between 1668 and 1673 over a length of 2,100 feet (640 m.) under Wren's direction with wharfage on either side. By 1732 it had become stagnant and choked with mud, and in 1737 was covered over from Holborn down to Fleet Bridge; the rest, being no more than a small, filthy inlet and dock, was covered in 1765.

The present Ludgate Circus was built in 1864 as part of a road-widening programme, and completed in 1875. Prior to then Fleet Street had continued over the bridge and up to the Ludgate. On the south side of the road, and afterwards on the Circus itself, from 1775 to 1950, stood an obelisk surmounted by a lamp standard with an inscription to the Right Honourable John Wilkes, Lord Mayor. Wilkes (1727-97) was a politician who championed parliamentary reform and the American colonial cause. He was twice imprisoned and prevented from taking his seat in Parliament for opposition to King George III.

On the north-western corner at Ludgate House is a tablet in bas-relief commemorating the life and work of Edgar Wallace. The inscription reads:

Edgar Wallace Reporter Born London 1875 Died Hollywood 1932 Founder member of the Company of Newspaper Makers. He knew wealth and poverty yet he had walked with kings and kept his bearing, and his talents he gave lavishly to authorship, but to Fleet Street he gave his heart.

Lud was the name of the Celtic god of water and rivers. Geoffrey of Monmouth (1100?-54) records that a gate to Roman Londinium

St Bride's, the journalists' church

was erected on this site in 66 BC and decorated with carvings depicting the head of Lud and his two sons. Such a tradition was kept alive by the Old King Lud public house, which was situated on the north-east corner of the Circus, now occupied by the Hogshead, from before the turn of the 20th century until the redevelopment of 1992. King Lud may still be seen on the topmost dormer floor of that building, and also on the balconies of the upper floor of Ludgate House.

2. Cross Ludgate Circus and proceed up Ludgate Hill to the second turning on the left, the Old Bailey. (For those wishing to see the restored Temple Bar – see p.41 – continue up Ludgate Hill and bear left at St Paul's Cathedral into the precinct of Paternoster Square. The gates of Temple Bar are open and the structure is on your left. Return the way you came.)

The presence here of a medieval gate into the City, some 100 yards (90 m.) up the present day Ludgate Hill, was recorded between 1100 and 1135. Called the Lutgata, the name may have derived from the personal name Luda or Lude, both presumably referring back to the god Lud, or more likely from the Old English word for postern, 'hlydgeat'. In 1260 its repair beautifying the images of King Lud and his sons is chronicled. Renewed in 1586, Ludgate escaped the Great Fire of 1666 and was eventually pulled down in 1760. The figures of Lud and his sons were donated to St Dunstan's School in 1935 by the Marquess of Hertford, into whose possession they came.

Seacoal Lane, recently renamed Limeburner Lane, reflects the cargoes coming up the Fleet River. In Seacoal Lane stood a hostel attached to St Sepulchre's Church, Newgate. This ancient lodging for students lay just within the City walls, and has been identified as the oldest of the Inns of Chancery, St George's Inn, whose members migrated in the latter part of the 15th century to a site at Wych Street, latterly called New Inn, but first called Our Lady Inn. (See chapter 2) The hill from the Ludgate to St Paul's Cathedral was known as Bowyer Row until 1359 when it became Ludgate Street. It took its present name at some point during the reign of Queen Elizabeth I. At the sign of the Hawk and Pheasant lived the diarist John Evelyn, 1658-9. Some 80 years later in 1731 James Ashley opened the London Coffee House at No. 42 on the north side, famous in its day for its book auctions, as a meeting place for Americans in London, and as the venue for a scientific society led by a Dr Priestley among whose prominent membership

The restored Temple Bar in Paternoster Square

was Benjamin Franklin. The 'London' is the place where Arthur Clennam spent one Sunday evening in Dickens's *Little Dorrit* becoming increasingly maddened by the local church bells.

Above:
The restored Temple Bar in St Paul's Churchyard precinct

Right: The Temple Bar in 1870 Illustrated London News

3. Proceed along Old Bailey to the Central Criminal Court, the public gallery of which is open from 10.30 a.m. to 4.00 p.m. on court sitting days.

Old Bailey: the name is famous across the globe and both more recognised and more inspiring than the Central Criminal Court, the building which has adopted by popular use the name of the street in which it stands. The *vetus ballium* was the name given to the space enclosed by the City wall between Ludgate and Newgate and the name was in use as such as early as 1241. By 1289 the area was known as 'the Baillie', though throughout the middle ages a row of tenement buildings at the northern end divided the enclosure into two courtyards, Great and Little Old Bailey, which were so divided until the close of the 18th century.

The present court building is on the site of Newgate prison, slightly to the south of Newgate itself, which was the principal western entrance to the City along the old Roman road of Watling Street. A record of 1285 describes the Chamberlain's Gate at this point, and the Domesday Book identifies a vineyard at 'Holeburn' belonging to William the Chamberlain. Five gates were constructed on the site between the reign of King Henry I (1100-35) and the demolition of the last in 1777. It was probably from the rebuilding after a fire of 1177 that it received the name 'the new gate', although there were equally substantial reconstructions in 1423, 1555, 1630 and 1672.

The upper part of the gatehouse contained a prison for felons and trespassers after 1189. This penal institution grew to absorb neighbouring buildings and became the principal prison for the county of Middlesex as well as the City of London. In 1334 an official enquiry found terrible conditions with torture a common practice. In 1381 Wat Tyler's rebels unsuccessfully tried to storm it, causing some damage. It was a place notorious for squalor and unsanitary conditions giving rise to typhoid, otherwise called gaol fever. In 1414 the keeper and 64 prisoners died of plague, and in 1457 there occurred a major gaol break-out.

Like the gate itself, the prison underwent destruction and rebuilding. The entire building was lost in the Great Fire of 1666 and reconstructed. Here Daniel Defoe was imprisoned for sedition in 1702-3. Some 20 years later the highwayman Jack Sheppard and his companion Edgworth Bess escaped for a third time. In 1724 they were recaptured and executed at Tyburn, having first been exhibited to the public for 1 shilling, as was then customary, for two hours before the execution.

Outside the debtors' door of Newgate Prison public executions took place from 1783 when the State's killing ground moved here from Tyburn. Some executions were more gruesome than others. Here in 1789 a woman was strangled and burnt for counterfeiting coinage, the last such execution in England. On 1 May 1820 the five Cato Street conspirators, who planned to assassinate the entire Cabinet of Lord Liverpool and form their own government in its place, were executed before Newgate, first being hanged and then beheaded. At the Magpie and Stump, formerly the King of Denmark public house, opposite the place of execution, window seats sold at 20 guineas to watch the execution of Franz Muller, a railway murderer, in 1864, when a crowd of 50,000 turned out in Smithfield and Old Bailey to watch. The last execution in public in England took place in May 1868 and was of the Fenian, Michael Barrett.

In June 1780 Newgate gaol was attacked in the 'No Popery Riots' and burnt down. However, the rebuilding work, to the designs of George Dance the Younger (1741-1825) was completed in 1783, comfortably in time to provide hospitality to the instigator of those same riots, Lord George Gordon, who was incarcerated here from 1787 until he died of gaol fever in 1793.

By 1813, although described by Dickens in *Barnaby Rudge* as a new building, it was found to be ill-ventilated, overcrowded and with no restraint between the mixed prisoners. Elizabeth Fry founded the Ladies Prison Visiting Association in 1817 as a result of the conditions found at Newgate and those conditions were condemned by an inspectorate of prisons in both 1837 and 1843. The opening of Holloway prison in 1852 led to the removal of some women prisoners. In 1857 the interior of Newgate was remodelled to provide for separate cells; and in 1861 a women's block was built. In 1880 Newgate ceased to be in use as a prison except for the sittings of the assize courts, and in 1902 it was demolished to make way for the Central Criminal Court which presently occupies the site.

The earliest court to sit here was open to the weather; with railed enclosures where prisoners were brought out of the prison for judgment. Between 1539 and 1774 the King's Commissions for the Peace of Oyer and Terminer and General Gaol Delivery of

Newgate for the City of London and the County of Middlesex were held at the Justice Hall in the Sessions House at Old Bailey eight times each year or more frequently if the prison needed clearing because of overcrowding or disease. The threat of disease spreading from the prison to the courtroom was a very real concern. In 1750 the Lord Mayor of London, two judges, an alderman, an under-sheriff and 50 others died from typhus contracted from a prisoner. Thus began the tradition whereby between 1 May and 30 September annually, on the first two days of each session and on red letter days, judges at the Old Bailey and the Sheriff's party who accompany them as a reminder of the jurisdiction of the City of London over its courts, carry posies of old English sweet-smelling flowers to smother the evil odours emanating from the neighbouring gaol, and the bench and ledge of the prisoner's dock are strewn with herbs.

The great door and portico of the Central Criminal Court on the site of the debtor's door of Newgate Prison

Fleet Street to Old Bailey

The single courtroom was destroyed in the Gordon Riots of 1780, but was rebuilt and subsequently enlarged in 1809. Under the Central Criminal Courts Act 1834 the court received its current name and status, namely, the venue for the principal criminal trials in England and Wales. It was to this building that W.S. Gilbert referred in *Trial by Jury*, *The Pirates of Penzance* and *Ruddigore*, and Dickens referred in chapter 52 of *Martin Chuzzlewit* and book 2, chapter 2 of *A Tale of Two Cities*, and where Oscar Wilde was tried in 1895.

The present building was constructed between 1902 and 1907 to a design by Edward Mountford. Faced in Portland stone, its world-famous feature is the bronze gilt figurine of Justice sculpted by F.W. Pomeroy which surmounts the lantern of the tower dome. She is 12 feet (3.6 m.) high, her outstretched arms have a span of 8 feet (2.4 m.) and her sword is sword is 3 feet 6 inches (1.07 m.) long. The ball upon which she stands is 95 feet (29 m.) from street level.

The other most prominent feature of the exterior is the great door, approximately where, in the old prison, the debtors' door led directly to the scaffold. Over the door Pomeroy's sculptures of Truth and Justice and the Recording Angel are featured, and the face of the building bears the inscription, 'Defend the children of the poor and punish the wrongdoer', taken from the Book of Common Prayer version of psalm 72.

The exterior of the building reflects the growth of the business of the courts during the 20th century. In 1967-8 an annexe of four courts was constructed across the road as the West Building, converted from a warehouse. Between 1965 and 1972 a major extension to the main building added a further 12 courts, making a total of 18 courts.

Occasionally the Central Criminal Court will sit at the Royal Courts of Justice building, and serious frauds were tried in the 1990s at a purpose-built court suite in Chancery Lane. Beneath the courts some 70 cells are available to hold prisoners who are brought daily for their appearances.

High Court judges attend to preside over the most serious criminal trials. The Central Criminal Court is the principal Crown Court of the south-eastern circuit but it belongs to the City of London: two sitting judges retain the ancient titles of the City's law officers: the Recorder of London and the Common Serjeant.

In each courtroom the centre chair on the bench is reserved for the Lord Mayor or an alderman of the City, a symbol of rank and status in these courts. Every morning and afternoon in courts 1 to 8 the judges are escorted into court by an alderman of the City, one of the two city sheriffs and the under sheriff. The Lord Mayor and his retinue do not, in fact, sit as judges, but by tradition the Mayor continues to receive the High Court Bench when he attends the court on its formal opening day each year.

The interior of the Old Bailey is redolent of the history of the English criminal justice system. The famous No.1 court has seen the trials of Dr Hawley Crippen in October, 1910 for the murder of his wife. Crippen, in fact an American doctor from Coldwater, Michigan, was caught by the first use of wireless telegraphy to alert the ship carrying him fleeing to Canada with his mistress Ethel le Neve, who was disguised as a boy; of Frederick Seddon in March 1912 for the murder of his wife. Famously he exchanged Masonic references in a conversation with the trial judge, Mr Justice Bucknill, before the latter passed the death sentence; of George Joseph Smith in June, 1915 who drowned his three wives in their baths; of Horatio Bottomley, the financier, in 1922 for corruption; of William Joyce ('Lord Haw-haw') in 1946 for treason, by broadcasting throughout the Second World War for the Germans; of John Christie in July 1953 for the murder of his wife at 10, Rillington Place, Notting Hill, which became the subject of a film; of Jeremy Thorpe, former leader of Britain's Liberal Party, who in June 1979 was acquitted of conspiracy to murder; and of Donald Nielson, who in July 1976 received five life sentences for luring young men back to his house in Muswell Hill to meet their deaths.

The Great Hall rises to the interior of the dome which is 67ft (20 m.) high. Beneath are large and highly coloured fresco panels by Gerald Moira painted in 1954. Here the symbolic figure of Justice is surrounded by figures representing religion, the law, work, the administration, the forces, the colonies, and maternity. Included are portraits of Edward Mountford and Sir James Eyre, who was appointed Recorder of London in 1763 and went on to become Chief Justice of the Common Pleas, inscribed 'The law of the wise is a fountain of life' (Proverbs 13:14.). A portrait of Caesar receiving a sword is placed above a cameo of William Beckford (1709-70), twice Lord Mayor, inscribed 'The welfare of the people is the supreme law' (Cicero, De Legibus). Cameos are here too of

Sir Heneage Finch, Earl of Nottingham, who was Lord Chancellor 1675-82, and George Dance, architect of Newgate, inscribed 'Poise the cause in Justice' equal scales' (Shakespeare, King Henry VI Part 2). There is also a fine cameo of Richard Whittington (1358?-1423), four times Lord Mayor of London, who provided funds for the rebuilding of Newgate during his mayoralty.

The interior of the dome
Reproduced by kind permission of Central Criminal Court, Old Bailey

The other panels depict Abraham, inscribed 'Right lives by law and law subsists by power'; Moses, bearing the inscription 'Moses gave unto the people the laws of God'; King John at Runnymede, rather more provocatively inscribed 'London shall have its ancient rights'; and a tribute to the Civil Defence workers in the City during the Second World War showing the Blitz. In 1940 German aerial bombing destroyed the Recorder of London's Court and on 10 May 1941 there was further damage by incendiary bombs. However, the administration of justice at the Old Bailey continued throughout the war, and the repair of the damage to the north-western corner is commemorated in a tablet engraved *Fiat justitia ruat Caelum* (Let justice be done, though the heavens fall), placed there in October 1952 by Lord Mayor Sir Leslie Boyce.

Four statues by Pomeroy stand beneath the dome: Mercy, Justice, Temperance and Charity. Looking up one sees the dome bearing the coat of arms of the City of London with figural representations of Labour, Art, Learning and Truth. The grand staircase leads to the original upper court floor. This is lit by stained glass bearing the arms of the City of London and of Middlesex below the royal cipher. In the oriel window are arms of former lord mayors and sheriffs of London.

The Great Hall and dome with the statue of Elizabeth Fry

In deference to the association of the court with the prison, the work of prison reformers is honoured in these precincts. Outside No. 1 court, with the famous inscription over its doorway, 'Poise the cause in Justice' equal scales', a tablet commemorates John Howard (1726-90) after whom the Howard League for Penal Reform is named. And in the vestibule of court No. 3 stands a statue of Elizabeth Fry (1780-1845) by Drury, inscribed with a verse by Robert Browning:

One who never turned her back but marched,
Breast forward,
Never doubted clouds would break,
Never dreamed, though right were worsted, wrong would triumph,
Held we fall to rise, are baffled to fight better,
Sleep to wake

On the wall adjacent to court 18 is a plaque which states that:

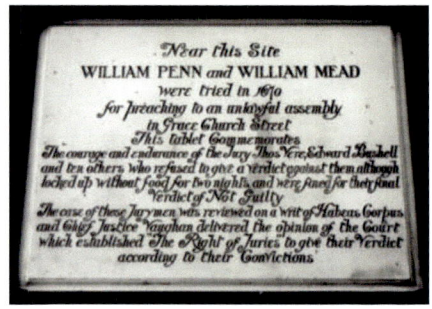

Near this site William Penn and William Mead were tried in 1670 for preaching to an unlawful assembly in Gracechurch Street. This tablet commemorates the courage and endurance of the jury, Thomas Vere, Edward Bushell and 10 others who refused to give a verdict against them although locked up without food for two nights and were fined for their final verdict of not guilty. The case of these jurymen was reviewed on a writ of habeas corpus and Chief Justice Vaughan delivered the opinion of the court which established the right of juries to give their verdict according to their convictions.

As one would expect, the building contains artefacts concerned with the history of the administration of criminal justice that the public does not see. A good example is to be found in the Old Bailey Bar Mess: a framed opinion, dated 27 July 1910 by Travers Humphreys as Crown counsel, in manuscript, establishes the right to arrest Dr Crippen upon his arrival in New York where he had fled by ocean liner, and by transferring him from one British ship to another, to execute the warrant for his arrest for murder. In fact Crippen landed and was extradited from Canada.

4. Proceed from Old Bailey turning right into Newgate Street. St Paul's Underground station is 300 yards (275 m.) ahead.

Chancery Lane with the former Public Record Office building on the left and the exterior of Old Buildings and Old Square, Lincoln's Inn, to the right foreground.

6. Chancery Lane

> *I stood in court, and there I sang him songs of Arcadee, with flageolet accompaniment – in vain. At first he seemed amused, so did the Bar; but quickly wearying of my song and pipe bade me get out. A servile usher then, in crumpled bands and rusty bombazine, led me, still singing, into Chancery Lane.*
>
> W.S. Gilbert, Iolanthe.

Chancery Lane

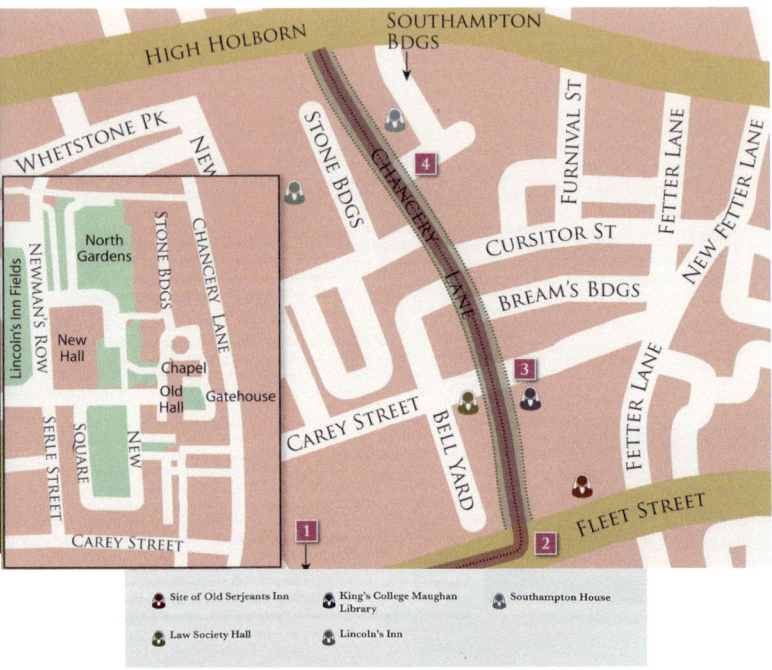

1. Underground to Temple station; from the station walk up to Strand and head east along Strand to the traffic lights at the southern end of Chancery Lane.

2. Proceed up Chancery Lane on the east side.

4. Cross Carey Street.

5. Cross to Southampton Buildings

1. Underground to Temple station; from the station walk up to Strand and head east along Strand to the traffic lights at the southern end of Chancery Lane.

Chancery Lane, which runs for a quarter of a mile (approx. 400 m.) directly north-south, links Holborn and Gray's Inn with the Temple and Strand. On the western side nearly two thirds of its length is the boundary of Lincoln's Inn. This ancient cart track, once called New Street, was such a dangerous and thorny quagmire in the reign of King Edward I (1272-1306), that for 10 years he ordered John Breton, custodian of London, to have it closed up and barred as a passageway at either end. It was only upon the petition of the bishop of Chichester to the sheriff of London that it was reopened.

By 1489 this turning is referred to in the Black Book of Lincoln's Inn as 'Chaunceleres Lane', and while there seem to be at least three candidates among the Lord Chancellors who might have lent it that name, the street's fortunes have been bound up with the history of the Court of Chancery for nearly 600 years.

Unlike the Exchequer, the king's chancellery continued to be part of the royal household for some 200 years after the Norman Conquest. The Lord Chancellor was a 'Pooh-Bah' minister, effectively incorporating the appointments of Home Secretary, Foreign Secretary, Minister of Justice, Minister for the Civil Service, and private secretary to the Sovereign. He was thus in close, if not constant, attendance on the king, and his secretariat was the writing office of the Curia Regis. Part of that office was responsible for the issue of writs, authorised under the Great Seal, of which he was custodian until the subsequent creation of a specific office of Lord Keeper. The secretariat of the royal chancellery also drafted charters and royal letters authenticated by the seal, and all such documents were copied out on parchment rolls, which survive as an unbroken series of State records from 1200. These rolls contained all the minutiae of centralised government and record the grants of land, the creation of nobles; appointments to offices, liberties, rights and privileges; instructions to royal officials, charters, incorporations and proclamations; as well as both public and private judicial and revenue matters.

The rolls of record and the secretariat which created and kept them became too unwieldy to travel with the king on

Chancery Lane

his progress out of London. Thus the Chancellor's scribes and officials would meet the royal party at designated centres on the tour. Here a large house would be commandeered as a billet to be 'the inn of the king's clerks in Chancery' for the duration of the royal stay, which could be for many months. However, by the death of Lord Chancellor Ralph Neville, Bishop of Chichester, in 1244, the body of clerks and scribes had even outgrown in size the royal household itself, and journeying into the provinces at all was too cumbersome and expensive. The king, Henry III, tried to administer the chancellery direct, and only appointed minor functionaries to deal with the various duties previously undertaken by the Chancellor. However, under pressure from the barons in 1258, a major reorganisation of the chancellery secretariat, or Chancery, was forced in 1260, and in 1306 King Edward I ordered it to remain at Westminster.

From the turn of the 14th century the bureaucracy of the Chancery expanded, with the Lord Chancellor being given the jurisdiction to issue his own writs 'in Chancery'. From about that time a new office was created to supervise the Chancery and administer its records. This functionary was the Custos Rotulorum, later to become known as the Master of the Rolls, and his immediate underlings were the 12 'clerks of the first form', in reality powerful men indeed and the predecessors to the modern masters in Chancery. The keeper of the records became deputy to the Chancellor and had custody of the Great Seal in his absence. He was usually a cleric until Thomas Cromwell was appointed to the post in 1534. From early in the 14th century, the Custos Rotulorum began to have charge of the household or inn ('hospitium' or hospice) of the clerks in Chancery.

Reflection of the former Public Record Office

At this time the junction of Chancery Lane with Fleet Street may have been a further 50 yards (48 m.) to the west. In this proximity on the western corner stood the house where Izaak Walton lived from 1627 to 1644, many years before the publication of his *Compleat Angler* in 1653. Attenborough's, the jewellers, moved here in 1843, having been founded in Holborn in 1696. On the eastern corner was for many years Hammick's law bookshop.

2. Proceed up Chancery Lane on the east side.

Set into the wall of 5 Chancery Lane is the blue plaque marking the site of Old Serjeants' Inn 1415-1910. Detailed records of this precinct go back to the 13th century, when the property was held by the see of Ely. In 1378 it was leased for 60 years to one Robert de Muskham, canon of York, a clerk in Chancery who, despite his ecclesiastical preferments, practised privately as a clerk and attorney. On his death 10 years later his executors surrendered the lease back to the bishop, whose next tenant, John de Scarle, was the Custos Rotulorum 1394-9 and thereafter Lord Chancellor. Thus this quarter was known as the hospitium Johannis de Scarle or Scarle's Inn 1391-6. His successor was Robert Faryndon (otherwise Farringdon), another clerk in Chancery and Custos 1399-1401, afterwards Treasurer of the Exchequer of Ireland until his death in 1405. Farringdon's Inn came into the possession of the serjeants by about 1416.

The Order of Serjeants-at-Law, or Order of the Coif so named after their headgear, provides the lawyers with their only direct link with the Knights Templar. The body of Servitors of the Knights Templar, or Lower Order, was known as the *fratres servientes* or frères serjens. The name of this order or brotherhood, since members addressed themselves as brother, was taken by the senior lawyers towards the mid 14th century, after which time they became so powerful that no judge could be appointed to the Common Law bench without having first been called to the Order of the Coif.

Serjeants' Inn, as it was called by 1484, comprised two courtyards containing chambers, set at north-south, with a chapel and hall. The inner courtyard was linked by a passageway into Clifford's Inn. All of its original buildings the freehold of their Inn and set about a total reconstruction which occurred in 1837-8 under the supervision of the architect Sir Robert Smirke (1781-1867).

However the days of the serjeants were numbered by the Supreme Court of Judicature Act 1873. Members of the Inn could no longer afford the upkeep of its buildings, and whilst students had been admitted in an attempt to defray expenses, too much was needed. In 1877 the serjeants sold their Inn to one of their number, Serjeant Cox, for £51,000, which provided each with a dividend of £900. 26 portraits were donated to the National Portrait Gallery, and the stained glass from the hall was removed to decorate Cox's own house at Mote Mount, Mill Hill. Long afterwards the arms of Serjeants' Inn were given as a decoration for the Law Society's hall and common room in 1926. The Inn was sold to the Royal Insurance Company in 1909 and the buildings were demolished and replaced by the office block which now occupies the site. Recently refurbished, this modern building at one time housed the Lands Tribunal and, during its short troubled life, the National Industrial Relations Court.

3. On the right: Clifford's Inn Passage.

The house that was subsequently called Clifford's Inn, and which became the first Inn of Chancery, was owned from 1290 by Malcolm de Harley a principal Chancery clerk who came from Shropshire. Here he took pupils into residence. Towards the end of May 1298, the property was escheated to the Crown in payment of debts owed by Harley. Between 1307 and 1309 the king granted it as a London residence to John de Britannia, Earl of Richmond. However, it was the next assignment of the property which gave it the name it still bears.

On 24 February 1310, King Edward II granted 'the messuage and appurtenances next St. Dunstan's in the West' to Robert de Clifford, 1st Baron Clifford, by way of service of one penny. De Clifford was a successful military commander, though he met his fate a mere four years later at Bannockburn, when Robert Bruce's Scots army defeated the English. His grandson inherited the property under age. Consequently his guardian, Isabella de Clifford, widow of the 3rd Baron, was able to lease it in 1344 to the *apprenticii di banco*, lawyers attached to the Court of Common Pleas, at an annual rent of £10. Their formal tenancy was only a short one, for on 27 November 1345 custody of the hospitium passed into the hands of David de Wollore, Keeper of the Rolls in Chancery, who converted it in about 1359 to an Inn of Chancery. De Wollore had charge of the Lord Chancellor's household, frequently being entrusted with the keeping of the Great Seal in his master's absence. He died in 1370, and after that date the *apprenticii di banco* began to leave the precincts of Clifford's Inn passing to the south of Fleet Street where they established themselves as the embryo Society of the Inner Temple. From the earliest times the two Inns were linked. The minute books of Clifford's Inn show that the three annual readers for the Inn were nominated by the Inner Temple.

The students of the clerks in Chancery remained in Clifford's Inn and as an institution it continued to thrive until modern times. Its original buildings, constructed in about 1310, included a hall and chapel. These divided up two of its three small courtyards and were extensively rebuilt in 1767. Subsequently a large part of the southern end of the Inn was hived off for the restoration of St Dunstans-in-the-West in 1830.

Governed by a principal and 12 aules, or rulers, with the juniors for some reason known as the Kentish men, the Ancient and Honourable Society of Clifford's Inn was endowed by Lord Clifford, Earl of Cumberland in March 1618. The Inn provided a serjeant from 1409 until the abolition of that appointment in late Victorian times. During the reign of Elizabeth I (1558-1603) the Society had over 100 members. Both Coke and Selden lived within its precincts. Here also, whilst living at No.15 Clifford's Inn, Samuel Butler (1835-1902) wrote *Erewhon* and *The Way of All Flesh*. At the turn of the 19th century George Dyer (1755-1841) had chambers here which were frequented regularly by Sir Walter Scott (1771-1832), Robert Southey (1774-1843), Samuel Taylor Coleridge (1772-1834), Charles Lamb (1775-1834), Sir Thomas Noon Talfourd (1795-1854) and other celebrated literati of the day. Charles Dickens refers to the Society in *Little Dorrit*, *Bleak House*, *Pickwick Papers* and *Our Mutual Friend*.

In legal history the most famous episode attaching to Clifford's Inn occurred after the Great Fire of 1666. The Chief Baron of the Exchequer, Sir Matthew Hale, sat in the Inn's hall together with 17 other judges as a commission to hear and settle property disputes arising out of the fire, and these afterwards became known as the fire judges.

Clifford's Inn was also the location of the writ office for the bills of Middlesex, the chambers of the attorneys of the Marshalsea Court, and after 1837 the hall was permanently fitted out at as an Exchequer Court, and occasionally used as an annexe for the High Court in Equity prior to the construction of the Royal Courts building.

The last member of the Society was admitted in 1877 and by 1899 only 16 remained. Of these 16, five wanted to sell the Inn, which gave rise to a lengthy action which is reported as *Smith* v *Kerr*. The Inn's property was eventually sold in 1903 for £100,000 of which £77,000 was put into trust for legal education. The purchasers were the British Optical Association, which used the hall as a library and museum for eight years, after which the Society of Knights Bachelor purchased the freehold of the hall, lodge, old courtyard and its adjoining buildings for £36,000. They held this interest until 1920, although during the First World War the War Office commandeered the Inn for use as the Army Spectacle Depot.

Clifford's Inn came back on to the market in 1925 when the Law Society was put under pressure by its members to purchase it as an Inn of Court for solicitors. Nothing came of that scheme and the property was eventually sold for redevelopment. By 1934 Clifford's Inn remained only in the name of a block of flats and offices built on the east part of the site, abutting New Fetter Lane. All that remains then and today of this ancient Inn is the gatehouse spanning Clifford's Inn Passage that lies behind St Dunstan's.

The Public Record Office building was erected from 1851 to 1902 from designs by Sir James Pennethorne at a cost exceeding £200,000. Augustus Hare (1834-1903), in his *Walks in London* describes it as 'a vast facade of feeble carpenter's gothic, with meaningless turrets and paltry ornaments'. This huge building was for nearly 90 years the national repository of records of government and the judiciary that are to be permanently preserved in a new purpose-built building opened at Kew in 1997. It is now occupied by the Maughan Library, the main university research library of King's College London which covers an important historical site, that of the Domus Conversorum or house of the converts 1232-1377, and the Court of the Master of the Rolls, together with his official residence and private chapel.

In 1232-3 King Henry III caused a house to be erected and administered by the monks of the Carthusian Order for the maintenance of converted Jews. This was gradually expanded to be come a group of almshouses collectively known as the Domus Conversorum. In 1278 the occupants were referred to in tally rolls

In 2003 the building was occupied by King's College, University of London and transformed into a state-of-the-art 21st-century library and information services centre, housing the collections of the College's Schools of Humanities, Law, Physical Sciences & Engineering, and Social Science & Public Policy. The work won a City Heritage Award for a conversion project described as 'a demonstration of how conservation can and should be done' and of 'stunning quality'.

as the *pauperes caelicolae christi*, and they received a substantial portion of the income confiscated from their former co-religionists by King Edward I, when he expelled the Jews from England in 1290. However, shortly after the expulsion, the Domus Conversorum was given into the custody of the Chancery clerks, since the then senior clerk, William de Osgodeby, was appointed its warden in 1307. A chapel had been attached to the principal house on the site at some time during the reign of King Henry II (1154-89). This was to become the Rolls Chapel.

By the petition of William de Burstall, Keeper of the Rolls, in 1377 King Edward II broke up the almshouses and attached the house and chapel to the office of Keeper in perpetuity; and for 460 years afterwards Rolls House, as it became known, was the official residence of the Keeper, later Master of the Rolls, together with his court, and a place for the storage of the kingdom's court records. The Rolls Chapel was rebuilt in 1617 by Inigo Jones, and at the

Chancery Lane

service for its consecration the sermon was preached by Dr John Donne.

Between 1837 and 1851 the buildings were gradually demolished and the site cleared to make way for the construction of the Public Record Office, as authorised by a statute of 1838. The control of the public records remained vested in the Master of the Rolls until as recently as 1959, when it passed to the Lord Chancellor.

Formerly in this building, but now at Kew, was a deposit of all governmental papers dating back to the middle ages; records of the court reports of England and Wales from 1189; treaties with foreign powers; log books of HM ships of the Royal Navy, and the dispatches of military commanders of historical importance; royal letters; and state papers, such as those of Oliver Cromwell and Thomas Wolsey. Upon its creation the Public Record Office brought together for the first time millions of documents contained in over 60 deposits, including those formerly housed in the Tower of London and the Chapter House, Westminster.

The public reading room of the Public Record Office normally allows free access to any public document over 30 years old. In addition, an Education and Visitor Centre was opened at Kew in April 2000 by the Lord Chancellor, Lord Irvine of Lairg, to replace the small museum formerly open in this building. Here there was for many years a permanent display of historical documents including the two thick volumes of Domesday Book of uneven size, dated 1086; letters patent granted to William Penn on his landing in America, 1681; 13th and 15th-century plea rolls from the High Court; the appointment of the Special Commission for the trial of Sir Walter Raleigh for treason, November 1603; minutes of the proceedings of the trial of the Tolpuddle Martyrs, March 1834; ratifications of the treaties of Vienna 1815 and Versailles 1919; official records of the military operations at Agincourt (1415), against the Armada (1588), at Trafalgar (1805), Waterloo (1815), at the Somme (1916) and the Battle of Britain (1940); the Royal Commission for the establishment of the Poor Law (1630); Shakespeare's will (1616); and the death duty account for Wordsworth (1850).

Other historical treasures available to readers on prior request included letters from every British monarch since Richard II; writings and letters by Chaucer, the Black Prince, William of Wykeham, Sir Walter Raleigh, Katharine of Aragon, Anne

Boleyn, Lady Jane Grey as Queen, Sir Philip Sydney, Essex to Elizabeth, Mary, Queen of Scots, Nelson and Bonaparte. Further documents included the indentures of Magna Carta, the log of HMS Victory, the confession of Guy Fawkes, the Treaty of Paris (1763), the earliest known document on paper, c. 1220, and the earliest map of New York.

The armorial stained glass which formerly ornamented the windows of the Rolls Chapel was brought to the Public Record Office museum between 1899 and 1901. A separate room near the museum was refurbished to house special exhibitions, and its windows, restored in 1959, contain not only the arms of 19 Masters of the Rolls, but in addition those of George I, Prince Henry and Lord Salisbury. Memorials from the Rolls Chapel are also housed here, and include the tombs of Sir Richard Allington, Master of the Rolls 1561, Lord Edward Bruce of Kinloss, Master of the Rolls 1611, and Dr John Yonge, Master of the Rolls 1516, whose sarcophagus of terracotta is by Pietro Torrigiano (1470-1528), the sculptor who had constructed the tomb of King Henry VII at Westminster Abbey and used for this memorial some of the frieze left over from the royal commission.

Opposite the Public Record Office building stands the Law Society's Hall, headquarters of the Incorporated Law Society of England and Wales, and home of the solicitors' profession which governs the 160,000 or so practitioners spread throughout

The Law Society's Hall

*The Reading Room
Law Society*

the country. The Law Society was formerly known as the Law Institute, founded in 1825 as a unifying body for attorneys and solicitors, and this hall was opened in 1830. A year later King William IV granted the Society a royal charter. As an institution it succeeded the Society of Gentlemen Practicers of the Courts of Law and Equity, which was founded in 1739.

The site upon which the hall stands is well documented, and an example of the way in which the town houses of single clerks in Chancery became known as their Inns. In the early part of the 15th century this land and the messuages on it were owned by one Nicholas Wymbush, a clerk in Chancery who also had a large practice as an attorney, so that he was effectively a civil servant dabbling also in the private sector. In 1454 the freehold was granted to Nocton Park Priory in Lincolnshire. Afterwards it became known as Harfleur or Harfleet Inn.

For some years after the turn of the 16th century a brewery occupied the site, but in 1611 offices for six clerks in Chancery were constructed here, and the name of this place became wholly associated with them for 250 years. In 1538 with the dissolution of Nocton Priory its estates passed to the Duke of Suffolk. Within a year he had sold this land to the six clerks who were created a corporation in order that they might hold the fee simple title. The senior of the six clerks, who gave his name to the 'Six Clerks' Inn' was Edward Kederminster. His memorial tablet was placed in the Rolls Chapel in 1607, and can today be found with artefacts from the Rolls Chapel housed across the road. The six clerks vacated much of the site in 1622 but retained a working office in the northern corner here until 1774 when they moved to purpose-built offices in the new Stone Buildings, further up Chancery Lane, within Lincoln's Inn.

4. Cross Carey Street.

At 93/4 Chancery Lane is the showroom and shop of Messrs Ede & Ravenscroft, the oldest bespoke tailors in the world. The firm not long ago celebrated its 300th anniversary, and proudly boasts a royal warrant held under 13 successive monarchs since its grant by William III and Mary in 1689. This establishment provides academic, court and ceremonial costumes, wigs and regalia throughout the Commonwealth, for the nobility, orders of chivalry, ecclesiastics, the legal world and the mayoralty. The firm has produced every kind of State ceremonial robe from the coronation robes of King William IV to the legal, court and peers' costumes to W.S. Gilbert's own specifications for the D'Oyly Carte Opera Company's original productions of Iolanthe and Utopia Limited. Messrs Ede & Ravenscroft formerly traded from premises in Serle Street, and moved to the firm's present address in 1894.

The inventive genius which brought Humphrey Ravenscroft into the ancient family tailoring business of Webb and Ede occurred in 1822. In that year Ravenscroft patented his forensic wig for the use of the Bar, which is still in use and tailor made at the rear of the premises. Until the end of the 16th century judges and barristers had worn red robes with a flat black coif on their head, reflecting the ecclesiastical roots of the profession. When wigs became fashionable, the judiciary and Bar adopted them as a court headdress and even after about 1750 when powdered wigs went out of fashion the Bar retained their use.

Ravenscroft's invention was to use fixed curls which would not unwind and therefore removed the need for frizzing regularly with pomatum to stop curls from falling out. These he made from horsehair, so that the wig did not have to be powdered: this was important, since wigs which were until then made from human hair had to be regularly powdered to keeping them looking white.

Facade of Ede & Ravenscroft

Ede & Ravenscrott:

Above and below: Barristers wigs in preparation

Furthermore, William Pitt had imposed a tax on wig powder to raise money to fight the War of American Independence. Ravenscroft blended in one black horsehair for every five white, which gave the appearance of a powdered human wig.

Ede & Ravenscroft have supplied the full-bottomed wigs of every Lord Chancellor since 1697, when one cost 6 guineas (£6.30). To give some idea of the pattern of inflation, in 1930 the barrister's forensic wig cost 7 guineas (£7.87). In 1989 the same article cost £209. By 1999 the cost had risen to £345. Today it may cost up to £560.

Within the shop a small exhibition of royal warrants, costumes and regalia is maintained for visitors, and legal or academic costumes are generally on show in the windows.

Between Ede's and the gateway to Lincoln's Inn are to be found two passageways, recently transformed by a modern office development centred on No. 81 Chancery Lane to house an annexe of the Central Criminal Court specialising in serious fraud trials. These alleyways, Chichester Rents and Bishop's Court, mark the site of the London town house of the bishops of Lincoln, constructed during the reign of King Henry III (1216-72), on a garden belonging to one John Herbertson. However, they are named not for the bishops of Lincoln, venerable men though they might have been. Rather the names of the courtyards are derived from the great Ralph Neville, who was bishop of Chichester from 1193 to 1244 and for much of that period Lord Chancellor of England.

In 1227 Neville built a mansion on the site now covered by Old Hall, Lincoln's Inn, Old Buildings and Hale Court. Its gardens, paddocks and coney garth, or rabbit warren, stretched up to the south side of Holborn. The two passageways, Chichester Rents and Bishop's Court, cut through the older houses to give access to Chancery Lane. The bishop's property was separated from Chancery Lane by a ditch together with a wall constructed of mud and reeds, which stood until 1422. A small wicket gate in the wall was situated near the entrance to Bishop's Court. Neville lived in his bishop's palace here until his death in 1244 when the building passed to the bishopric. Successive bishops of Chichester lived here until 1412, and one of their number was again Lord Chancellor. This was John de Langton, Chancellor from 1292 to 1302 and 1307 to 1310. More than Neville, it was probably from de Langton's period in office that the name Chancery Lane is derived.

Between 1412 and 1422 the Society of Lincoln's Inn came to occupy what by then was known as the bishops' house, and afterwards continued to pay rent to the diocese of Chichester until the confiscation of ecclesiastical property by the State in 1538 (the Dissolution).

On the east side of Chancery Lane, to the north of the Rolls Chapel, stood a small Inn of Chancery known as Symond's Inn. This may have been founded in the first half of the 15th century, but its origins are obscure. It appears to have only functioned as an

Inn between 1468 and 1540, and certainly it had disappeared by the time of Sir Edward Coke (1552-1634). Its buildings, however, were not demolished until 1873-4, and until that time the Inn housed a variety of High Court offices, including those of the masters and registrar in Chancery, and the Affidavit Office, precursor to the Chancery Chambers Registry of today.

A little further up Chancery Lane and to the right, Cursitor Street leads down to Took's Court. In the immediate vicinity stood Cursitors' or Bacon's Inn, which was founded as a satellite of Gray's Inn by Sir Nicholas Bacon (1509-79), then the Lord Keeper of the Great Seal, and father of Francis Bacon, Viscount St Albans (1561-1626). It has been suggested that the name 'cursitor' is a corruption of 'chorister', another link between the law and its ecclesiastical past. Certainly the Inn grew out of the Cursitor's Office, which was either an office concerned with the City of London's own courts, or a semi-independent office for issuing writs out of the High Court of Chancery, depending on which source is read. It is known that Lord Eldon, who was Lord Chancellor 1801-6 and 1807-21 had lodgings here when he first came to London, having eloped with his bride from Newcastle and tried his luck in Oxford en route.

In Took's Court stood another device of the 18th century's privatisation of penal institutions: a private debtor's prison or sponging-house known as Sloman's. In 1814 the dramatist Richard Brinsley Sheridan was incarcerated here for debt by the brewer Whitbread. The place appears in Disraeli's *Henrietta Temple* and Thackeray's *Vanity Fair*.

Returning to Chancery Lane, on the back wall of Old Square is the blue plaque commemorating John Thurlow, 1616-68, a bencher of Lincoln's Inn from 1654 and who lived in Old Square at various times until his death there. Thurlow was Cromwell's Secretary of State under the Commonwealth.

The exterior wall of Old Buildings and Old Square, Lincoln's Inn is bisected by the famous gatehouse to Lincoln's Inn, originally constructed between 1517 and 1521 from bricks baked in the Inn's own kilns on the site of the former coney garth. The design of the gateway follows that of St James's Palace, the priory of St. John's Clerkenwell and Lambeth Palace. The gate contained a guardhouse, afterwards a small set of barristers' chambers. Above the gate itself is a stone tablet containing three armorial

Chancery Lane

Lincoln's Inn Gatehouse

devices. In the centre is the royal coat of arms of King Henry VIII, and to the right that of Henry de Lacy, Earl of Lincoln, after whom the Society is named. The arms to the left are those of Sir Thomas Lovell, who paid for the erection of the gateway. During the time it was under construction Lovell served as member of Parliament for Northampton, Chancellor of the Exchequer and Speaker of the House of Commons. In 1520 he became 'gubernator' or governor of the Society.

Due to the increase of heavy traffic using Chancery Lane, and the substantially deteriorating condition of the original gatehouse, it was demolished in 1968. The present gatehouse is a replica, although the heavy oaken doors date from 1564.

Through the gateway the little gardened courtyard of Old Buildings and Old Hall can be seen, where the Lord Chancellor himself sat in the 1820s and 1830s, atmospherically recorded by Dickens in *Bleak House* and *Our Mutual Friend*.

Passing up the Lane, on the east side, is the narrow passageway leading into Quality Court. This has been for many years the home of firms of chartered patent agents, because nearby Southampton Buildings was the headquarters of the Patent Office, which is now in Newport, South Wales, and of the British Library's Science and Reference and Information Service, which is now in the new British Library building at 96 Euston Road.

Immediately beyond at 48/9 Chancery Lane is the present home of the legal industry's National Pro Bono Centre, which houses the profession's national clearing houses for legal pro bono work delivered in England and Wales: the Bar Pro Bono Unit, LawWorks (the Solicitors' Pro Bono Group) and ILEX Pro Bono Forum. The Centre is designed to be a "hub" for pro bono charities in the sector and helps individuals and community groups all over England and Wales.

5. Cross to Southampton Buildings.

Southampton Buildings occupied the site of the original Temple, which housed the Order of Knights Templar from 1118 to 1184. Here the order built its first church on land granted to Richard de Hastings, the Master of the Order, who was a close friend of Thomas à Becket. As the order grew in numbers and stature the land occupied by the commandery, residence, refectory and stables became insufficient to provide for the needs of the knights. Work on a new Temple church and commandery was commenced on land purchased between Fleet Street and the Thames, and from 1160 a steady migration of knights left this area known as the Old Temple. Immediately adjoining it, and later to absorb its buildings, was the bishop of Lincoln's Inn, founded by Robert de Curars in 1147. Successive bishops of Lincoln made this their London headquarters, including John Russell, who was Lord Chancellor to Richard III.

After the dissolution of the monasteries by King Henry VIII, the buildings passed to the earldom of Southampton, and had become known as Southampton House by 1549. In the 17th century a major clearance of the site made way for the erection of tenement buildings which were named Southampton Buildings. Here one of London's early coffee houses was founded in 1650. Some 170 years later Dr George Birkbeck (1776-1841) founded a mechanics' institute here in 1823, for the 'dissemination of useful knowledge among the industrious classes of the community', an idea which was to be satirised by W.S. Gilbert in *The Sorcerer*. Birkbeck's London Institute became Birkbeck College in the University of London. From 1820 to 1824 the essayist William Hazlitt (1778-1830) lived at 9 Southampton Buildings, where he wrote, taught and entertained the residual members of Charles and Mary Lamb's set.

Towards the northern end of Chancery Lane two classical-style buildings face each other. To the west is the rear frontage of Stone Buildings, Lincoln's Inn, constructed between 1774 and 1785 and accommodating the headquarters of the Inns of Court and City Yeomanry, the Territorial Army, and several sets of chambers for the Bar. Slightly before it is the wrought-iron gate between Stone Buildings and Old Square, Lincoln's Inn, surmounted by magnificent carriage lamps, and affording a splendid view of New Hall and the Library.

On the opposite side of the road is the much more modern Chancery House. In its vicinity stood the homes of two great men of history. Hereabouts was the house of Cardinal Wolsey (1475?-1530), who would daily travel in state procession down Chancery Lane, where he would cross Fleet Street, pass down Middle Temple Lane and take the boat from Temple Stairs to Westminster Hall. His near neighbour, but a century later, was the Earl of Strafford (born 1593), impeached and executed for treason in 1641.

Chancery Lane emerges into Holborn at its northern end, with Chancery Lane Underground Station some 250 yards (230 m.) along Holborn to the east. Opposite, Warwick Court leads to the City University School of Law, and Gray's Inn beyond.

New Square, Lincoln's Inn in the snow

7. Lincoln's Inn and the Fields

And hard by Temple Bar, in Lincoln's Inn Hall, at the very heart of the fog, sits the Lord High Chancellor in his High Court of Chancery.
　　　　　　　　Charles Dickens, *Bleak House*, Chapter 1

Lincoln's Inn & Fields

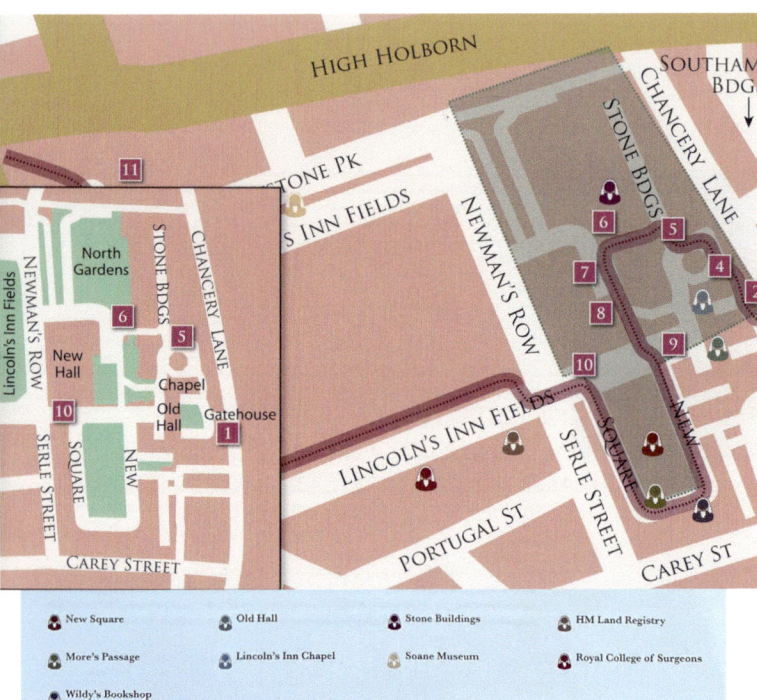

1. The tour of Lincoln's Inn commences at the gatehouse in Chancery Lane.
2. Proceed through the arcade by Old Hall.
3. Turn right along the frontage of Old Hall.
4. Proceed from the undercroft into Old Square.
5. Pass between 10 and 11 Old Square to Stone Buildings.
6. Proceed into the gardens by passing between Stone Buildings and 10 Old Square.
7. Turn left. There is a vista of New Square ahead, to the right of New Hall, elevated on its terrace, and diagonally to the left of the chapel and the frontage of Old Hall.
8. Proceed towards New Square.
9. Proceed in a clockwise direction around New Square from No. 12 around to No. 11 by the gate to Lincoln's Inn Fields.
10. Leave the precincts of the Inn and cross into Lincoln's Inn Fields.
11. Cross to the north-west corner of Lincoln's Inn Fields to the traffic lights on Holborn Kingsway. Holborn Underground Station is 150 yards (140 m.) to the right.

The name of surely the most beautiful of the Inns, Lincoln's Inn, is generally thought to derive from Henry de Lacy, Earl of Lincoln, and a King's Justice between 1289 and 1292, since the Inn used his coat of arms for at least three centuries. From those arms, a lion rampant survives as part of the upper left quadrant of the Inn's coat today. He is not, however, the only candidate, and the good earl himself is not likely ever to have occupied the land on which the Inn was built. His town house stood some half mile (750 m.) away at the north-eastern corner of Shoe Lane, purchased from the Friar Preachers (Dominicans) otherwise known as the Black Friars, in 1286. This building stood on the site formerly occupied by the Church of the Black Friars which became surplus to requirements after 1276 when the Mayor and City of London gave them a piece of ground between Baynard's Castle on the riverside and Lud Gate to build a new monastery and church.

De Lacy died at Shoe Lane on 5 February 1311, by which time he had established his staff of justices' clerks and students at a hostel opposite his house which became known as Thavies Inn. De Lacy's daughter had married his cousin Thomas, Earl of Lancaster, who was steward to King Edward I and the beneficiary of the manor of Holbourne. Records of the accounts of the Duchy of Lancaster show that even after de Lacy's death huge amounts of legal business were transacted out of the house in Shoe Lane. In 1314-15 alone, 129 dozen parchments for the issue of writs were delivered there together with 1,714 pounds (777 kg.) of wax with vermilion dye to make the red wax seals which were attached to the writs.

Unfortunately Thomas of Lancaster, who led the barons' opposition to King Edward II, was executed for treason in 1322. The property in Shoe Lane passed through his widow on her remarriage to one Ebulo le Strange and it became known as Strange's Inn. It is not known whether the Honourable Society of Lincoln's Inn was descended directly from the occupants of Strange's Inn, because the issue becomes confused in 1344, when a Society of Lincoln's Inn appears to have been established by a serjeant called Thomas de Lincoln at a property on the east side of Chancery Lane between Holborn and the Rolls Chapel.

At that time the opposite side of Chancery Lane was occupied by the London mansion and gardens of the bishops of Chichester. This land had been escheated and made forfeit to the Crown when William de Haverhill, treasurer to King Henry III was convicted of treason, and the property given to Ralph Neville, who was bishop of Chichester from 1193 to 1244 and for much of that time Henry's Lord Chancellor. He built a large house in 1227 and lived here until his death in 1244. It afterwards became the residence of John de Langton, who was bishop of Chichester under King Edward II.

By the turn of the 15th century this property was showing distinct signs of decrepitude. Bishop Reade, the last bishop to live at the mansion, died in 1415. Within the next seven years the Society of Lincoln's Inn appears to have crossed the Lane, occupying the mansion. The see of Chichester continued to own the property until the beginning of the 16th century when it was sold to an Essex gentleman named Sulyard. In 1579 his family conveyed it to William Kingsmith and other benchers of the Honourable Society of Lincoln's Inn for £520.

The records of the present Honourable Society of Lincoln's Inn commence in 1422, the earliest complete records of any of the Inns of Court, and are referred to as the Black Books. These indicate that the gardens on the northern part of the site where Old Square and Stone Buildings now stand, then called Cottrell's Garden, were leased from the Hospital of St Giles-in-the-Fields, itself held from the Knights Hospitaller of the Order of St John of Jerusalem, the great rival order to the Knights Templar. To the west of Cottrell's Garden was an area of waste ground known as Backside which was later developed into the coney-garth or rabbit warren of the Inn. The southern part of the Inn, which now comprises New Square, was part of what is today Lincoln's Inn Fields, an open area then called Fickett's Field, used by the Templars for archery practice and jousting, and separated from Backside by a ditch.

Lincoln's Inn Library, Detail

The Black Books show that the earliest control of the Society lay with the masters of the bench, all of whom were

Entrance to the Inn between 3 and 4 New Square by Wildy's bookshop

utter barristers, meaning they had held rights of audience in the common law courts for seven years. Late in the 16th century, utter barristers were those who had previously held the office of reader, and in the 19th century the term was used to distinguish between those called within the Bar – the 'inner barristers' or Queen's Counsel – and the outside or 'utter' Bar. Between 1424 and 1574 the masters of the bench elected annually four governors to conduct the administrative affairs of the Inn, and appointed: the treasurer (from 1456), who was titular head of the society; the reader (from 1464), whose function was to control the moots, preside over bolts – legal argument in law French – and give discourses on the law to students after dinner in hall; the dean of the chapel; the butler; the keeper of the Black Books (from 1513); the marshall (from 1455), whose concern was to secure attendance at hall and chapel and to punish disorderly conduct; the pensioner (from 1427), whose function was to collect each member's pension or subscription, from which was paid the rent, chaplain's salary and expenses, and the chapel servants' wages; the butler and the steward for Christmas (from 1422); the master of revels; and the escheator, who levied fines. By the mid 16th century the Inn also had a master of walks and a master of the library.

As with Gray's Inn, whose early fortunes were bound up with the history of one family, the Bacons, so Lincoln's Inn had its famous early dynasty. In 1464 the butler to the Inn was one John More, who six years later became steward. For his service as an officer he was rewarded with membership of the society and went on to become reader in 1489 and again in 1495. His son was Sir Thomas More, who knew the Inn man and boy for over 40 years. Thomas was educated in Old Hall before going to Oxford and specially admitted in 1496 at the request of his father. His rise to high office after the death in 1509 of King Henry VII, whose enmity he gained by proposing a reduction in the privy purse voted by Parliament to the king, was inexorable. In 1510 he became an under sheriff of the City of London, and shortly afterwards was the autumn reader for 1511 and the Lent reader 1516. He attracted the attention of King Henry VIII, becoming a close confidant, and was appointed to the Privy Council in 1518 and knighted in 1521. He was elected Speaker of the House of Commons two years later, became under treasurer of the Exchequer, and in 1529 Lord Chancellor upon the fall of Cardinal Wolsey. More was the first layman to hold the Great Seal, but he resigned his office in 1532 since he could not support the king's attack on the papacy over the refusal of the pontiff to consent to a divorce from Katharine of Aragon. In 1534 Sir Thomas More refused to swear the oath of supremacy to the king, was tried for high treason and executed at Tower Hill on 6 July 1535. He was canonised by the Roman Catholic church exactly 400 years later. A statue of More is set in the wall of the Inn at the corner of Carey Street and Serle Street.

Lincoln's Inn did not attract the notoriety of either Gray's or the Middle Temple during the Elizabethan age as a society venue. It was staunchly loyal to the king during the Civil War 1645-9, despite the fact that three of the regicides were members of the society and Thurlow, Cromwell's Secretary of State, had his chambers here. King Charles II came to the Inn on three occasions after the restoration in 1660, and it is said that on one of those visits everyone dined so well that they could not stand to drink a toast and he granted members of Lincoln's Inn the privilege of drinking the loyal toast seated, in perpetuity. No official evidence of this appears to exist. In 1892 Prince George, later King George V, was elected an honorary bencher, and he became treasurer in l904. His consort, Queen Mary, became the first woman bencher of any of the Inns in November 1943. By 1860 the Inn was firmly, almost exclusively, associated with practice in the High Court of Chancery. Having outgrown the facilities at Westminster, the Chancery courts and offices were scattered throughout the precincts of the Inn and its immediate surrounds. The Chancery writ office was at Rolls Yard; the Vice-Chancellor's court sat in Old Hall; the masters of the Exchequer were at Stone Buildings; the Queen's Remembrancer, then an officer of the Court of Chancery, was in Chancery Lane and the masters in lunacy sat at an office in Lincoln's Inn Fields. Even today the Chancery practitioners, dealing mainly with property, companies, insolvency, trusts and settlements, are to be found principally in Lincoln's Inn.

The Inn has had many distinguished members and is particularly proud to have produced nine former male prime ministers: Sir Robert Walpole, William Pitt the Younger, Henry Addington (later Viscount Sidmouth), Spencer Perceval, George Canning, Viscount Melbourne, Benjamin Disraeli (later Earl of Beaconsfield), W.E. Gladstone, and Herbert Henry Asquith (later Earl of Oxford and Asquith); the first female prime minister, Margaret Thatcher; and the recent incumbent, Tony Blair. The Inn has had over 20 Lord Chancellors among its members, in particular, Lords Bathurst, Erskine, Herschell and Hailsham of St Marylebone. Perhaps the most distinguished judge of the 20th century, Lord Denning, was a member of this Inn for nearly 80 years. It extended the election of honorary bencher to several allied commanders of the Second World War, notably General, afterwards President, Dwight D. Eisenhower, Admiral of the Fleet Lord Cunningham of Hyndhope, and Earl Alexander of Tunis, and to United States Secretary of State Dean Acheson.

Lincoln's Inn has also had its fair share of literary and artistic talent. David Garrick (1717-79), the great actor manager, was entered as a student of the Inn in 1737, and the writers Charles Kingsley (1819-75) in 1839, and Wilkie Collins (1824-89) in 1846. The historian Lord Macaulay (1800-59), and the writers Charles Reade (1814-84), Thomas Hughes (1822-96), Horace Walpole (1717-97) and H. Rider Haggard (1856-1925) all had chambers here. Sir Francis Burnand (1836-1917), dramatist and editor of *Punch* 1880-1906 was called to the Bar of the Inn in 1862.

1. The tour of Lincoln's Inn commences at the gatehouse in Chancery Lane.

The frontage of Lincoln's Inn runs for 500 feet (150 m.) along Chancery Lane. The original gatehouse was built between 1518 and 1521 and bears a panel of three coats of arms over the gateway. These are to the left, those of de Lacy; in the centre the royal arms of Henry VIII, dated 1518, and to the right the arms of the treasurer for 1521, Sir Thomas Lovell, who had fought for Henry VII, then Henry Tudor, at the battle of Bosworth in 1485, and was made Speaker of the House of Commons. The red brick was ornamented by inlaid brickwork of different colours, in the style of the famous gatehouses at Hampton Court Palace and St James's Palace. The bricks were manufactured at the brick kiln in the Inn's own coney-garth. It is recorded that one Fuller, a bencher of the Inn, reputedly came upon the dramatist Ben Jonson working as a bricklayer on the construction.

The gatehouse and Old Buildings at the turn of the 20th century

Despite its ancient appearance, the gatehouse is a reconstruction of 1968, when the original was demolished and extensive rebuilding took place over the period 1966-9 in Old Buildings to enable the construction of Hale Court to take place at the rear. The oaken gates are original, though, and date from 1564.

As is common throughout the Inns of Court, building works are marked by the date and initials or arms of the treasurer for that year. Thus, for example, it can be seen that the interior of the right-hand side of the gatehouse, which formed No. 1 Old Buildings, was reconstructed in 1956 during the treasurership of John M. Daynes; and on the gatehouse facing westwards into the Inn are the arms of Lord Upjohn, Edward Bide and Princess Margaret, treasurers in 1965, 1695 (recognising an earlier restoration) and 1967 respectively.

The western side of the courtyard into which one emerges, Old Buildings, was originally a 1524 extension to the kitchens of what is now Old Hall. The south side was first erected in about 1562. Chambers were in use at No. 27 shortly after that date to the left of the gatehouse, but these were removed during substantial alterations to the eastern side of the Inn abutting Chancery Lane, which were carried out in 1880-1, and which account for the appearance of the Inn's exterior today.

The original Nos. 21-24 Old Buildings were raised in 1609. At No. 21 were the chambers of Lord Chancellor Henley in 1760 when, on the accession of King George III, the title Lord Keeper of the Great Seal, an office also held by Henley since 1757, became merged with the Chancellorship. Number 25 was built earlier, in 1601, and became the chambers of Lord Denman, Chief Justice of the King's Bench 1832-50. The corner turret at No. 21 was rebuilt in 1954 and again in 1969.

John Thurlow, 1616-68, lived at 24 Old Buildings from 1646 to 1659 and for the following two years at No. 13. He was a bencher of the Inn from 1654 and became Secretary of State to Oliver Cromwell in 1650 and for the 10-year period of the Commonwealth. Cromwell was a frequent visitor at his chambers.

Other famous occupants of Old Buildings in their day included the poet Edmund Waller in 1628, Benjamin Disraeli as a pupil in 1824, and the early Victorian author and historian, A.W. Kinglake in 1837.

2. Proceed through the arcade by Old Hall.

Between 21 Old Buildings and Old Hall an arcade with an embossed ceiling, built in 1926, passes the entrance into Old Hall and emerges into the open courtyard formed by 16-20 Old Buildings, formerly called Kitchen Garden Court.

Number 14 Old Buildings was known as the Library Staircase, that being the site of the original benchers' library on the first floor. Number 16 was built in 1535 and three centuries later was occupied by the chambers of Lord Cottenham, the Lord Chancellor between 1836 and 1846. Numbers 18-20 were erected even earlier, in 1525.

Old Hall, Lincoln's Inn is only the third building upon the site. The first hall was that of the bishop of Chichester, and appears to have remained unaltered for some 70 years after the society acquired the bishop's house. Sir John Fortescue, Chief Justice of the King's Bench 1442-60, is known to have dined here throughout his office.

In 1489 work commenced on a new hall for the Inn which was 70 feet (21 m.) long, 30 feet (9 m.) broad and 32 feet (10 m.) high. It opened in 1491, although work was not completed until 1507. A gallery was added in 1565. This hall had an open hearth in its centre with a smoke louvre above. It was the only fire in the Inn, since chambers did not have fireplaces before the mid-17th century. It was glazed with windows in 1454 and lit until 1609 by six candle plates and one great candlestick holding two candelabra. After renovations of 1625, 1657 and 1806, the hall was lengthened in 1824 to provide for the addition of two more Bar messes.

Members of the Inn were summoned to their meals, or 'taking commons', which occurred at strictly observed times, by the blowing of a horn in the courtyards. Breakfast of bread and ale was served at 7 a.m.; at midday the principal meal of beef or mutton with ale followed by cheese was given; and a supper of bread and cheese was provided at 6.00 p.m. Gradually over the centuries the dinner hour moved through the afternoon until it was 4.00 p.m. and then effectively merged with supper. In 1908 it was fixed at 7 p.m. and each of the Inns now dines at this hour, although the menu, having been extended by 1800 to include two cooked dishes, is somewhat broader now.

No 20 Old Buildings

At the northern end of hall was a raised platform for the masters of the bench, the 'benchers', with two perpendicular side tables allotted to the Bar. One was called the ancient syde where the mess of eight ancients, the senior members of the Inn who had not been elected as benchers, dined; the other table ran along the wall to the buttery and here the rest of the Bar sat. Students were placed on the opposite side of the hall. In the south-west corner a recessed table was used by the clerks of the benchers, and the other clerks sat at the lower end of hall. The readers delivered lectures from the ancient syde, and the barristers conducted their exercises, which comprised readings, moots and bolts, then the only form of practical legal education, from the Bench end of the Bar table.

Old Hall

Between 1605 and 1646 there were about 140 in commons. During that period the readers' feasts, and pensioners' suppers became famous for riotous behaviour and disturbances. The messes engaged in a pastime called mock hunting. Up to 1629 members played cards and dice in hall on Saturday nights, a practice suppressed with the onset of Puritanism in middle-class society. However, after the Restoration much of the gaiety for which the Inn was known in the 17th century returned. King Charles II attended the Christmas revels of 1661 and 1670 in hall. His third visit, recorded in the diaries of both Samuel Pepys and John Evelyn, was to a masque on 27 February 1672, on which occasion he was accompanied by his brother, the Duke of York, afterwards King James II, their cousin Prince Rupert, the Royalist cavalry commander during the Civil War, and, ironically, Charles's illegitimate son the Duke of Monmouth, who a little over a decade later led an insurrection against James, his companion on that evening.

Old Hall looking towards the screen

Old Hall was and remains dominated by William Hogarth's painting of Paul before Felix, which was undertaken between 1746 and 1748, having been commissioned by the benchers at the suggestion of William Murray, then the Solicitor-General, but afterwards better known as Lord Mansfield, Chief Justice of the King's Bench 1756-88. A bequest of £200 was available and the scene is from chapter 24 of the Acts of the Apostles. The painting was restored in 1970.

From 1428 to 1739 a buttery linked hall and chapel and this became a withdrawing room when hall was put into use as a courtroom. In 1717 the Rolls Court in Chancery Lane was undergoing repair and the Master of the Rolls, Sir Joseph Jekyll, moved his court into hall. The success of this temporary move, and the pressure for space at the Courts of Westminster Hall led the then Lord Chancellor, Lord Talbot, to approach the benchers of Middle

Temple in 1734 to request the use of their hall out of the dining term. They refused, but in doing so did the Temple a considerable disservice, because once the Lord Chancellor's Court had removed as an alternative, by agreement, to Lincoln's Inn hall, the greatly increased demand for chambers here led to a twentyfold increase in the Society's rental income. The Lord Chancellor's Court sat in hall from 1734 to 1875, and a clear and accurate picture is provided of it by Dickens in the opening chapter of *Bleak House* in which he describes the court in the Chancellorship of Lord Eldon at the turn of the 19th century.

The masters in Chancery had sat here in 1655 at the request of the Recorder of London. In 1819 the Court of the Vice-Chancellor was added by building a partition to enclose the north-western corner of hall; and in 1841 the judicious use of a further partition screened off the eastern end to house a court for the Lords Justices of Appeal. In 1874 both partitions were removed and for a year afterwards the Lord Chancellor resumed sitting alone while work on the Royal Courts of Justice building commenced.

3. Turn right along the frontage of Old Hall.

In 1926 the hall was demolished and replaced by an exact reconstruction dating from 1928. At the far end of Old Hall the roadway passes beneath the storey which links hall with the chapel. Here, set into the brickwork is a tablet bearing the inscription 'This hall was built in the fifth year of Henry VII rebuilt and restored in the 18th year of the reign of George V. Opened by Queen Mary in November 1928'. The only noticeable difference in the rebuilt hall is that the former carved stone corbels were replaced with heraldic shields bearing the emblems of Henry VII and George V.

For two centuries after 1422 the lawyers used the domestic chapels of the bishops of Chichester, the Chapel of Our Lady and the Chapel of St Richard. It is recorded that the Chapel of St Richard was one of the many meeting places of the Curia Regia in the reign of Henry III, but this would not be unusual when Bishop Neville was Lord Chancellor. In 1609 the society resolved to construct a new chapel but had to wait a few years to ensure that the busy achitect who was to be commissioned could supervise the building works personally. This was Inigo Jones (1573-1652), whose work in the 'perpendicular gothic' style was erected 1620-23. Once again there is a legend that one of the stonemasons was Ben Jonson. The opening sermon on 22 May 1623 was given by Dr John Donne, Dean of St Paul's and poet, who also held the post of preacher to the society from October 1616.

In 1685 Sir Christopher Wren (1632-1723) carried out repairs. The chapel was restored and altered by Wyatt in 1797 and in 1820 the present organ installed. The building was extended and the exterior put into Victorian gothic in 1882-3 by Salter after the demolition of two adjacent sets of Jacobean chambers, including those of Thurlow at No. 13 Old Buildings.

Lincoln's Inn chapel

The interior contains sculpted heads of Bishop Neville and Queen Victoria. A monument stands in the vestibule to Spencer Perceval who was prime minister 1809 to 1812, and treasurer of Lincoln's Inn, but is now remembered mainly for the manner of his death: he was murdered in the House of Commons in 1812, the only prime minister ever to be assassinated, although a determined attempt was made on the life of Margaret Thatcher, another Lincoln's Inn premier, in October 1994.

The south window contains the arms of readers from 1586 to 1677, and the east window, the arms of treasurers from 1680 to 1862. The chapel is open to worship and services are held on every Sunday during the law terms. Its bell, which for centuries tolled for curfew at 9 p.m. and on the death of a bencher between 12.30 and 1.00 p.m., was brought from a sacking of Cadiz by the Earl of Essex in 1596.

The undercroft (crypt) under the chapel was made open as an ambulatory for students to walk and confer in their studies. It is mentioned by Samuel Butler (1612-80) in *Hudibras*, and Pepys records walking here in 1663. A similar custom developed at the Round in the Temple Church. The undercroft has a Victorian vaulted ceiling, and on the left-hand side at its western end a plan on the wall indicates the layout of gravestones dating back to 1667. Here is to be found the tomb of John Thurlow.

The undercroft of Lincoln's Inn chapel

4. Proceed from the undercroft into Old Square.

As late as 1536 no building was situated to the north of Old Hall. In that year the predecessor of Old Square, Gatehouse

Court, was erected, a place where Lord Mansfield first studied law. Here Dickens set Kenge and Carboy's offices in *Bleak House* and the chambers of Serjeant Snubbin in the *Pickwick Papers*. Thomas Hughes, afterwards a county court judge, member of Parliament and author of *Tom Brown's Schooldays*, was an occupant between 1848 and 1854. He formed a close association with fellow member Charles Kingsley, author of *Westward Ho!* and *The Water-Babies* and the two men led the Christian Socialist movement in the 1860s, Kingsley also being a leading Chartist.

The block of buildings on the site of 8-15 Old Square was enlarged in 1566 and rebuilt in 1607. Its present red-brick, gabled, Queen Anne revival style derives from a reconstruction of Nos. 8-10 in 1872-5, No. 11 in 1878, No. 13 in 1880 and the remainder in 1882-3. The section of Old Square now numbered 8-10 and adjacent to the garden stands on the site of a group of chambers called Garden Court or Garden Row. Its four most famous occupants were William Lenthall (1591-1662) the Speaker of the Long Parliament, who resisted the attempt of King Charles I to have five members of Parliament arrested, and who afterwards became Master of the Rolls; Sir Matthew Hale, an immense legal luminary of the Inn, a serjeant, Justice of the Common Pleas in 1654-8, member of Parliament 1658-66, Chief Baron of the Exchequer 1666-71 and President of the Fire Commissioners, and Chief Justice of the King's Bench 1671-6; the philosopher Jeremy Bentham (1748-1832); and Lord Brougham, who was Lord Chancellor 1830-4, and a great law reformer who was responsible for the abolition of various obsolete courts, the creation of both the Central Criminal Court and the Judicial Committee of the Privy Council, and the passage of the Great Reform Act of 1832 which created for the first time in Britain a limited form of universal suffrage through Parliament.

The building which replaced Garden Row has also produced eminent lawyers, notably at 9 Old Square, Viscount Buckmaster, Lord Chancellor 1915-6; Viscount Simonds, Lord Chancellor 1951-4 and a distinguished editor-in-chief of *Halsbury's Laws of England*, and Sir Robert Megarry who was Vice- Chancellor 1976-85 and Lord Hoffmann. At No. 10 Viscount Haldane, the Lord Chancellor 1912-15 and 1924-5, who masterminded the reform of English land and property law in 1925, had chambers.

5. Pass between 10 and 11 Old Square to Stone Buildings.

Stone Buildings have a distinctive and imposing late Georgian façade. Nos. 3-6 were raised in 1774 from the design of Sir Robert Taylor and were part of a plan to rebuild the entire Inn in stone rather than brick. Nos. 1, 2 and 7 were built in 1845, by which time the plan had, fortunately, been abandoned. At No. 2 Lord Macnaghten was in chambers from 1869 to 1887 when he achieved the unusual distinction of passing from silk directly into the House of Lords to sit as a Lord of Appeal in Ordinary without first having held high judicial office, a remarkable feat replicated by Lord Sumption KC who was appointed to the Supreme Court in 2012 directly from practice at the Bar. At No. 3 were the chambers of Frederick William Maitland (1850-1906), the great jurist and legal historian who became Downing Professor of the Laws of England at Cambridge in 1888 and was the driving force behind the founding of the Selden Society for the study of English legal history.

The garden façade of Stone Buildings

No 10. Stone Buildings houses the regimental headquarters of the Inns of Court and City Yeomanry, formerly the Volunteer Rifle Corps. Military service by lawyer volunteers has a long and honourable history dating back to 1585 when 95 lawyers entered a solemn pledge to defend Queen Elizabeth I from the threat of invasion by Spain. King George II gave the regiment the title 'the Devil's Own'.

On the roadway in front of No. 10 is a stud. A tablet on the front of No. 10 relates how a bomb falling at that point from a German aircraft on 18 December 1917 at 8.10 p.m. struck the ground and exploded, shattering the windows of Stone Buildings and causing structural damage that can still be seen: shrapnel holes pockmark the walls of Nos. 10, 4 and 5. A second memorial at No. 10 also reveals that this part of Stone Buildings was erected in 1774 to accommodate the Six Clerks of the King's High Court of Chancery after their removal from the office that they occupied in Chancery Lane at the corner of Carey Street. This was an ancient administrative department which was abolished in 1842.

At No. 4 Stone Buildings William Pitt the Younger (1759-1806) occupied a set of chambers in 1780; in 1782 he became a bencher, the year in which he was appointed Chancellor of the Exchequer, and held also the society's offices of keeper of the Black Book in 1789 and dean of chapel the following year. In commemoration of his treasurership in 1794, on the garden façade of Stone Buildings a sun-dial was placed with the inscription *Qua redit nescitis horam* (You do not know the hour when he returns), possibly attributable to the Book of Revelations 3:3. In 1796 he became master of the Walks. Following his father both into politics and to becoming prime minister, Pitt led the government in two ministries, from 1783 to 1801 and 1804 to 1806. He restored British confidence and prosperity after the American War of Independence, and became a strong war leader in the struggle against revolutionary France.

First World War shrapnel holes, Stone Buildings

6. Proceed into the gardens by passing between Stone Buildings and 10 Old Square.

The North Gardens of Lincoln's Inn, otherwise called the Walks, are on the site of the former coney-garth, or rabbit warren, owned by William Cotterell. The presence of rabbits is mentioned in the Black Books between 1452 and 1555. Rabbits were a valuable source of income in the 15th century, not as food but for their skins. Rabbits were used in banqueting, but never appeared to be the cheap source of food that one might suppose. The Inn's records show that many members were expelled for poaching rabbits. In 1572, as the value of the rabbits fell and the rabbit population became a nuisance, an order was given to destroy the warrens and level the area prior to quarrying for red clay, and within a few years a large portion of the coney-garth was turned over to builders constructing chambers in the Inn to use as a brick kiln.

In 1594 alone 400,000 bricks made of burnt clay were quarried there. In 1566 a wall was built along the western boundary of the gardens and this was extended in 1588 to the northern side. In 1571 the upper end of the gardens still contained three archery butts in obedience to an ordinance of Henry VIII in promoting archery made over 50 years earlier. The Walks were laid out as formal gardens in 1584 when the elms were planted which today

The garden in front of New Hall

are such an imposing feature. The Great Garden, so called for it size, was laid out in 1663 and a contemporary description can be found in the diary of Samuel Pepys for 27 June of that year recording his visit. At its southern end a private enclosure was created in 1724 to make a benchers' garden, and by the southern extremity of the garden memorial gates were erected 1872 in memory of Colonel Brewster, the commander of the Inns of Court Volunteers.

The library, standing to the right of and perpendicular to New Hall, was built by the architect Philip Hardwick (1792-1870) in 1845. Originally 80 feet (24 m.) in length, it was extended by a further 50 feet (15 m.) in 1873 to a design by Sir George Gilbert Scott (1811-78). The existence of a library at Lincoln's Inn is recorded from 1475, making it probably the earliest in London. The first library was housed in Kitchen Garden Court, afterwards moving to 14 Old Buildings in 1508-9, where it remained until 1787 when it moved to 2 Stone Buildings. It contains a fine collection of manuscripts bequeathed by Sir Matthew Hale.

The Library building:

Right: interior
Below: exterior

7. Turn left. There is a vista of New Square ahead, to the right New Hall, elevated on its terrace, and diagonally to the left the chapel and the frontage of Old Hall.

By the end of the 1830s Old Hall was too small for the requirements of the Inn and a new hall, designed by Philip Hardwick, was opened on 30 October 1845 in the presence of Queen Victoria and Prince Albert. A painting of the ceremony hangs in the vestibule at the south end. In an ornamental niche in the apex of the south gable between large square towers, some three storeys in height, is a statue of Queen Victoria, and the initials of the architect appear on the south frontage in diaper-work.

The interior of New Hall is 120 feet (36 m.) in length, 45 feet (14 m.) broad and 62 (19 m.) feet high. The southern end is divided off by a screen of carved oak. The stained glass of its windows depicts as much of the series of royal arms and arms of the members of the society 1450-1843 as was preserved after the windows were blown out by the explosion of a landmine in the nearby Fields in 1941. The roof bears a decorative octagonal louvre with weathervane.

The upper portion of the north wall is covered by the huge fresco by G.F. Watts entitled *Justice, a Hemicycle of Law-Givers*. It contains 33 figures, including symbolic representations of Justice, Mercy and Religion. Depicted are such diverse characters as Moses, Zoroaster, Pythagoras, Confucius, Minos of Crete, Muhammad, Charlemagne, Attila (on the basis that presumably the Victorians did not give him such a bad press), Alfred, Edward I, the Earl of Salisbury and Archbishop Stephen Langton. Watts also used some contemporaries as portrait studies: thus Minos is the poet Alfred, Lord Tennyson, Justinian is William Harcourt who was Solicitor-General 1873-4, and Bishop Ina of Northumbria is the artist Holman Hunt. On the east wall hangs the painting *Short Adjournment* produced by Norman Hepple RA in 1958, which depicts the seven Lincoln's Inn benchers who were then in the nine-man Court of Appeal: Lord Denning is shown walking to the door to represent his recent elevation to the House of Lords.

The oak panelling contains the arms of treasurers, preachers in the chapel, and the holders of high offices of State who have been members of the Inn. The window in the west bay contains the royal arms of King George V and his brother Prince Albert Victor, Duke of Clarence, who were both benchers. Portraits and busts in hall depict a number of Lord Chancellors who were members of the Inn, namely, the first Earl of Shaftesbury, (Lord Chancellor 1762-3), Lord Lyndhurst (1827-30, 1834-5 and 1841-6), the first Earl of Selborne (1872-4 and 1880-5), and the first Viscount Haldane (1912-15 and 1924). There are portraits too of King George V, Herbert Asquith, who was prime minister 1908-16 and later Earl of Oxford and Asquith, and heads of Inigo Jones, William Pitt and Sir John Fortescue.

Between New Hall and the library are the benchers' apartments comprising a spacious vestibule, the council chamber and the drawing room. The vestibule contains a collection of engravings of famous lawyers and jurists together with statues of Lord Eldon, Earl Cairns and Francis Henry Goldsmid, the first Jew to be called to the Bar, in January 1833.

New Hall

There is a fine portrait of Baroness Thatcher and a deed chest of about 1548. The benchers' rooms are hung with portraits by Gainsborough, Reynolds, Kneller, Singer Sargent, G. F. Watts and Orpen among others.

The building of the new Hall and library substantially reduced the gardens, renowned for their graceful elms. On 30 October 1945 Queen Mary planted a walnut tree to celebrate the centenary of the opening of New Hall and the library.

8. Proceed towards New Square.

Immediately on the left is the Inn's war memorial unveiled in March 1921 by Asquith, in the year of his treasurership. He was rare among prime ministers, a barrister who, after serving as prime minister, returned to private practice at his chambers at 1 Paper Buildings, Temple. He was ennobled as the first Earl of Oxford and Asquith in 1925 and took a seat on the Judicial Committee of the Privy Council.

New Square

9. Proceed in a clockwise direction around New Square from No. 12 around to No. 11 by the gate to Lincoln's Inn Fields.

New Square, originally part of Fickett's Field, was owned in 1680 by Henry Serle, a bencher of Lincoln's Inn, and it was he who erected the first houses here between 1682 and 1693 and named it Serle's Court. Until that time the southern boundary of the Inn had stood at the location of the modern No. 13 New Square. The centre of the square was laid to gravel with a Corinthian column in the centre bearing a vertical sundial, which remained until 1817. Having been grassed over in 1843, the garden was laid out in 1845 when a small pond was placed where the column once stood. The entire square was covered over in 1866-7 when a temporary building housed a public exhibition of designs for the Royal Courts of Justice building architectural competition.

The gates at the northern end of New Square are all of the filigree wrought-iron work that was saved from being contributed to the war effort in 1940. The fine railings which surrounded the rest of the garden were given up to be melted down for ammunition.

Hale Court leading to the modern Hardwicke Building

New Square comprises, from left to right, Nos. 12 and 13, which were formerly 15 and 17 Old Buildings respectively and themselves once part of Kitchen Garden Court; the garden of what was 14 Old Buildings, leading to modern Hale Court; then east Nos. 1-3, south Nos. 4-6, and west Nos. 7-11.

Between Hale Court and 1-3 New Square was a gateway called Back Gate which was opened in 1697 by the then treasurer, William Dobbins. It was the only carriageway entrance into the square.

New Square still has a captivating outlook which has attracted many of the finest lawyers to its chambers. For example, at No. 2 Sir Samuel Romilly, the great advocate of reform of the criminal justice system, was in chambers 1802-6, then moving only as far as No. 6 from 1808 to 1818.

Beneath No. 4 is the passageway by Wildy's, perhaps the most famous legal bookshop in the world. It leads into Carey Street below the chambers of Lord Camden, the Lord Chancellor 1766-70, and below the two large coats of arms over the archway. These are Henry de Lacy's lion of Lincoln and the arms of Henry Serle. The name Carey Street is itself famous, lending its name to a popular phrase taken from the sittings of the High Court of Bankruptcy along towards Portugal Street in the l9th century. Originally a carriageway flanked by two footpaths for pedestrians, in 1830 the footpaths were blocked in and occupied by Wildy's. It is said that the Duke of Wellington, whilst prime minister, had a narrow escape from an angry pursuing mob by cutting through this archway.

Immediately to the west of the gate into Carey Street stood Serle's Coffee House, which, by the turn of the 18th century, had achieved some notoriety as a haunt of lawyers. Here on 29 March 1829 a meeting of solicitors took place as a result of which it was agreed to form a Law Society, whose purpose was declared to be to keep in order the black sheep of the profession.

At No. 5 New Square Robert Raymond, Chief Justice of the King's Bench, had chambers from 1710 to 1733. They were subsequently occupied by Lord Cairns, who was Lord Chancellor 1866-8 and 1874-80.

More's Passage

Beneath No. 7 is More's Passage, named for Sir Thomas More. After its construction in 1694 the building housed the Stamp Office. At that time a little further on, a postern gate stood between Nos. 9 and 10 New Square with shops on either side which were eventually converted into chambers, with the gate, too, being blocked up and the building enclosed.

No. 8 was occupied by one William Lamb, the last practising barrister to become prime minister (1834-41) before Asquith. He inherited the title Viscount Melbourne and became Queen Victoria's close and favourite adviser. Next door at No. 9 Lord Westbury, who was Lord Chancellor 1861-5, had chambers.

No. 11 housed the chambers of two former Lord Chancellors, Lord Eldon 1801-6 and 1807-27, believed to have been Dickens's Chancellor in *Bleak House* and Viscount Selborne, 1872-4 and 1880-5, who steered the Supreme Court of Judicature Act 1873 through Parliament, so sweeping away the existing courts and replacing them with the Supreme Court of Judicature, and presiding in his second term of office over the opening of the Royal Courts of Justice building and supervising the removal of the machinery of justice from Westminster to Strand.

The new gateway into Lincoln's Inn Fields dates from 1845. It bears the arms of the architect Philip Hardwick above a gable on the Fields side. On the side facing the Square are the arms of the then Treasurer, Sir Francis Simpkinson.

10. Leave the precints of the Inn and cross into Lincoln's Inn Fields.

At 12 acres (4.9 ha.), Lincoln's Inn Fields, which, of course, derives its name from the Inn, is the largest square in London and was reputedly laid out by Inigo Jones. This tract of land was itself part only of Fickett's Field, which included the entire area bordered by Holborn, Chancery Lane and Strand. Until the 14th century a portion was divided off and known as the Campum Templarorium, for the use of the Knights Templar. Here, a farrier called Walter le Brun established a forge in 1235 to shoe the Templars' horses and repair the arms used in martial exercises. The Exchequer pipe roll for that year records the payment of a quitrent of six horseshoes for the land to the parish authorities of St Clement Danes. The forge was still in existence at its location in the Fields in 1446. Its rental income has a place in the ceremony of quitrent still held at the Royal Courts of Justice each Michaelmas term, and this is believed to be the oldest surviving custom in London.

By 1562 Fickett's Field was confined to the area between Portugal, Carey and Serle Streets. To the north the presentday area of Lincoln's Inn Fields was divided into the Cup Field and the

Purse Field, reached from Holborn respectively by the passages of Little and Great Turnstile, names which still survive. The public execution of commoners was occasionally carried out here in the reign of Queen Elizabeth I (1558-1603).

To the north-west, Gate Street, and Whetstone Park were already established by 1549 when the Ship Tavern opened and became a notorious gambling house, together with others in that vicinity. Portugal and Sardinia Streets are named for the embassies of those countries to be found there between 1700 and 1780.

By 1641 nearly all of the sides of the Fields were bordered by houses. Nell Gwynne, the actress and mistress of King Charles II, had her residence here, and the open area, unenclosed until 1735, was a popular place of recreation for bowls and tennis. However, after the turn of the 18th century this became a place to avoid after dark. In 1716 John Gay wrote that the Fields represented a considerable danger after dark. It became the headquarters of London's beggars, called the mumpers and rufflers. The problem became so serious for its residents that a private Act of Enclosure was sponsored in Parliament to enable the householders to enclose the Fields. The preamble to the Act read:

> *Whereas the square has become a receptacle for rubbish dirt nastiness of all sorts and many wicked and disorderly persons have frequented and met together therein, using unlawful sports and games, and drawing in and enticing young persons into gaming, idleness and other vicious courses; and vagabonds, common beggars and other disorderly persons resort therein, where many robberies, assaults, outrages and enormities have been and continually are committed.*

View across the Fields

The Act caused the Fields to be barred with an iron palisade on a stone plinth. Within, though, grass and gravel walkways were laid out with a large basin filled with water in the centre. This was filled in in 1790. Early in the l9th century the gardens were landscaped as they appear at present, and in 1894 they were reopened to public for the first time since 1735.

There are important and imposing buildings surrounding the square. These include the former headquarters of the Land Registry at No. 32, and that of the Royal College of Surgeons of England at Nos. 35/43. This was erected 1835-6 by Sir Charles Barry, and contains the famous Hunterian Museum of pathology. This collection holds the remains and skeletons of several 17th and l8th-century celebrities. On the northern side of the Fields at No. 13 is a private collection which is open to the public and very much worth a visit. Sir John Soane's Museum is the 1837 town house of the eccentric architect of the Bank of England, Egyptologist and collector, Sir John Soane (1753-37). It contains Hogarth's The Rake's Progress, and works by Reynolds, Canaletto, Goya, Turner and Eastlake. In addition there are illuminated manuscripts, plaster models of Greek and Roman buildings, Soane's own drawings, and a host of antiquities.

The Fields as they are seen today, a broad green space for the recreation of Londoners, were very nearly lost to the public. Between 1832 and 1836 there was very considerable support in Parliament for the Fields to be the location of the planned concentration of the Royal Courts upon their removal from Westminster. What a good thing that these 12 acres of greenery escaped the great and powerful Victorian urge to redevelop.

11. Cross to the north-west corner of Lincoln's Inn Fields to the traffic lights on Holborn Kingsway. Holborn Underground Station is 150 yards (140 m.) to the right.

Staple Inn

8. Holborn and the Northern Inns of Chancery

Reason to rule, but mercy to forgive:
The first is law, the last prerogative.
                    John Dryden, *The Hind and the Panther*.

Holborn & Northern Inns

1. Commence at Chancery Lane Underground station or follow on from the chapter on Chancery Lane.
2. From the top of Chancery Lane, opposite Warwick Court, turn right towards the City.
3. Cross to the south side of Chancery Lane Underground station at the corner of Staple Inn Buildings.
4. Return into High Holborn and turn right towards Holborn Circus.
5. Cross to enter the site of Furnival's Inn.
6. Cross to the site of Barnard's Inn.
7. Cross New Fetter Lane to the site of Thavies Inn.
8. Return to Chancery Lane Underground station.

1. Commence at Chancery Lane Underground station or follow on from the chapter on Chancery Lane.

The name Holborn is bound up with the wretched last passage of convicted criminals, drawn slowly and publicly in procession along its entire length, from Newgate gaol to the execution ground at Tyburn, where modern-day Edgware Road meets Marble Arch. It is a name derived from the principal tributary of the Fleet River, possibly an alternative name for the Fleet itself above the Holborn bridge, and mentioned in the Domesday Book as the Holeburne or burne of the hollow. From the late middle ages what little stream was left was called the Old Bourne.

During the reign of King Richard I the Lion-heart (1189-99) the Old Bourne stream was abutted by the meadow of the nunnery of St Mary Clerkenwell and the gardens of the Knights Hospitaller of St John of Jerusalem. The road that followed its course was paved over in 1417 at the expense of King Henry V, and afterwards became the principal highway from the Tower of London and Newgate to the gallows at Tyburn, and indeed from the City of London to Westminster.

This substantial and important London route is historically divided into three distinct parts. First, where Holborn Viaduct now passes over Farringdon Street, a stone bridge called the Old Bourne Bridge once crossed the Fleet River. From there to Fetter Lane the highway was called Holborn Hill, a landmark often used by Dickens and to be found in *Martin Chuzzlewit*, *Pickwick Papers*, *Great Expectations*, *Barnaby Rudge*, *Bleak House* and *Oliver Twist*. Secondly, from the present Holborn Circus to Brooke Street, a turning just short of Gray's Inn Road, the highway was just called Holborn. Thirdly, from Brooke Street to Drury Lane, the remainder was and is known as High Holborn.

The Newgate Street side of Holborn Hill was too steep to take the carts of condemned prisoners on their final journey. Thus they travelled via the Church of the Holy Sepulchre in Giltspur Street, Smithfield and Cock Lane, fording the stream and back up to Holborn Bars. The passage of such vehicles led to Holborn Hill being given the nickname of Heavy Hill, and it was referred to as such by William Congreve, John Dryden and Ben Jonson. On 22 May 1685 John Evelyn recorded in his diary the passing of Titus

Oates, being whipped at a cart's tail from Aldgate to Newgate and afterwards to Tyburn.

2. From the top of Chancery Lane, opposite Warwick Court, turn right towards the City.

On the northern side of High Holborn next to an ancient tavern which presently bears the name 'Citie of Yorke' stands the gatehouse to Gray's Inn. The Holborn gate was originally erected in 1594 but was regrettably 'Victorianised' in 1867 when its red bricks were covered with cement. Between the gatehouse and the entrance into South Square, Gray's Inn, is a lane of some 80 yards (73 metres) in length. Just inside the gateway stood John's coffee house in 1656. This remained until the 1830s and was used by Dickens, who worked close by, as the Gray's Inn coffee house in *David Copperfield*. By 1720 an assortment of taverns and alehouses, coffee houses and places of entertainment filled this passageway to cater for the occupants of Gray's Inn, traditionally a raucous lot.

3. Cross to the south side of Chancery Lane Underground station at the corner of Staple Inn Buildings.

The small obelisk surmounted by the City griffin marks the boundary of the Liberties of the City of London at, or very close to, the site of Holborn Bars. The Bars were toll gates where the Corporation of London received a tax of one or two pennies for the carts or carriages of non-freemen entering the City. The broad expanse of Holborn was for 250 years clogged by a block of houses constructed where the central island and war memorial now stand. The traffic had to pass around these houses until they were demolished in 1865. This was Middle Row, and marked the site of the Bishop of Ely's fair in the 13th century.

Immediately behind the City marker is the famous Tudor frontage of the buildings at 337/8 High Holborn, which form the northern elevation of Staple Inn. The shop front was built in 1586, and immediately inside the gateway is a map of the City and plaque bearing the inscription:

Holborn & Northern Inns

The Holborn frontage of Staple Inn

Original building erected 1545-89 by Vincent Enghame and another. Rear elevation was cased in brick, 1826. The front, after various alterations, was restored to its original design in 1886. The entire building was reconstructed in 1937 the old front being retained.

This little square is a jewel. It was reconstructed after the Blitz to epitomise the sense of proportion and quietude once typical of an Inn of Chancery. Its restoration has been so successful that Dickens's description of Staple Inn in *The Mystery of Edwin Drood* is still recognisable:

Behind the most ancient part of Holborn . . . where certain gabled houses some centuries of age still stand looking on the public way, as if disconsolately looking for the Old Bourne that has long run dry, is a little nook composed of two irregular quadrangles, called Staple Inn. It is one of those nooks, the turning into which out of the clashing street, imparts to the relieved pedestrian the sensation of having put cotton in his ears, and velvet soles on his boots. It is one of those nooks where a few smoky sparrows twitter in smoky trees, as though they call to one another, 'Let us play at country', and where a few feet of garden-mould and a few yards of gravel enable them to do that refreshing violence to their tiny understandings . . . Moreover, it is one of those little nooks which are legal nooks; and it contains a little Hall, with a little lantern in its roof.

Staple Inn is so called after its long medieval association with the wool trade. At the turn of the 14th century it was the site of a warehouse where wool was brought for the assessment of excise duty. By the Statute of Staple of 1353 Westminster became one of the staple towns which held the monopoly licence to export wool. In 1375 the Society of Merchants of the Staple moved here from Westminster and conducted business until about 1413, although the society was itself only here for three years and its members drifted away afterwards.

By 1415, only two years after the wool merchants finally left, Staple Inn had become established as an Inn of Chancery, attached to Gray's Inn. The parent Inn of Court was granted the freehold in 1529 by King Henry VIII, to be held on trust by the principal and 12 Ancients who governed Staple Inn. In its heyday during the reign of Queen Elizabeth I (1558-1603). Staple Inn attracted the largest membership of any Inn of Chancey with an average of 145 students in term and 69 out of term. A gradual decline set in during the 18th century and by 1761 it was no longer in use as an Inn. Only two years previously Dr Johnson moved here from his more well-known house in Gough Square, and wrote *The History of Rasselas, Prince of Abyssinia*.

Staple Inn became independent of Gray's Inn in 1811 and for the next 70 years was taken over by solicitors. Indeed, upon its dissolution in 1884, when the freehold was sold to a firm of auctioneers, the principal and remaining seven ancients were all solicitors. Two years later the government acquired the southern courtyard where in 1843 the chambers of the Chancery taxing masters had become situated. These were demolished to make way for an extension of the Patent Office building which stands there today, though the Patent Office has moved out.

The north courtyard was purchased by the Prudential Assurance Society who engaged Alfred Waterhouse (1830-1905) to restore the buildings and lay out the small garden next to the hall. His work was undone in September 1944 when a German flying bomb destroyed much of the Inn. Restoration work for the Society of Actuaries, who had leased the Inn in 1887, took until 1955, and the appearance of the courtyard and garden have remained much the same ever since.

Staple Inn Hall and south courtyard

The hall clock, dated 1757, some armorial glass in the hall windows dating back to 1500, and the original stone lintels over the doorways are all that remain of pre-war Staple Inn. The lintels are marked with the initials of the principals, just as the treasurers are marked in the four Inns of Court. Thus the principalship of Thomas Leech (1753-9) is recorded over the door to the hall, Robert Jenkin (1729-31) over Nos. 7 and 9, and John Thompson (1747) over No. 10, where Dickens placed the chambers of Mr Grewgious in *The Mystery of Edwin Drood*.

4. Return into High Holborn and turn right towards Holborn Circus.

On the north side of High Holborn, covering the entire block between Brooke Street and Leather Lane stands the enormous former headquarters of the Prudential Assurance Society on the site of Furnival's Inn. On the east side of the main entrance is set a blue plaque denoting the demolition in 1897 of that Inn; on the west, a bust of Charles Dickens, who lived here from 1834 until he moved to 48 Doughty Street in 1837. Here he wrote the *Posthumous Papers of the Pickwick Club*, his very successful first novel. The property has now been refurbished as an office development known as Waterhouse Square.

The great court of the former Prudential Assurance building

5. Cross to enter the site of Furnival's Inn.

Originally the town mansion of the Lords Furnival, it is recorded that within its precincts Sir William Furnival had two messuages and 13 shops in the sixth year of the reign of Richard II (1382-3). By 1408 it had become an Inn of Chancery, occupied by migrating students who came up the road from Thavies Inn. By 1422 it had become attached to Lincoln's Inn by virtue of a lease granted to its benchers, and in 1547 that honourable society purchased the freehold.

Furnival's was probably the largest of all such satellite inns, comprising as it did a substantial courtyard surrounded by buildings, an inner courtyard and large gardens to the north. Sir Thomas More was reader here for the three years from 1498 to 1501, and Inigo Jones designed several of its buildings around 1640. As with other Inns, it gradually fell into disuse and its chambers became residential apartments or otherwise let for other enterprises. One such became famous in the 1720s and 30s when a corner block was occupied by the great pastry chef Edward Kidder, who ran a cookery school from it. By 1817 with the membership of Furnival's Inn having shrunk to six ancients and about 16 juniors, the benchers of Lincoln's Inn refused to grant a further lease. Furnival's was disestablished and a building lease was granted to Henry Peto who cleared the site within a year.

Almost wholly consigned to residential apartments, the site contained a hotel called Wood's, to which Mr Grewgious crossed over for dinner in *The Mystery of Edwin Drood* (1870). Dickens described the Inn in *Martin Chuzzlewit* (1843-4):

> *It is a shady, quiet place, echoing to the footsteps of the stragglers who have business there; and rather monotonous and gloomy on summer evenings.*

The Holborn frontage of Furnival's Inn

6. Cross to the site of Barnard's Inn.

On the opposite side of High Holborn stand Dyers' Buildings, formerly the almshouses of the Dyers' Company. A little beyond lies the concealed entrance to Barnard's Inn, which has in very recent years undergone a major redevelopment. This tiny precinct, smaller even than Staple Inn, was an Inn of Chancery attached to Gray's Inn from 1549 until 1888, by which time it had become little more than a dining club. Its foundations and history are well documented since they are bound up with the diocese of Lincoln Cathedral.

These quarters were owned in 1451 by Dr John Mackworth, Dean of Lincoln, and, as Mackworth's Inn, the property was bequeathed by the good doctor to the Dean and Chapter of Lincoln Cathedral in 1454. Some 19 years earlier, in 1435, a group of lawyers headed by one Lionel Barnard took occupation of the premises, and over the passage of years until their lease was acquired by Gray's Inn this small Inn of Chancery became known as Barnard's Inn.

Administered by a principal, a 'gubernator', and 12 'antients', this was the only Inn of Chancery to have its own library. Built in 1540 and carefully restored in 1932, its hall was, and remains, the smallest of all the historic dining halls in London, being only 36 feet (11 m.) by 22 feet (6.7 m.) and 30 feet (9 m.) high. Yet size means little: upon the roll of its principals are to be found the names of the eminent statesman William Cecil, Lord Burghley (1520-98), and Francis Bacon, Viscount St Albans (1561-1626), Lord Coventry (1578-1640), who was appointed Lord Keeper of the Great Seal in 1625, and Sir John Holt (1642-1710), who was Chief Justice of the King's Bench from 1689 until his death. In Elizabethan times 112 students could be found dining in term and 24 out. Barnard's Inn contained the residence of the Astronomer Royal, Edmund Halley, in 1737. However Dickens writes of it in *Great Expectations* as 'the dingiest collection of shabby buildings ever squeezed together in a rank corner as a club for Tom-cats!'

Although still flourishing at the beginning of the 19th century, the number of admissions collapsed soon afterwards; there were only 40 from 1800 to 1870. In 1855 the Society of Barnard's Inn numbered only 18 and that included the principal, antients and companions. As a society it dwindled from 1851 when it was decided that no more ancients would be appointed. The buildings by then were in considerable want of repair, the cost of which vastly exceeded their rental income. In 1877 the Dean and Chapter of Lincoln vested their freehold in the Ecclesiastical Commissioners who mortgaged the reversion of the lease back to the society for £23,000. With just seven antients and four companions left, the society in 1883 formally resolved to wind itself up as soon as a purchaser for their interest could be found, and some 18 months later abolished the ancient categories of membership.

In 1892 the senior livery company of the City, the Mercers, purchased Barnard's Inn for £43,000, and over the course of the following two years erected a school for the sons of its freemen. The old hall became the school refectory but had to be demolished in 1931. The Mercers' School left Barnard's Inn in 1959 and the precincts of the Inn were leased to the Prudential for office development.

Immediately behind Barnard's Inn stood a house in the mid 15th century belonging to one Serjeant Thomas de Lincoln. Little is known about it but the building had a frontage on Holborn and gardens that ran along Fetter Lane. At some point

The tiny hall of Barnard's Inn reconstructed in 1932

around the era when lawyers were moving east from Holborn towards Chancery Lane, and much to the confusion of historians, this was known as Lincoln's Inn.

Across Holborn again is the passageway up to one of London's most popular lunchtime street markets, Leather Lane. A public house there is named for Queen Elizabeth I's Lord Chancellor, the wit, scholar and dramatist Sir Christopher

Hatton (1540-91). His name is more readily familiar to those associated with London's jewellery trade, which is centred on the next turning on the left, Hatton Garden. Holborn Circus is the junction of six streets formed in 1869 as a result of the completion of the new Holborn Viaduct leading to Newgate and the Old Bailey across Farringdon Road. At the west end of the viaduct New Fetter Lane was cut through to Fleet Street to the south. In the centre of Holborn Circus stands an equestrian statue of Albert, Prince Consort unveiled 9 January 1874 as an anonymous gift to the Corporation of London.

7. Cross New Fetter Lane to the site of Thavies Inn.

On the right between New Fetter Lane and St Andrew Street a modern-day Lloyds Bank is housed in a building called Thavies Inn House. Beyond it to the left under an archway is an equally modern courtyard surrounded by office buildings called Thavies Inn. There a public house called the White Hart has a Thavies Bar. Thus is the name remembered of a former Inn of Chancery attached to Lincoln's Inn in 1422, and purchased by that society in 1549.

It was over two centuries earlier that lawyers first came to this precinct, and indeed the roots of the association that later became the Honourable Society of the Inner Temple lie here. Shortly before the turn of the 14th century a large building to the south-west of St Andrew's Church was let as a lodging house to the *apprenticii di banco*, those students of the law whose principals had achieved sole rights of audience in the royal courts after 1292. This building was owned by John Thavie, an armourer, who died in 1348 bequeathing his rents to the church. Between 1350 and 1397 a Chancery clerk and receiver resided here, and it may be that the name of this place was properly Davy's Inn. Whichever is the case, it was from this place that the capital's first class of professional lawyer emerged; in 1340 a dramatic expansion in the business of the courts meant a migration away from Thavies Inn down to the new Temple to be nearer to the river ferry for Westminster. Equally a group left to join Furnival's Inn about 1380, and onwards to the Bishop of Chichester's hostel from 1412 to 1422.

The ancient buildings which surrounded a small northern courtyard were destroyed by a fire of 1804. From that time Thavies

Inn became effectively a cul-de-sac. It had long lost its connections with the law. The Society of Thavies Inn could not meet the new rents that Lincoln's Inn required on its lease renewal in May 1769, and the parent Inn evicted its satellite. In July 1772 the buildings of Thavies Inn were sold for £4,100 and that money was used in constructing Stone Buildings, Lincoln's Inn.

Beyond Thavies Inn to the east, for some years in the first half of the 15th century, Henry de Lacy, Earl of Lincoln, had a house also called Lincoln's Inn. When that nobleman's name became associated with the present Lincoln's Inn, this precinct became known as Strange's Inn, but that too had disappeared, with little else known of it, by 1450.

The site of Thavies Inn

St Andrew's Church stands on the corner of St Andrew Street and the green in front of Holborn Viaduct. It was constructed by Sir Christopher Wren in 1686 replacing a church that stood here since at least 1297 in the gift of the Earl of Southampton. At the dissolution of the monasteries the then earl was Lord Chancellor Wriothesley. He was buried here in 1550. St Andrew's escaped the Great Fire of 1666 but was rendered unsafe. The stained glass at the end of its south aisle represents the arms of John Thavie. Also buried here is Dr Henry Sacheverell, who in 1709 preached against the government of the Earl of Godolphin, leading to its downfall, and who died as rector of St Andrew's in 1724. A further claim to fame is that the jurist Sir Edward Coke married Lady Elizabeth Hatton, daughter of William Cecil, Lord Burghley here in 1598. St Andrew's is called the poet's church because Thomas Chatterton (1752-70), and Henry Neele (died 1828) are to be found in the graveyard.

Next to St Andrew's, on the north side of the present Holborn Viaduct, stood Union Court, formerly called Scroop's Court. This was originally the town house of the Scrope family of Bolton, let to serjeants-at-law from 1483 until 1498 when it was demolished. It had flourished as Scrope's Inn from about 1459. By 1800 its name had become Scroop's Court, and all trace of even that was obliterated by the 1862-7 development of Holborn Viaduct.

8. Return to Chancery Lane Underground Station.

Gray's Inn Hall

9. Gray's Inn

A Gray's Inn man is better than any other man and no damn nonsense about other things being equal.
F.E. Smith K.C., Earl of Birkenhead.

Gray's Inn

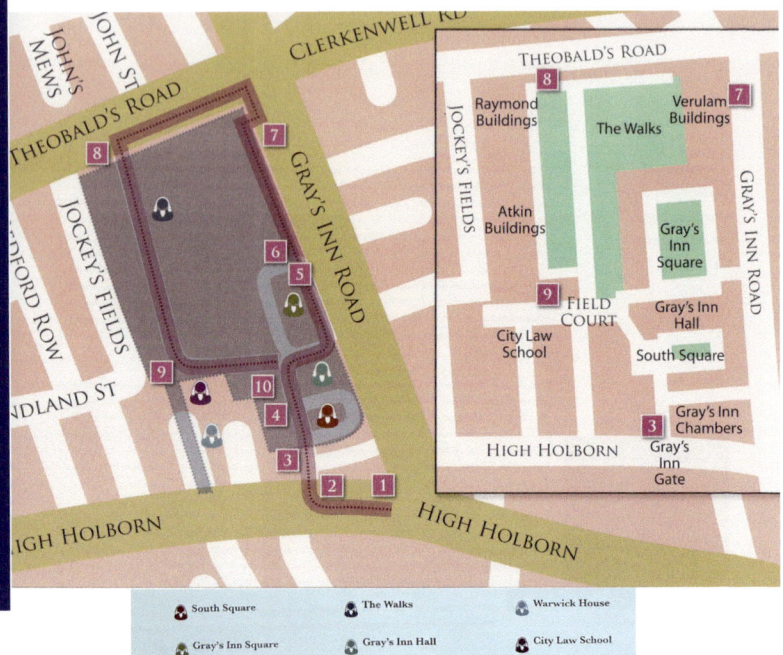

1. From Chancery Lane Underground station proceed west along High Holborn to the entrance gateway of Gray's Inn.
2. Proceed down the private roadway along to precincts of the Inn passing, on the right, the modern Gatehouse Chambers.
3. Proceed under the second archway into South Square.
4. Proceed to the north-west corner of the square passing 10 South Square which houses Gray's Inn Common Room, on the site of the former Bacon's Buildings, and the passageway which runs from here into Field Court, and pass into Gray's Inn Square.
5. Proceed anticlockwise around Gray's Inn Square to the north-east corner.
6. Proceed through the passageway in the north-east corner under No. 9 which leads to Verulam Buildings.
7. Proceed beyond Verulam Buildings out of the Inn into Gray's Inn Road. At the traffic lights turn left into Theobalds Road and walk along the boundary of the Inn.
8. At the end of the railings turn left back into the Inn.
9. Turn left and pass No. 3 Gray's Inn Place along Field Court towards Gray's Inn Square.
10. Proceed through the passage and turn right into South Square and back to the start.

1. From Chancery Lane Underground station proceed west along High Holborn to the entrance gateway of Gray's Inn.

The most northerly of the Inns of Court, Gray's Inn, is situated within the medieval manor of Portpoole, a name meaning the market by the pool, which refers to the bishop of Ely's fair held in the 13th century at Holborn Bars nearby. A turning off Gray's Inn Road still bears the name Portpool Lane. Residing here at the time were the de Greys, a family of great eminence in the law under the Plantaganets. Walter de Grey was Lord Chancellor 1206-14 under King John, his nephew became a justice in eyre in 1260, and his nephew's son Reginald was Chief Justice of Chester under Edward I and the first Lord Grey of Wilton.

By Lord Grey's death in 1308 the manor of Portpoole consisted of a large house with outhouses, dovecote and windmill, although shortly afterwards the family moved out. By 1370 the manor house was being described as a *hospitium*, an inn for clerks and officers of the courts, with some satellite law students. A William Skipworth is mentioned as the reader for 1355 and Gray's Inn may therefore pre-date either Temple as an honourable society. Its existence is certain during the reign of Edward III (1327-77). However it was not until the early 16th century that the property was sold by Edmund, Lord Gray (sic) of Wilton. A conveyance of August 1505 provides for the transfer to Hugh Denny Esq. of the manor of Portpoole, otherwise called 'Gray's Inn', four messuages, four gardens, the site of a windmill, eight acres (3.2 ha.) of land, 10 shillings of free rent and an advowson of the chauntry of Portpoole. Between 1513 and 1539 the freehold was held by the priory and convent of East Sheen. At the dissolution of the monasteries the convent's holding was escheated to the Crown. Quite typically, the lease was regranted and the lawyers now found themselves paying their 10 shillings rent and £6 13s 4d fine annually to the royal treasury rather than the monks of Sheen.

Over the next 30 years a body of students joined Gray's from Barnard's and Staple Inns, and the modern records of the Honourable Society of Gray's Inn date from 1569. These show a structure that remained relatively unchanged over the succeeding centuries. The Inn was governed by the masters of the bench. Its members comprised, in order of seniority: the readers, senior members of the Bar who undertook the legal education provided by the Inn in the form of lectures, moots and bolts (discourses on pleadings in Norman French); the inner barristers of over seven years' seniority including the Grand Company of Ancients who held the right to practice at the superior courts of law at Westminster; the 'utter' or outer barristers of under five years' seniority; and students.

Life in Gray's Inn under the Tudors and Stuarts (1485-1688) was austere, with the only relief being revels after supper, masques and grand week. The society ran as a strict collegiate system in the 16th and early 17th centuries. Chambers were assigned to members of the Inn by the benchers with a condition of residence. The men had to be 'in commons', lunching together at midday and dining together at 6 or 7 p.m. Their attendance at chapel, both morning and evening, was observed, as was their compulsory attendance at moots, bolts and other exercises. Fines were levied for nonattendance and expulsion threatened.

By 1570 the society had four serving officers: the steward, butler, dean of chapel, and master cook. The dean was the master of the bench responsible for securing attendance at chapel, which was compulsory for all of the occupants of the Inn, not just the Bar, and for receiving and distributing the alms and taxes levied as a stipend for the benefit of clergy.

Gray's Inn was in its heyday about 1585. At that time the number of its students was double the total of the other three Inns of Court together. Its more famous members, literary, military and naval, had no intention to practise in the law, but saw the conviviality of hall much as a gentlemen's club for the sons of the nobility and the merchant class. Between 1520 and 1550 a substantial part of the nobility of England was admitted to Gray's, including Thomas Stanley, Earl of Derby, John Dudley, Duke of Northumberland, Charles Brandon, Duke of Suffolk, Edward de Vere, Earl of Oxford, Charles Radcliffe, Earl of Sussex,

Stained glass window, detail

Francis Russell, Earl of Bedford, Henry Neville, Earl of Westmorland, and Edward Seymour, Earl of Hertford. For those more studious, the buildings of the Inn stood at the very northern fringes of the city, 'airy, commodious and quiet, and free from the fogs which in the winter season afflicted the region near the river'. Its outbuildings stood in fields which ran away northwards to Middlesex, while the Inn still consisted of only four small courtyards: Coney, Chapel, Field and Holborn Courts.

Until very late in the 16th century the only entrance to the Inn was by a gateway in Gray's Inn Lane (now Gray's Inn Road). The growth of chambers in Holborn Court made it essential for an entrance to be made from Holborn, in the proximity of the Citie of Yorke, a public house established in 1431. A gatehouse was erected here in 1594 during the treasurership of Francis Bacon, subsequently Viscount St. Albans, when a house was purchased from George Fullwood, demolished and a passage cut through to Holborn Court. The gatehouse also contained two shops, the rents from which were to defray the expense of a gate porter. One of these shops became occupied by bookseller Henry Tomes, who afterwards became Bacon's publisher. In 1603 Archbishop Whitgift, Bacon's former tutor, petitioned the society for permission to build chambers over the gateway.

The porter of Gray's Inn gatehouse became a well-known officious character. He occupied a lodge built inside the gateway on the west side in 1714, which remained until 1770 when the passage into the Inn was paved with Purbeck stone from Coney Court. The times of closing the gate were recorded in the annals of the Society: in 1709 gates were closed at 10 p.m; by 1720 this was reduced by an hour. However, in 1730 members fortunate enough to arrive in coaches could enter up to midnight, even though posts had been set in the middle of the lane against coaches and carts in 1723.

Between 1776 and 1794 Gray's Inn owned and operated two very successful coffee houses called, respectively, Weldon's and Abington's, situated nearby, to the east of the gate. The gatehouse today still occupies its original location, though it was unfortunately Victorianised in 1867 when the original red brick was covered over with cement. The huge gate is undated.

2. Proceed down the private roadway along to precincts of the Inn passing, on the right, the modern Gatehouse Chambers.

Over the archway into the Inn stands the sign of a griffin in the position described by heralds as 'segreant', which is the same stance as a lion rampant. Since the turn of the 17th century the society's arms have been a gold griffin segreant on a black field. Before then the coat of arms of Lord Grey de Wilton was adopted after his death in 1308. The present arms are derived from the family arms of Richard Aungier, a bencher and three times treasurer of Gray's, who was murdered in the Inn in 1598. A confession was exacted from his son and a porter and the pair were hanged at Tyburn. Aungier's arms were themselves derived from those of the ancient Counts of Angers.

The griffin of Gray's Inn

3. Proceed under the second archway into South Square

South Square, formerly called Holborn Court, was an open field until the reign of Queen Elizabeth I (1558-1603). By 1588 it was known as South Court and contained more chambers than its northern neighbour. The courtyard was formed by nearly contiguous blocks of chambers named after their founders. To the immediate west of the archway stood Irish Rents in 1577. These were demolished and rebuilt as Downe's Buildings in 1611. Beyond them stood Fuller's Buildings.

Number 10 South Square was built in 1970-2. Between 1629 and 1905 it was the site of Davenport's Buildings named for Sir Humphrey Davenport, who was called to the Inn in 1590, was reader for 1613, became a serjeant of 1623 and went on to become a justice of the Court of Common Pleas, 1630, and eventually Chief Baron of the Exchequer in 1631. He sat as the presiding judge in the Ship Money case (1637) and for doing so and upholding the view that the king may impose a tax without consulting Parliament, was impeached by the Long Parliament. He joined King Charles I at Oxford for the raising of the standard which marked the commencement of the English Civil War and died in 1645.

At what is now Nos. 11 and 12 South Square, Humphrey Purefoy constructed buildings in 1572 from these, north to the gate leading to what is now Field Court but was then a meadow. Purefoy's Buildings were rebuilt in 1655. Next to them, where No. 13 stands, were Howland's and Cage's Buildings constructed between 1572 and 1577. These were all demolished and rebuilt in 1685 to bring the buildings into conformity as a square.

Although South Square was entirely reconstructed as a result of the Blitz, one original building survived, this being No. 1, immediately to the right-hand side when entering the Square. On this site stood Gerard's Buildings, which were constructed about 1555 and named for Sir Gilbert Gerard, reader of the Inn in 1553, treasurer in 1555, and Attorney-General upon the accession of Elizabeth I. Gerard became Master of the Rolls in 1581. The present building was constructed in 1759 during the treasurership of John Waple. Here Charles Dickens was engaged as a clerk to Ellis and Blackmore, attorneys, in 1827.

After Dickens became famous Edward Blackmore wrote:

He was a bright, clever-looking youth and I took him as a clerk. He came to me in May 1827 and left in November 1828 . . . . Several instances took place in the office of which he must have been a keen observer, as I recognised some of them in his Pickwick and Nickleby; and I am much mistaken if some of his characters had not their originals in persons I well remember.

Gray's Inn

South Square

For his part Dickens does not give anywhere a happy account of the 18 months at the attorneys' offices, but he mentions South Square. In *David Copperfield* Traddles's chambers are at the top of No. 2 South Square (referred to by its old name, Holborn Court, in the novel), and in *Pickwick Papers* the chambers of the junior barrister Mr Phunky are also at Holborn Court.

More of the flavour of life at Gray's in the 18th and 19th centuries is conjured up by the names of its occupants and their activities. The former Nos. 2-4 South Square were constructed in 1738 on the site of a ramshackle group of buildings, Chyswold's, Blower's and Lenton's. At No. 3 W.S. Gilbert held court each Saturday night with a group of dramatists and writers known, ironically, as 'the serious family', after he moved here from Clement's Inn in late 1866 or early in 1867. The members of this private association, whose dinners were intended to rival the lunches of the *Punch* editorial board, paid a two-guinea subscription and the list included Tom Hood, who was 'head of the family', Henry Byron, Clement Scott, Arthur Cecil, Tom Robertson, Artemus Ward, E.L. Blanchard, Jeff Prowse, Henry Leigh, Paul Gray and several others. This stable of writers produced much of the light entertainment of Victorian London throughout the 1860s and 70s.

1 South Square where Dickens was engaged as a clerk in 1827

Gray's Inn

The names of the buildings here have all but disappeared: Higgens' built 1620; Stanhope's, 1578; Hale's, c. 1542; New, 1568-70, incorporating Wade's and Tatersall's; and Denny's, 1628, which projected into the Square from hall. At No. 7 stood the office of the Court of Star Chamber between 1602 and 1645 when that unhappy institution was abolished. Its use as a political tool by King James I and afterwards even more blatantly by Charles I caused that great turbulence resulting eventually in revolution and civil war. After the Commonwealth it was re-established for 30 years as the Fine or Pipe Office. Next door, No. 8 was used as an extension to the Inn's library. It really formed part of the old Osbaldestone's Buildings, where the great author Thomas Babington Macaulay (later Lord Macaulay) took chambers from 1829 to 1834.

The reconstruction of South Square as it appears today was completed in 1958. The central statue of Francis Bacon was unveiled by Arthur Balfour in 1912 and is by Frederick W. Pomeroy (1856-1924), who also sculpted the Lady of Justice on the Old Bailey and W.S. Gilbert's memorial medallion on the Embankment. Bacon is acknowledged as the Inn's greatest son. Entered as a student in 1576 he was called in 1582. He became reader in 1588, dean of chapel in 1589 and treasurer of the Inn from 1608 to 1617. He was appointed Solicitor-General in 1607, Attorney-General in 1613,

Gray's Inn

and, having been ennobled as Baron Verulam, served in the office of Lord Keeper of the Great Seal in 1617, and as Lord Chancellor 1616-22. He was made Viscount St Albans in 1621. He had grown up in the precincts of the Inn for his father Sir Nicholas Bacon, admitted as a student in 1532, made an ancient by 1536 and bencher in 1550, was himself Lord Keeper. William Hepworth Dixon, in his *Story of Lord Bacon's Life*, describes the progress in state of Francis Bacon on 7 May 1617, from Gray's Inn to Westminster to open the courts as the new Lord Keeper:

He rode from Gray's Inn, which he had not yet left, to Westminster Hall, to open the courts in state, all London turning out to do him honour, the Queen [Anne consort of King James I] sending the lords of her household, Prince Charles [the future King Charles I] the whole of his followers – the lords of the Council, the judges, and serjeants composing his immediate train. On his right hand rode the Lord Treasurer, on his left the Lord Privy Seal, behind them a long procession of earls and barons, knights and gentlemen. Everyone who could procure a horse and a footcloth fell into the train, so that more than 200 horsemen rode behind him, through crowds of citizens and apprentice boys from Cheap, of players from Bankside, of the Puritan hearers of Burgess, of the Roman Catholic friends of Danvers and Armstrong; and he rode, as popular in the streets as he had been in the House of Commons, down Chancery Lane and the Strand, past Charing Cross, through the open courts of Whitehall, and by King Street into Palace Yard. He wore on that day, as he had worn on his bridal day, a suit of purple satin. Alighting at the gates of Westminster Hall, and passing into the Court, he took his seat on the bench; when the company had entered, and the criers commanded silence, he addressed them on his intention to reform the rules and practices of the court.

Gray's Inn Library, which now covers much of the eastern end of the square, was formed out of bequests made in 1555, although it did not occupy its present site until 1884, having formerly stood in Coney Court. In 1927 a bequest was made following the death of Sir John Holker, a Lord Justice of Appeal who had been one of the last serjeants and was Attorney-General 1876-80, and the library was named for him. That fine building was burnt out in the Blitz with the loss of 30,000 volumes, including Walton's *Biblia Polyglotta* (Polyglot Bible) of 1657. The interior of the present library boasts a vaulted ceiling with dome, and panelling and bookcases of old English oak. It houses, among its fine collection, the records of the Inn. These are called Pension Books, the title of the oldest office holder of the society, the pensioner, a post dating from before 1577. The pensioner received the subscriptions to pay the Inn's rents.

In the north-eastern corner of the Square is Gray's Inn Treasury built in 1952. It contains the modern Pension Chamber, a meeting room for discussion of the affairs of the society. The Chamber has been situated here since 1778 when it replaced the Duchy Office, which was constructed to abut the south side of the chapel in 1641 and was named after Sir Edward Moseley who was then attorney to the Duchy of Lancaster. To commemorate its role the small Pension Room still has its ceiling decorated with the embossed seal and red rose of Lancaster.

Gray's Inn Hall looking from the screen to the bench table

To the left can be seen the hall of Gray's Inn, which was reconstructed 1950-1 on the site of its predecessor, which, together with the library and chapel, was entirely destroyed by incendiary bombs on the night of 11 May 1941. The interior is a detailed restoration of the original, which was built between 1556 and 1560 during the treasurerships of Nicholas Bacon and Gilbert Gerard at a cost to the Inn of £4,000. On the site of the former hall of the manor house of Portpoole, Gray's Inn Hall was said to be a little inferior to that of Middle Temple but more handsome than either

Inner Temple or Lincoln's Inn. The hall is 75 feet (23 m.) long, 35 feet (11 m.) wide and 47 feet (14 m.) high. Its walls are panelled in oak with armorial bearings of successive readers and treasurers which were saved from destruction together with some armorial glass dating back to 1355 mounted in the windows. Its original oak screen depicting victory over the Spanish Armada and bench tables were presented by Queen Elizabeth I, who is said to have been a frequent visitor. The screen was saved by the bravery and exertion of the rooftop firewatchers. Above the screen is an elaborately carved minstrel gallery.

Until the 18th century the floor of the hall was strewn with rushes. The bench table and cupboard were situated as in Middle Temple. The room was heated by an open central fire, the smoke from which was emitted through a Tudor louvre, although ventilation and the atmosphere must undoubtedly have improved when the Victorians added a wooden 'pigeon-house' lantern on the roof. Nineteenth- century taste also led to a coating of stucco to the Tudor red brickwork of the hall, chapel and library, and the addition of unnecessary Gothic crenellations to the exterior in 1826.

Thus the leading men of their particular day came to a hall that had no sanitary facilities, a room that was smoke, not particularly warm and had very poor lighting. It did, however, have detailed bench table rules for both dining and the 'wearing of apparel'. In 1560 the wearing of hats in hall incurred a penalty of 3s 4d, a not inconsiderable sum in those days. By 1600 there were bans on riding boots and spurs and on rude noises during eating or the exercises that followed; and no member could stand with his back to the fire. For all that, hall was the centre of the daily life of the Inn. In term time after dinner the reader, supported by the elite of the house, gave a reading upon a statute, and the 'cupboard-men', those sitting at the square table immediately below the bench table, would argue the cases. The important ceremonies in hall took place at the cupboard. Here oaths were taken by newly called members, and the Inn's plate was displayed.

The original hall was hung with fine portraits of its benchers who held high judicial office and of the Sovereign, commissioned from leading artists of the day. These included portraits of Queen Elizabeth I, King Charles I, King Charles II, King James II, Sir Nicholas Bacon, Francis Bacon, Lord Raymond, who was Chief Justice of the King's Bench 1725-33, Sir John Turton, a baron of the Exchequer 1689, Sir Edward Coke, Sir James Eyre who was Chief Baron of the Exchequer 1787-93, Sir Christopher Yelverton, a justice of the King's Bench 1602, William Cecil, whom Elizabeth elevated as Lord Burghley and Bishop Gardiner, who was Lord Chancellor 1553-5. The modern hall contains, in addition, pictures of F.E. Smith, the Earl of Birkenhead, who was Lord Chancellor 1919-1922 and Lord Atkin, who was a Law Lord from 1928 to 1944.

Gray's Inn Hall looking from the bench table to the screen

The new hall was opened by HRH the Duke of Gloucester, a royal bencher, on 5 December 1951. Shortly afterwards a dinner was given to the 70 or so workmen from Trollope & Coles who had laboured on the project for two years. The architect, Sir Edward Maufe (1883-1974), was elected an honorary bencher. He had used 160 selected English oaks, each 30 feet (9 m.) in length, for the undertaking. To mark a generous donation from the American Bar Association to Gray's the arms of the United States were placed in a new south window. Indeed the Inn has had a long, if somewhat tenuous, connection with America. On 29 July 1918 at their first meeting Franklyn D. Roosevelt and Winston Churchill both became benchers of this Inn.

The entertainment in Hall was of considerable renown. Serjeants' feasts and banquets were sumptuous affairs, and masques were given throughout the calendar. The first recorded masque at Christmas 1527 caused grave offence to Cardinal Wolsey whom it satirised. One of the first performances of Shakespeare's *The Comedy of Errors* was performed here on Holy Innocents' Day (28 December) 1594. This was part of the 'Prince of Purpoole's revels', riotous and wildly expensive entertainments and feasting that lasted from 20 December 1594 to 3 January 1595 with much of the nobility, including the Queen, attending them. Revels at Christmas continued to be celebrated

The U.S. arms in the south window of Gray's Inn Hall

in Gray's Inn Hall until 1773. At the masque of Allhallowtide (1 November) 1633, King Charles I was present; and in November 1956 a masque was given in the presence of Queen Elizabeth II.

Over the centuries there have been many famous Gray's men who would have been readily familiar with hall, even as it is today. Examples abound, such as Sir William Gascoigne (1350?-1419), Chief Justice of the King's Bench, who is said to have committed the then Prince of Wales, afterwards King Henry V, to prison for contempt of court. His descendant George Gascoigne (1525-77), a member of this Inn, was a well-known Elizabethan poet and dramatist.

Thomas Cromwell (1485-1540), was admitted in 1524 and became an ancient in 1534. In the same year, as the architect of the scheme devised to help his master's finances, King Henry VIII appointed him Vicar General for the Dissolution of the Monasteries. Cromwell's lust for power in the short years before his doom led him to become Secretary to the Privy Council, Chancellor of the University of Cambridge, Master of the Rolls and Lord Privy Seal. But in June 1540, having outlived his usefulness, and only a few weeks after he was made Earl of Essex, Henry had him committed to the Tower, impeached for corruption before Parliament, and beheaded at Tower Hill on 28 July.

Sir Thomas Gresham (1519-79) was admitted in 1535. In 1566 he founded the Royal Exchange, which was modelled on the Antwerp Bourse. William Cecil, Lord Burghley (1520-98) was admitted in the year of Thomas Cromwell's execution and became an ancient and pensioner in 1547. His second son by his second marriage was Robert Cecil, Earl of Salisbury (1563-1612) who was especially admitted in 1580. He became chief minister of both Queen Elizabeth I and King James I, and swapped his father's house, Theobalds, at Cheshunt, for the royal palace at Hatfield, which he rebuilt as Hatfield House. Thomas Wriothesley, first Earl of Southampton, was admitted in 1534, becoming Lord Chancellor a mere 10 years later. Upon his appointment he acquired Lincoln House at Holborn, formerly the town house of the bishops of Lincoln, and changed its name to Southampton House. His grandson, the third Earl, who was admitted in 1588, became the patron of William Shakespeare and is one of the best-known candidates for addressee of the sonnets. His political machinations, together with those of the then Earl of Essex were reflected in

Richard II. There was a great split among members of Gray's Inn during the Civil War, intensified by the fact that Bradshaw, an ancient of the Inn, presided over the State trial of King Charles I in 1649. Gray's Inn also had its literary connections. Sir Philip Sidney (1554-86) wrote *The Arcadia* here and Samuel Butler (1612-80) had chambers in the Inn, as did Oliver Goldsmith (1730-74) in 1764. William Camden (1551-1623), the antiquary, lived here. William Cobbett (1763-1835) of *Rural Rides* and the *Political Register* was a clerk in chambers here; and in more modern times Hilaire Belloc (1870-1953), Sidney Webb (1859-1947), Sir Robert Menzies (1894-1978) and Sir Edward Heath (1916-2005) have been members of the society, although the latter two are not usually thought of foremost as literary figures.

4. Proceed to the north-west corner of the square passing 10 South Square which houses Gray's Inn Common Room, on the site of the former Bacon's Buildings, and the passageway which runs from here into Field Court, and pass into Gray's Inn Square.

In early Elizabethan times what is now Gray's Inn Square was divided into two courtyards, the smaller of which was called

Gray's Inn Square and the chapel

Chapel Court. This was bounded by the hall and the chapel on its south side, two rows of buildings running northwards, and enclosed buildings on the east and west. To the east of the hall an open field was adjacent to the houses abutting Gray's Inn Road. To the north were gardens called Green Court, so named for the turfing over of the site of gallery buildings erected to disguise the difference in level between the two courtyards. To the west lay another but much larger open field, which was later to become the Walks. At some time early in the 1560s a new building called Coney Court was constructed on the former rabbit warrens, a little to the west of the present square.

A plaque on the wall at the entrance to the square recounts:

The Great War 1914-1918: In this square were trained the men raised by Gray's Inn and Holborn for service in the 6th Bttn Volunteer regiment under the command of Lt Col Sydney Ashley VD.

A chapel is known to have stood on this site since between 1305 and 1316. A chauntry is referred to in the grant by Reginald, the first Lord Grey, of the lands and manor of Portpoole to the convent of St Bartholomew the Great in Smithfield. This was an annual stipend for providing a priest to celebrate divine service daily at the manor chapel, reportedly on this site. As a building it suffered with the dissolution of St Bartholomew's in 1541. Nine years later, during the reign of King Edward VI, the chapel's finery was stripped by Protestants requiring austerity in worship. However, it was restored not long after under Queen Mary Tudor, in 1553. A substantial reconstruction took place between 1619 and 1624 and a further repair in 1689. Throughout that century it remained collegiate with no women or boys admitted. In 1702 a ladies' gallery was constructed for the wives of judges, serjeants and benchers and by 1754 visitors were permitted to attend the services. A last major reconstruction prior to the Blitz took place between 1893 and 1897 when Tudor windows were discovered, these having been covered by plaster. A magnificent east window, inaugurated in 1899 contains figures of Archbishops Thomas à Becket, Whitgift, Laud, Wake and Juxon, with Laud depicted on the scaffold at Tower Hill.

Although the chapel no longer plays an important feature in the life of the Inn, its historical importance is immense. From at least 1600 attendance at services was compulsory for all gentlemen. A fine of 4d was imposed every time they failed to receive communion in a term, and failure for a year could lead to expulsion. Each evening for over three centuries the chapel bell would be tolled 40 times to announce the 9 o'clock curfew.

Gray's Inn has been particularly associated with eminent churchmen also admitted as students of the law. Stephen Gardiner, Lord Chancellor to King Henry VIII in 1555, and a great rival of Thomas Cromwell, was also bishop of Winchester. Those commemorated in stained glass are the martyred Archbishop Laud and William Juxon who ministered to King Charles I at his execution. Whitgift became archbishop of Canterbury in 1593. Some 70 years later Gilbert Sheldon, who had been a student at Gray's Inn, became archbishop and, as Chancellor of Oxford University, builder of the Sheldonian Theatre.

The vast majority of the buildings in Gray's Inn Square were reconstructed after Second World War bombing, although where possible old brickwork was used, particularly at Nos. 1, 6, 7, 8 and 12 north, which dates back to 1676. Many of the original door lintels were incorporated into the rebuilding. Numbers were first painted over the staircases in 1693. At about that time the whole square became known as Coney Court but the numbering was the same as the present Gray's Inn Square. It is thus less these buildings than their addresses that call famous occupants of the Square to mind.

At No. 2 lived the 19th-century author and journalist Edward Dicey. Lord Merrivale (1855-1939), who was President of the Probate, Divorce and Admiralty Division from 1919 to 1933, had chambers at No. 4. The old Pipe Office was situated at No. 5 in the early years of the 18th century, and from this address Shelley wrote to Southey in March 1816. At No. 6 the great penal reformer, Sir Samuel Romilly took chambers between May 1779 and December 1791: in that final month he wrote, 'the moment the sun peeps out I am in the country. A cold country it is, for having only one row of houses between me and Hampstead and Highgate a north-west wind blows full against my chambers'. And at No. 7 the eminent architect, Sir George Gilbert Scott (1811-78) practised from rooms on the ground floor.

The buildings on the western side of the square abut the gardens and were formerly part of the original smaller block which was called Coney Court, although they were once known as Bacon's chambers since three generations of that august family practised here from 1570 until 1626 when Viscount St Albans died. This famous set, situated at library staircase, 1 Coney Court, was burned down in the fire of 6 January 1684 when revels to entertain King James II got a little out of hand, and a bonfire destroyed Coney Court in its entirety, the original library of the Inn founded in 1568 and housed in the rooms directly below Bacon's chambers, and many other Tudor buildings. From 1555 until the 19th century the original Pension Rooms of the Inn were situated here in what became Finch's and Denny's Buildings.

5. Proceed anticlockwise around Gray's Inn Square to the north-east corner.

Under the main window of the chapel, as a second reminder of the Inn's contribution to the First World War, a plaque is set in the wall between two free-standing ornamental urns on pedestals:

> *In glorious memory of the gallant officers, NCOs and men of the 1st and 2nd London Welsh Battalion, Royal Welch Fusiliers, who laid down their lives at the call of King and Country in the Great War 1914-1918 mewn anghof ni chant fod (never forgotten). These battalions were recruited at Gray's Inn.*

Running south of the gatehouse, past the former chapel and into Holborn Court, as it then was, stood Osbaldestone's Buildings, erected 1630-2 and destroyed in a fire in January 1687. On the first stairway south of the gate were the chambers of Sir John Holt, an eminent Chief Justice of the King's Bench 1689-1710.

The gatehouse in Gray's Inn Square was raised approximately on the site of the original gate of the manor house of Portpoole. Until Elizabethan times it was the only entrance into the Inn and Bacon gave the rooms over the gate as a residence to his tutor, Whitgift. From 1587 alms were given to the poor three times weekly at the gate, but this generosity appears to have consisted solely of providing the remnants from hall table. The present edifice was built after the Second World War with funds provided by Inner Temple. In a graceful tribute the archway bears not the arms of Gray's Inn, but the Pegasus of Inner Temple.

Sir Henry Yelverton, eldest son of Sir Christopher, was Solicitor-General in chambers here in 1613. He succeeded Francis Bacon as Attorney-General in 1617. As a result of outrageous fortune he was sent to the Tower in 1620, fully expecting the block for royal disfavour, but was restored to become a justice of the Court of Common Pleas 1625-30.

The old gate dates from about 1688 when Chapel and Coney Courts were reconstructed. Here Jacob Tonson (1656-1736) had his bookshop, held, according to the records, upon a 21-year lease from Lady Day (25 March) 1725, and he afterwards took the shop at Holborn Gate as well. Tonson was a well-known Whig and secretary of the Kit-Kat Club. He purchased the copyright of *Paradise Lost*, published the works of John Dryden and Joseph Addison and was satirised by Alexander Pope.

To the north of the gatehouse stood Shute's Buildings, named after Robert Shute who was treasurer in 1576, a baron of the Exchequer in 1579 and justice of the Queen's Bench in 1585. Erected between 1567 and 1576 these were pulled down in 1627 and rebuilt as Cooper's Buildings. Further along, where 10 and 11 Gray's Inn Square now stand, was Ellis Buildings, constructed in 1579. The north side was completed as a square by Sir Edward Stanhope in 1580.

3 Verulam Buildings, detail

On the west side of the square were Daniel's Buildings 1566-79, afterwards known simply as 'West Side'. From this projected two ancient stone buildings called respectively Long Gallery and Lower Gallery, which were part of the outhouses of the original manor. These ran into the square parallel with the hall, and effectively split Chapel Court from the rest of what is the present-day square. In 1685 these were demolished together with a four-storey building to the west of Long Gallery known as 'the House'.

6. Proceed through the passageway in the north-east corner under No. 9 which leads to Verulam Buildings.

This discreet terrace was originally known as Panyerman's Close in 1579, and often suffered from flooding due to the inadequate drainage of Gray's Inn Lane, as Gray's Inn Road was then called. From 1608 it contained a bowling alley and a summer house for the benchers. However, in 1677 the area was returned to use as gardens, and remained so for a further 120 years. This lovely Georgian terrace, named for Francis Bacon who held the title of Baron Verulam, was constructed in two parts: Nos. 1-3 during the treasurership of Romilly in 1803, and Nos. 4-5 (which protrude slightly) during that of Isaac Espinasse in 1811.

The novelist William Makepeace Thackeray (1811-63) took chambers here in 1861 and in 1866 W.S. Gilbert spent some of his short time in practice at No. 1.

7. Proceed beyond Verulam Buildings out of the Inn into Gray's Inn Road. At the traffic lights turn left into Theobalds Road and walk along the boundary of the Inn.

The old police station building near the corner of Theobalds Road was built in 1896 and designed by John Dixon Butler (1861-1920), a well known architect of police stations and magistrates' courts of that era. It is now the Metropolitan Police Traffic Warden Centre.

On the north side of Theobalds Road, opposite Gray's Inn Walks are King's Mews and John Street which leads into Doughty

Street where at No. 48 the Dickens Museum and Library are located. This was Charles Dickens's first house after he married and in the two years while he was resident, 1837-9, he wrote *Oliver Twist* and *Nicholas Nickleby* here. He also finished *Pickwick Papers* and commenced *Barnaby Rudge*.

The railings on the south side of Theobalds Road mark the northern boundary of Gray's Inn and open to view are the Walks bordered clockwise by Verulam Buildings, Gray's Inn Square, Field Court, Gray's Inn Place, Atkin Building and Raymond Buildings.

Raymond Buldings

8. At the end of the railings turn left back into the Inn.

The terrace of Raymond Buildings is named after Lord Raymond, who was called to the Bar in 1697. As Sir Robert Raymond he became Solicitor-General in 1710, Attorney-General in 1720, and went on to become Chief Justice of the King's Bench from 1725 to 1733. The coachway alongside was cut after 1790 and was originally intended to run to the west end of the hall. The wall abutting Bedford Row was erected in 1722 at the same time as the gates to the Walks were raised. Number 2 covers the site of the folly called Bacon's Mount and his summer house. At No. 5 Rupert Brooke (1887-1915), the war poet, had chambers.

Attached to the end of Raymond Buildings, Atkin Building, named for the leading jurist of the first half of the 20th century, Lord Atkin (1867-1944), was constructed in 1987-8 on the site of Gray's Inn tennis club, and is used principally by the City University School of Law.

From the end of the terrace a pathway leads into Gray's Inn Place and back into Holborn. Although now in modern buildings, the former Inns of Court School of Law was established as the principal college for Bar vocational training by the Council of Legal Education in 1883, and the School maintained a near monopoly in such training until relatively recently when the Council of Legal Education was abolished and the General

The Walks

Council of the Bar licensed its vocational training to other educational establishments in London and the provinces. The School is now a faculty of City University. Its site, though, is of greater historical interest.

In 1570 the then Reader, William Allington, constructed a walled house and gardens here. In 1622 this came into the possession of Robert Rich, second Earl of Warwick, and became his town residence, known as Warwick House, which still stands today, on the right. The garden of the house extended to the ground now occupied by 6, 7 and 8 Warwick Court and to the area which became Gray's Inn Place in 1793. Warwick, who died in 1658, was Lord High Admiral of the Commonwealth navy and a promoter of many ventures that led to New England settlements, some of which were planned and organised from this house.

9. Turn left and pass No. 3 Gray's Inn Place along Field Court towards Gray's Inn Square.

The Walks is the name of the gardens of the Inn laid out by Francis Bacon on the site of the meadows and the coneygarth (a warren where rabbits were bred for the kitchens) in 1598-1600. The Pension Books record that 71 elms, eight birches, 16 cherry trees, 125 roses, pinks, violets, primroses and vines were planted. Bacon also constructed a delightful folly, his fairies' mount, some 30 feet (9 m.) high and itself surmounted by the Banqueting House. The mount was removed in 1755. The gardens, now open to the public between 12.00 and 2.30 p.m. on weekdays, remained as laid out by Bacon for nearly two centuries. During the reign of King Charles II they became a fashionable place for social promenade on summer evenings, offering uninterrupted views, at least until 1663, of the rising ground leading to Hampstead and Highgate. Samuel Pepys came here in 1661 and 1662, as did Joseph Addison and John Dryden, who also placed their literary characters in the Walks, and the evangelist John Wesley. Charles Lamb wrote of them:

> *They are still the best gardens of any of the Inns of Court – my beloved Temple not forgotten – have the gravest character, their aspect being altogether reverend and law-breathing. Bacon has left the impress of his foot upon their gravel walks.*

Entrance gates to the Walks

Gray's Inn

The elaborate gates to the Walks, erected in 1723 during the treasurership of Sir William Gilbey, are directly opposite Field Court gate, which is itself surmounted by two stone griffins, and leads into Fulwood Place, formerly Fulwood's Rents. This was named after Fulwood House, which was built in 1580 as the home of Sir George Fulwood. Once a fashionable turning leading to the Walks, by the 1720s it contained an assortment of taverns, ale and coffee houses and places of entertainment to cater for the occupants of the Inn, together with overflow chambers. Of these, John's Coffee House established in 1656 was the most popular with members of hall. Also to be found at Fulwood Rents were Squire's, frequented by Addison, and Fuller's, home of the Whig Club after the Restoration.

To the right of the archway passing back into Gray's Inn Square stood Page's Buildings 1620-1894, although its name became 1 and 2 Field Court in 1731. By the side stood a barber's shop, used by Pepys. To the east of the Field Court gate a hall and lecture rooms were constructed in 1905 with a large common room connected to the minstrel gallery of the hall by a corridor over the archway. This stood on the site of Grimston's Buildings, one of the earliest in the Inn, occupied by Sir Francis Walsingham, principal

Secretary of State to Queen Elizabeth I, with his brother-in-law, Sir Walter Mildmay, Chancellor of the Exchequer.

Gray's Inn Hall, detail of stained glass window

10. Proceed through the passage and turn right into South Square and back to the start.

Bibliography

Barber, Malcolm, *The Trial of the Templars*, Cambridge University Press, Cambridge, 1991.
Bellot, Hugh H.L., *Gray's Inn and Lincoln's Inn*, Methuen, London, 1925.
Bellot, Hugh H.L., *The Temple*, 5th edn, Methuen, London, 1930.
Besant, Sir Walter, *The Fascination of London* (series), A & C Black, London 1903-8.
Birkenhead, 1st Earl of, *Famous Trials*, Hutchinson, London, 1946.
Cecil, Lord David, *The Cecils of Hatfield House*, Constable, London, 1953.
Collins Dictionary of Biography, William Collins, London, 1971.
Gilbert, W.S., *The Savoy Operas*, Oxford University Press, London, 1962.
Daniell, Timothy, *Inns of Court*, Wildy's, London, 1971.
Denning, Lord, *The Family Story*, Butterworths, London, 1981.
Dutton, Ralph, *London Homes*, Allan Wingate, London, 1952.
Goodman, Andrew, *Gilbert and Sullivan's London*, Faber & Faber, London, 2000.
Goodman, Andrew, *The Royal Courts of Justice Guide*, Longman Professional, London, 1985.
Hare, Augustus J.C., *Walks in London*, 2 vols., George Allen, London, 1901.
The Harmsworth Encyclopeadia, Thomas Nelson, London, 1903.
Kelly, Bernard W., *Famous Advocates and Their Speeches*, Sweet & Maxwell, London 1921.
Kent, William, *An Encyclopeadia of London*, J.M. Dent, London, 1951.
Kiralfy, A.K.R., *Potter's Outlines of English Legal History*, Sweet & Maxwell, London, 1958
The London of Charles Dickens, Dickens Fellowship, London Transport, London, 1970.
Marjoribanks, Edward, *Life of Lord Carson*, Victor Gollancz, London, 1932.
Marjoribanks, Edward, *Life of Sir Edward Marshall Hall*, Victor Gollancz, London, 1930.
Milsom, S.F.C., *Historical Foundations of the Common Law*, Butterworths, London, 1969.
Mr Punch in Wig and Gown, *Punch Library of Humour*, ed. J.A. Hammerton, Educational Book Co. Ltd, 1921.
The Oxford Dictionary of Quotations, Oxford University Press, London 1953.
Pannick, David, *Advocates*, Oxford University Press, Oxford, 1992.
Service, Alastair, *London 1900*, Granada, London, 1979.
Thornbury, Walter, *Old London*, 7 vols., Alderman Press, London, 1987.
Walker, David M., *The Oxford Companion to Law*, Clarendon Press, Oxford, 1980.
Worley, George, *The Temple Church. A short history and description*, G. Bell & Sons, London, 1911.

Wrottesley, Frederick J., *Letters to a Young Barrister*, Sweet & Maxwell, London, 1930.

Pamphlets, periodicals and journals

Central Criminal Court Journalists Association, The Old Bailey, Corporation of London, 1976.
Davis, G.R.C., *Magna Carta*, British Library, 1992.
High Court Journalists Association, *Royal Courts of Justice Illustrated Guide*, London, 1977.
The Honourable Society of the Middle Temple, *Middle Temple Ordeal*, Pitman & Sons Ltd, 1948.
Inner Temple Yearbooks 1986-99
The Journal of Legal History, vols 1 (1980), 10(1990), 12 (1992) to 19 (1999), Frank Cass, London.
Life and Times of King John, George Weidenfeld & Nicholson, London, 1972.
Macassey, Sir Lynden, *Middle Templars' Associations with America*, Middle Temple, London, 1998.
Megarry, Sir Robert, *Inns Ancient and Modern*, Selden Society, 1972.
Royal Courts of Justice Illustrated Handbook 1883, reprinted by Wildy's, London, 1977.
Royal Courts of Justice, An introduction for visitors, South Eastern Circuit Office, London, 1981.

Index

Page numbers in italics refer to illustrations. Some textual material may occur on the same pages.

A

Abinger, Lord (James Scarlett) 104
Abington's coffee house 239
Abraham, Henry 50-1, 53, 120
Acheson, Dean 199
Addington, Henry (Viscount Sidmouth) 199
Addison, Joseph 39, 51, 117, 255, 260
Affidavit Office 188
Albert, Prince Consort 43, 213, 232
Aldwych/Kingsway development 26, 30, 33
Alfred (King) 35, *73*, 77
Alienation Office 101, 104
All-Hallows Barking-by-the-Tower 12
Allington, William 260
Alverstone, LCJ 113
American Bar Association 123, 248-*249*
Anderson, Jacob 142
Anne (Queen) 27, 40, 51, 123
Anne (Princess Royal) 100
Anne of Cleeves 113
Anne of Denmark 27
Anti-Corn league 157
Apollo Club 39
Arbuthnot, Dr John 51
Armstead, Henry 58, 93
Armstrong, Sir Thomas 40
Arne, Dr Thomas 114
Arundel House 29
Ashley, James 162
Ashley, Robert 82
Ashmole, Elias 51, 112
Asquith, Herbert Henry 100, 199, 215
Atkin, Lord 248, 259
Atkin Building 257, 259
Attenboroughs, jewellers, 177
Aula (Curia) Regis 6
Aungier, Richard 240
Australia House 30, 33
Automobile Association 151

B

Babington's Rents 106
Backside, 196
Bacon, Francis (Viscount St Albans) 188, 230, 239, 243, *244*, 245, 247, 255
Bacon, Sir Nicholas 188, 245, 247
Bacon's Chambers 254
Bacon's Mount (folly) 258
Bail Court 13
Baker, Sir John 110
Balfour, Arthur 243
Ballantyne, Serjeant 141
Bankruptcy court 13
Bar Pro Bono Unit, 190
Barbon, Dr Nicholas 117, 119
Barnard, Lionel 230
Barnard's Inn 147, 229, 231
Barrett, Michael 166
Barry, Sir Charles 4, 5, 220
Barry, E.M. 52
Bath's Inn 29
Bathurst, Lord Chancellor 199
Baynard's Castle 195
Beaumont, Francis (dramatist) 39, 95, 105
Beaumont, Francis (justice) 104
Becket, Thomas à (saint) 27, 130
Beckford, William 169
Beerbohm, Sir Max 34, 158
Bell Yard 147
Belloc, Hilaire 251
Bencher's Walk 89
Benjamin, Judah Philip 107
Bentham, Jeremy 208
Besant, Sir Walter 116
Bethell, Richard 50

Bide, Edward 201
Big Ben 5
Birkbeck, George 191
Birkbeck College 191
Birkenhead, Earl of (F.E. Smith) 248
Bishop's Court 187
Black Books, 196
Black Buildings 101
'Black cap' 68
Black Friars 195
Black Prince 182
Blackfriars 12
Blackfriars Bridge 160
Blackstone, Sir William 113-115, 126
Blair, Anthony 102, 199
Blair, John 84
Blanchard, E.L. 242
Blom, Richard 142
Blomfield, Arthur 58
Bloody Assizes 98
Blower's Buildings 242
Board of Inland Revenue 28
Boden, George 140
Boleyn, Anne 39, 183
Bolt Court 156
Bonaparte, Napoleon 183
Boswell, James 41, 140, 141, 153, 157
Bottomley, Horatio 169
de Bouillon, Godefroi 129
de Boulogne, Baudouin 129
du Bourg, Baudouin 129
Bouverie Street 156
Bow Street Runners 16
Bowyer Row 162
Boyce, Sir Leslie 170
Bradshaw (ancient of Gray's Inn) 251
Bradshaw, Henry 106
Bradshaw's Rents 106
Bramwell, Lord 88
Brandon, Raphael 53
Breton, John 175
Brewster, Colonel 212
Brick Court 84, 112, 114, 116
Bridewell 88
Bright, John 157

British Library Science and Reference and Information Service 190
British Optical Association 180
Brooke, Rupert 258
Brougham, Lord Chancellor 65, 208
Brown, Sir Stephen 98, 99
Browning, Robert 95, 171
Bruce of Kinloss, Lord Edward 183
le Brun, Walter 218
Buckingham, Duke of (Henry Stafford) 9
Buckmaster, Lord Chancellor 208
Bucknill, Mr Justice 169
Buller, Charles 50
Burges, William 53
de Burgh, Hubert (Earl of Kent) 131
Burghley, Lord (William Cecil) 230, 234, 248, 250
Burke, Edmund 127, 141, 144, 150
Burnand, Sir Francis 199
Burney, Charles 141, 157
de Burstall, William 181
Bush House 30
Butler, John Dixon 256
Butler, Samuel 100, 136, 152, 179, 207, 251
Butler-Sloss, Dame Elizabeth 98
Byfield, John 138
Byron, Henry 242
Byron, Lord 153

C
Caesar, Sir Julius 107
Caesar's Building 107
Cage's Buildings 241
Cairns, Earl (Lord Chancellor) 66, 217
Camden, Lord Chancellor 217
Camden, William 100, 251
Campum Templarorium 218
Canadian Bar Association 123
Canning, George 101, 199
Carlyle, Thomas 157
Carpmael Buildings 85
Carr, Baroness, 99

Carson of Duncairn, Lord Edward 142
Cassels, James 122
Catherine of Braganza 27
Cato Street conspirators 166
Caxton, William 153
Cecil, Arthur 242
Cecil, Robert (Earl of Salisbury) 125
Cecil, William (Lord Burghley) 125, 248
Central Criminal Court *see* Old Bailey
Chambers, Sir William 27
de Champagne, Godefroi 129
Chancellor of the Exchequer 21
Chancery Chambers Registry 188
Chancery Courts 11, 12, 49, 175, 199
Chancery House 191
Chancery Lane 147, 156, 173, 173-191, 195, 223
Chancery Writ Office 199
Chapel Court 239
Charles I 10, 27, 40, 97, 105, 123, 125, 156, 208, 241, 243, 247, 250, 251
Charles II 20, 26, 27, 38, 40, 67, 96, 123, 148, 151, 198, 203, 219, 247, 260
de Charney, Geoffroi 133
Chatterton, Thomas 234
Chaucer, Geoffrey 121, 147, 182
Chester Inn 26
Chesterton, G.K. 158
Chichester Rents 187
Chief Whip 21
Child and Co. 39, 40
Child's Place 40, 114
Chilton, George 101
Christie, John 169
Chronicle House 158
Church Court 107, 108, 131
Churches
  All-Hallows Barking-by-the-Tower 12
  Blackfriars 12
  Church of the Holy Sepulchre 223
  Domus Conversorum 12
  St Andrew's, Holborn 138, 233

St Bride's 158-159, *161*
St Clement Danes 25, *37*, 218
St Dunstan's-in-the-West 147, *152*, 179
St Mary-le-Strand 12, 28-29
St Paul's Cathedral 162
St Sepulchre's, Newgate 162
Southwark Cathedral 12
Whitefriars 12
see also Temple Church
Churchill, Sarah (Duchess of Marlborough) 103
Churchill, Sir Winston 11, 248
Churchyard Court 142
Chyswold's Buildings 242
Cibber, Colley 41, 103
Cipriani, G.B. 31
Citie of York public house 224, 239
Clachan Pub 154
Clare Market 34, 35
Clarke, Sir Edward 66
Clarke, George Somers 53
Clement V, Pope 132, 133
Clement's Inn 34, 35, 36, 53, 242
Clement's Inn Passage 36
de Clifford, Isabella 178
Clifford, Lord (Earl of Cumberland) 179
de Clifford, Robert 178
Clifford's Inn 91, 147, 152, 177
  gatehouse 152, *153*, 180
Clifford's Inn Passage 152, 178
Cloister Court 110, 137
Cloisters 110, 112
Cobbett, William 157, 251
Cobden, Richard 157
Cobham, Eleanor, 78
Cock and Bottle 151
Cock Tavern 151
Cockburn, Sir Alexander 65, 81
Cohen, Arthur 139
Coke, Sir Edward 33, 94, 97, 105, 179, 188, 234, 248
Coleridge, LCJ 115
Coleridge, Samuel Taylor 141, 154, 179

Collins, Wilkie 158, 199
Colman, George 141
Common Pleas, Court of 6, 11, 13, 155, 241, 255
Common Serjeant 168
Conan Doyle, Sir Arthur 158
Coney Court 239, 245, 252, 254
Congreve, William 51, 127, 157, 223
Cooper's Buildings 255
Cottenham, Lord Chancellor 202
Cotterell, William 211
Cotton, John 100
Cottrell's Garden 196
Courtauld Institute 30
Courts
  Bail 13
  Bankruptcy 13
  Barons of the King's Household 6
  Chancery 12, 13
  Common Bench 6
  Common Pleas 6, 11, 13, 155
  Exchequer 6, 13, 140
  Exchequer Chamber 13
  High Court Divisions 30
  Principal Registry of the Family Division 30
  High Court of Admiralty 13
  King's Bench 6, 12, 13, 155
  Lady Chief Justice of England's Court *66, 69*
  Master of the Rolls 13
  Middlesex Crown Court 17
  Probate and Divorce Court 13
  Requests 4
  Star Chamber 6
  Vice-Chancellor's 13
  see also Royal Courts of Justice
Covent Garden 28
Cowper, William (Lord Chancellor) 70, 123, 126
Cowper, William (poet), 113, 127, 128
Cowper-Temple, William 54
Cox, Serjeant 178
Crippen, Dr Hawley 169, 172
Crockford's eating house 52
Cromwell, Oliver 10, 27, 29, 35, 42, 182, 188, 201
Cromwell, Thomas 176, 250, 253
Crown Office Row 85-86, 87, 90
Cruikshank, George 158
Cunningham, 'Praise-God Barebone' 155
Cunningham of Hyndhope, Lord 199
De Curars, Robert 190
Curia Regis 6, 7, 159, 175, 205
Cursitor's Inn 188
Cursitor's Office 188
Custos Morum 7
Custos Rotulorum 176

D

Daily Express 158
Daily Mail 156
Daily News 156
The Daily Telegraph 158
Danby, Dick 11
Dance, George (the Younger) 166, 170
Daniel's Buidings 256
Dare, Virginia 159
Davenport, Sir Humphrey 241
Davenport's Buildings 241
Davis, Jefferson 107
Daynes, John M. 201
De la More, Walter 134
De Montfort, Simon 3, 27
Deane, Thomas 53, 54
Dean's Yard 14
Defoe, Daniel 44, 165
Denman, Lord 64, 201
Denning, Lord *70, 199*, 213
Denny, Hugh 237
Denny's Buildings 243
Derwentwater, Lord 10
Devereux, Robert (Earl of Essex) 10, 38, 97, 116, 206
Devereux Chambers 117
Devereux Court 117
Devil's Tavern *41*
Diana, Princess, 126
Dicey, Edward (Lord Merrivale) 253

Dickens, Charles 12, 31, 33, 35, 40, 44, 49, 52, 75, 79, 89, 100, 102, 111, 118, 119, 127, 142, 156, 163, 166, 168, 179, 190, 193, 205, 208, 218, 223, 224, 225, 227, 229, 230
 as clerk 241-2, 243
 Museum and Library 257
Dickens, John 31
Dickinson, John 84
Digby, John 120
Dispatch 157
Disraeli, Benjamin 49, 52, 55, 189, 199, 201
Dixon, William Hepworth 249
Domus Conversorum 12
Donne, John 152, 182
Dowding, Air Chief Marshal Lord 37
Downe's Buildings 241
Downing, Sir George 20
Downing Street 20-21
Dowson, Ernest 158
D'Oyly Carte Opera Company 185
Dr Johnson's Buildings 139, 141, 142
 library 141
Drake, Sir Francis 51, 96, 124, 125
Drury Lane 28, 32, 223
Dryden, John 40, 51, 155, 223, 255, 260
Du Maurier, George 160
Ducane, Sir Edward 22
Duchy of Cornwall Office 150
Dudley, John (Duke of Northumberland) 238
Dudley, Robert (Earl of Leicester) 94, 104, 105, 116
Duke, John 115
Dyer, George 179
Dyers' Building 229

E
Earl Godwin 27
Economic Assurance Society 156
Ede & Ravenscroft, Messrs 184-*185*, *186*-187
Edgworth Bess 165
Edward the Confessor 3, 27, 147

Edward I 6, 11, 92, 175, 176, 181, 195, 213, 237
Edward II 8, 35, 38, 78, 116, 147, 181, 195
 Templars and 132, 133, 134
Edward III 7, 92, 140, 148, 237
Edward IV 6
Edward VI 9, 29, 42, 252
Edward VII 32, 93, 126
Edward VIII, 123
Edwards, Martin 122
Eisenhower, Dwight D. 199
El Vino 154, 155
Eldon, Lord Chancellor 123, 126, 188, 205, 214, 218
Eliot, George 31
Elizabeth I 38, 42, 78, 84, 95, 107, 110, 116, 122, 123, 124, 125, 153, 162, 179, 210, 219, 226, 240, 247, 250
 statue *154*
Elizabeth II 142, 250
Elizabeth the Queen Mother 81, 126
Elizabeth Tower, *4*,*5*
Ellenborough, Lord 97, 101
Ellis Buildings 255
Elm Court 112, *127*
Erle, Sir William 101
Ermsted, Rev William 110
Erskine, Lord Chancellor 89, 97, 199
Essex, Earl of (Robert Devereux) 10, 38, 97
Essex, Earl of (Thomas Cromwell) 176, 250, 253
Essex Court 114, *116*, 117, 120
Essex House 38, 116
Essex Stairs 79
Ethelred 52
Eugenius III, Pope 129
Evelyn, John 9, 79, 116, 127, 162, 204
Evening Standard 158
Exchequer Chamber Court 13
Exchequer Court 6, 13, 49, 88
Exchequer Office 140

269

Excise Office 157
Exeter Inn 38
Eyre, Sir James 169, 248

F
Falconer, Lord 98
Farrar's Building 139, 140
Farringdon's Inn 177
Faryndon (Farringdon), Robert 177
Fawkes, Guy 10, 183
Al Fayed, Mohamed 160
Fetter Lane 154
Fettor Lane 154
Fickett's Croft 133
Fickett's Field 35, 133, 196, 215, 218
Field Court 239, 257, 261
Fielding, Henry 16, 113, 127
Fielding, John 16
Fig Tree Court 85, 91, 108, 127
Finch, Sir Heneage 97, 170
Fine Office 243
Fine Office Court 140
Fire judges 94
Fisher, St John 9
Fleet Bridge 160
Fleet Street 147-172
Fleet Street Inn 155
Fletcher, John 41, 95
Forster, John 158
Fortescue, Sir John 202, 214
Fountain Court *118*, 127
Fountain Court Chambers 119
Fountain tavern 150
Fox, Charles James 101
Francis Taylor Building 106
Franklin, Benjamin 163
Frost Fair 78-79
Fry, Elizabeth 166, *171*
Fuller's Rents 104-106
Fullwood, George 239
Fulton, Sir Forrest 119
Fulwood, Sir George 261
Fulwood Rents 261
Furnival, Sir William 228
Furnival's Inn 147, 227-228, 229

G
Gainsborough, Thomas 214
Gandhi, Mohandas Karamchand 98, 109
Garden Court, Lincoln's Inn 208
Garden Court, Temple 82, 84, 117, 119
Garden Row, Lincoln's Inn 208
Gardiner, Stephen (Lord Chancellor) 248, 253
Garling, Henry 53
Garrick, David 141, 157, 199
Gascoigne, George 250
Gascoigne, Sir William 250
Gate Street 219
Gay, John 150, 219
Geoffrey of Monmouth 160
George I 11, 123, 183
George II 20, 94, 123, 210
George III 160, 201
George IV 12
George V *92*, 198, 205, 214
George VI 93, 104
George tavern *38*
George's coffee house 38
Gerard, Sir Gilbert 241, 247
Gerard's Buildings 241
Gibbon, Edward 141, 157
Gibbons, Grinling 108, *109*, 137
Gibbs, James 37
Gibson, James 16
Gibson, John 53
Giffard, Hardinge Stanley, Earl of Halsbury 94, 101
Gilbert, W.S. 33, 36, 38, 79, 113, 168, 173, 185, 191, 242, 243, 256
Gilbey, William 261
Gillett and Bland clockmakers 73
Gladstone, W.E. 49, 52, 93, 100, 113, 199
Godmaston, John 8
Goff of Chievely, Lord 98, *99*
Goldsmid, Francis Henry 214
Goldsmith, Oliver 84, 89, 113, 114, 141, 142, 143, 144, 157, 251
Goldsmith Building 121, 142

Goodfellowe, Christopher 96
Gordon, Lord George 166
Gordon Riots 40, 144, 168
Gosforth, Lord Taylor 66
Goslings Bank 151
Gough Square 158
Graham and Tompion clockmakers 157
Gray, Edmund (Lord Gray of Wilton) 237
Gray, Paul 242
Gray's Inn 235-262
  Bacon statue 243, *244*
  Bacon's folly 258
  Bacon's Mount 258
  Blitz damage 245, 252
  chapel *238, 251*
  Chapel Court 239, 252
  coffee houses 239
  Coney Court 239, 245, 252, 254
  entertainment 249
  famous members 238, 250-252
  Field Court 239, 257, 261
  gatehouse 224, 239
  Gatehouse Chambers, 240
  Green Court 252
  griffin *240*
  Hall *238, 246, 248, 249*
  Holborn Court 239
  library 245
  Long Gallery 256
  Lower Gallery 256
  Pension Chamber 246
  South Square 240, *242, 243*
  Square *25*
  Walks 257, *258-259*, 260, *261*
Gray's Inn Place 257
Green Court 252
Gresham, Sir Thomas 250
Grey, Lady Jane 183
de Grey, Reginald (Lord Grey of Wilton) 252
Grimston's Buildings 261
Gunpowder Plot 97
Gwynne, Nell 40, 219

H
Haggard, H. Rider 199
Hailsham of Marylebone, Lord Chancellor 66, 199
Hal, Frans 126
Haldane, Viscount (Lord Chancellor) 208, 215
Hale, Sir Matthew 64, 94, 179, 208, 212
Hale Court 187, 200, *216*
Hale's Buildings 243
Hall, Sir Benjamin 5
Hall, Sir Edward Marshall 79, 119
Hall Court 118
Hall of the Military Knights 91, 111, 121, 127
Hall of the Priests 91
Halley, Edmund 230
Halsbury, Earl of (Hardinge Stanley Giffard) 94, 101
Halsbury's *Laws of England* 101
Hammick's law bookshop 177
Hampden, John 14, 99
Harcourt, Sir Simon 81, 94
Harcourt, Sir William 63
Harcourt, William 213
Harcourt Buildings 81, 84
Hardwick, Philip 52, 212, 218
Hardwicke, Lord Chancellor 123, 126
Hardwicke Building *216*
Hare, Augustus 180
Hare, Nicholas (nephew to Sir Nicholas) 140
Hare, Sir Nicholas (the elder) 113, 140
Hare Court 91, 112, 113, 139
Hare Place 154
Harfleur (Harfleet) Inn 185
De Harley, Malcolm 178
Harold I (Harefoot) 36
Harris, Sir Arthur 37
Harrison's Buildings 101
Hastings, de, Richard 190
Hastings, Warren 11, 97
Hatherley, Lord Chancellor 64, 93
Hatton, Sir Christopher 51, 95, 125,

231-2
Hatton, Lady Elizabeth 234
Hatton Garden 95, 232
de Haverhill, William 196
Hawk and Pheasant 162
Haydon, Benjamin Robert 141
Hazlitt, William 141, 154, 191
Heath, Sir Edward 251
Heavy Hill 223
Henderson, W. Craig 122
Henley, Lord Chancellor 201
Henrietta Maria (Queen) 14
Henry I 165
Henry II 130, 133, 136, 181
Henry III 3, 90, 131, 133, 176, 180, 187, 196
Henry IV 7, 155
Henry V 223
Henry VI 78, 147
Henry VII 6, 85, 108, 153, 183, 198, 200, 205
Henry VIII 3, 7, 8, 10, 27, 41, 116, 140, 156, 189, 190, 198, 211, 227, 250
Hepple, Norman 213
Heraclius (Patriarch) 133, 136
Herbertson, John 187
Herrick, Robert 41
Herschell, Lord Chancellor 58, 199
Hertford, Earl of (Edward Seymour) 239
Heyward, Edward 99
Heyward, Thomas jr. 83
High Court
  Divisions 30
  Principal Registry of the Family Division 30
High Court of Admiralty 13
High Court of Justice 11
High Holborn 224
       See also Holborn
Hind Court 156
Hoare's Bank 153
Hogarth, William 107, 108, 204, 220
Hogshead 161
Holborn 195, 221-234

Holborn Bars 41, 223, 224, 237
Holborn Court 239
Holborn Hill 223
Holborn Viaduct 160, 223, 232
Holeburne 223
Holker, Sir John 245
Holloway prison 166
Holt, Sir John 230, 254
Honorius II, Pope 129
Hood, Thomas 141, 158
Hopwood, Charles Henry 84
House of Lords' Judicial Committee 13, 21
Howard, John 171
Howard, Thomas 116
Howard, William 125
Howard League for Penal Reform 171
Howland's Buildings 241
Huddlestone, Mr Baron 66
Hughes, Thomas 199, 208
Humphreys, Travers 172
Hunt, George 55
Hunt, Holman 213
Hyde, Edward (Lord Chancellor) 126

I
ILEX Pro Bono Forum, 190
India House 32
Ingersoll, Charles Jared 84
Inner Temple 179
  benchers' rooms 90
  Blitz damage 81-83
  Cloisters 110, 112
  famous members 83, 98
  gardens 88, *89, 90, 91*
  gateway 150
  Hall Chambers 91
  library 106-108
  Master's House *109*, 110
  Niblett Hall 104
  paintings 123
  Parliamentary Chamber 108
  Pegasus symbol 93, *94,* 109, 131
  Privy Garden 104
  statues 92

Treasury 99, *100*
Inner Temple Hall *88*, 92, *94, 96, 97*, 112
   Blitz damage 81-83
   dramatic presentations 93
   paintings 94
   Pegasus symbol 93, *94*, 109, 131
Inner Temple Lane *143*, 144
Innocent III, Pope 130
Inns of Chancery 12
   see also individual Inns e.g. Clifford's Inn
Inns of Court and City Yeomanry 191, 209
Inns of Court School of Law 261
Irish Rents 240
Irvine of Lairg (Lord Chancellor) 98, 102, 182
Isaacs, Rufus (Marquess of Reading) 119

J
James I 10, 29, 39, 42, 52, 89, 97, 110, 142, 150, 243, 250
James II 10, 42, 68, 98, 123, 204, 247, 254
Jeffreys, Lord George (hanging judge) 39, 94, 98, 108, 113, 138
Jekyll, Sir Joseph 204
Jenkin, Robert 227
Jessel, Sir George 66
Jewel Tower (little) 4
Joe's Coffee House 154
John Bull 156
John (King) 159, 170, 237
John of Gaunt, 27
John Murray bookshop 153
John's Coffee House 224, 261
Johnson, Dr Samuel 37, 43, 114, 140, 153, 156-158, 226
Johnson, Thomas 156
Johnson's Court 156
Jones, Horace 45
Jones, Inigo 29, 42, 150, 181, 205, 214, 218, 228
Jones, Sir William 141
Jonson, Ben 41, 100, 137, 200, 205, 223
Joyce, William 169
Judge's Gate 117, *118*
Judicial Committee
   House of Lords 13, 21
   Privy Council 21
Juxon, Archbishop William 252, 253

K
Kat, Christopher 51
Katharine of Aragon 182, 198
Kederminster, Edward 185
Keene, Charles 160
Kelly, Fanny 141
Kemble, Charles 141
Kenmure, Lord 10
Kenyon, Lord Justice 123
Kidder, Edward 229
King of Denmark public house 166
Kinglake, A.W. 201
King's Bench Court 6, 12, 13, 155
King's Bench Office 101
King's Bench Walk 85, 88, 89, 101, *102*, 104, 105
King's Champion 7
Kingsley, Charles 199, 208
Kitchen Garden Court, 201, 212, 216
Kit-Kat Club 51, 255
Kneller, Sir Godfrey 39, 94, 123, 214
Knights Hospitallers 131, 132, 134, 196, 223
Knights Templar, Monument *111*

L
de Lacy, Henry 189, 195, 200, 217, 233
Ladies Prison Visiting Association 166
Lamb, Charles 85-86, 90, 106, 141, 154, 155, 179, 191, 260
Lamb, Mary 106, 191
   Lamb, William (Viscount Melbourne) 199, 218
   'Lamb and Flag' 121
   Lamb Building 107, 108
   Land Registry 220

273

Lands Tribunal 178
Langton, Bennett 157
de Langton, John 187, 196
Langton, Stephen 213
Laud, Archbishop 252, 253
Law, Edward (Lord Ellenborough) 97
Law Society 183
  common room 183
  Hall *183*
  reading room *183*
LawWorks, 190
Le Neve, Ethel 169
Leather Lane 231
Lee, Arthur 84
Leech, John 158, 160
Leech, Thomas 227
Legal costume 66-67
Leicester, Earl of (Robert Dudley) 94, 104, 105, 116
Leigh, Gerald 95
Leigh, Henry 242
Lemon, Mark 159
Lenton's Buildings 242
Liddell, Frederick 140
Limeburner Lane 162
Lincoln, Abraham (statue) *15*
Lincoln's Inn 187, 193-220
  administration 196-98
  benchers 203
  buttery 204
  chapel 205, *206, 207*
  Cottrell's Garden 196
  crypt *207*
  gardens 196, *211*
  gatehouse 188, *189, 197*, 200
  Gatehouse Court 207
  gates 216
  Kitchen Garden Court 201, 212, 216
  library 196, 212
  Library Staircase 201
  members 202
  New Hall 191, *213*, 214
  New Square *193*, 213, *215*, 216, 217
  Old Buildings 187, 200, 201, *202*
  Old Hall 187, 198, 201, 202, *203, 204*, 205, 213
  Old Square 188, 191, 208
  paintings 204
  records 196
  Stone Buildings 191, *209, 210*, 233
  taking commons 203
  Walks 207, 210, 211
  see also individual courts e.g. Hale Court
Lincoln's Inn Fields 49, 218, *219*
  gateway 188
Lintot(t), Bernard 150
Little Turnstile Passage 219
Littleton, Sir Thomas 96
Littleton Chambers 101
Livingstone, William 84
Lloyd George, David 142
Lockwood, Henry 53
London Coffee House 162
Lord Chancellor 6, 175
see also individual Lord Chancellors
Lord Chancellor's Court 205
'Lord Haw-Haw' 169
Lord Keeper of the Privy Seal 6, 175
Lord Treasurer 6
Lords of Appeal in Ordinary 13, 16
Louise (Princess) 93
Lovell, Sir Thomas 189
Lud 160
Ludgate 153
Ludgate Circus 158, 160
Lushington, Henry 106
Lynch, Thomas jr. 83
Lyndhurst, Lord 214
Lyon's Inn 33
Lyttleton, Sir Edward 105

M

Macaulay, Thomas Babington (Lord) 157, 199, 243
Mackay of Clashfern, Lord Chancellor 98, 99
McKean, Thomas 83
Mackworth, Dr John 230

Mackworth's Inn 230
Macmorran, Kenneth 81
Macnaghten, Lord 209
Maenan, Lord 106
Magna Carta 6, 11, 131, 183
Magpie and Stump public house 166
Maitland, Frederick William 209
Malcolm, Sarah 107
Manners, Lord John 55, 67
Manningham, John 125
Mansfield, Lord (William Murray) 102, 204, 208
Margaret (Princess) 201
Marriot, Richard 152
Martin, Alfred George 139
Mary Queen of Scots 95, *148*, 158, 183
Mary Tudor 42, 110, 252
Master of the Rolls 176
  court 13
Masters, Rev Dr 137
Mathews, Sir Charles 88
Matthews, Henry 22
Maufe, Sir Edward 81, 113, 249
Mayhew, Henry 159
Mead, William 172
Megarry, Sir Robert 208
Melbourne Place, 33
Mendoza, June 98
Menzies, Sir Robert 251
Mercers' School 231
Metropolitan Police Traffic Warden Centre 256
Middle Temple
  American Law Collection 83, 84
  Blitz damage 81-83, 93, 96, 120, 137
  buttery 92
  clerks commons 124
  emblem *121*
  gardens 120
  gatehouse *149*
  library 81, 82, 120
  Parliament Chamber 85, 93, 108, 126
  Pump Court 81, 90, *110*, 111-113, 126, 127
  Strand Inn 28
  Treasury 84
Middle Temple Hall 111, 121, *122*-126
  paintings 123
Middle Temple Lane 80, 81, 85, 114, *115*, 148
Middlesex Crown Court 15
Middlesex Guildhall 15, 17
Middleton, Arthur 83
Mildmay, Sir Walter 262
Millbank Penitentiary 14
Milton, John 152, 159
Mitre Court 154
Mitre Court Buildings 106
Mitre Court Chambers 154
Mitre Tavern 153
Moira, Gerald 169
de Molay, Jacques 132
Monk, General George 29
Montague, Ewen 16
Montague, Oliver 112
More, John 198
More, Sir/St Thomas 9, 198, 217, 228
More's Passage 217
Morning Advertiser 147
Mortimer, John QC 144
Motte, Benjamin 148
Moulton of Bank, Lord Fletcher 120
Mountford, Edward 168, 169
Muller, Franz 166

N

Nando's coffee house 149
National Industrial Relations Court 178
National Pro Bono Centre, 190
Neele, Henry 234
Nehru, Jawaharlal 98, 109
Nelson, Horatio 183
Neville, Bishop and Lord Chancellor 206, 175
Neville, Ralph 176, 187
New Court 117, 118, 119
New Inn 33, 35, 162

New Square 193
Newgate 165
Newgate prison 165, 166, 223
News of the World 156
Newton, Sir Isaac 29
Niblett, William 104
Niblett Hall 104
Nielson, Donald 169
Norman Shaw Building 21-22
North, Francis (Lord Gifford) 126
Northcliffe, Lord 153
Northcliffe House 156
Northcote, Sir William 89
Northumberland, Earl of 9
Norton, Thomas 95
Norwich Union 156
Nugent, Dr 141

O

Oates, Titus 6, 37, 41, 98, 223
O'Connor, T.P. 158
Offa 3
Old Bailey 165-172, *167, 170, 171*
 serious fraud trials annexe 187
Old Bell public house 159
Old Boar's Head 156
Old Bourne Bridge 223
Old Essex Court 117
Old King Lud public house 161, 138
Old Serjeant's Inn 177
Old Temple 190
Order of the Coif 155, 177
Osbaldestone's Buildings 243, 254
de Osgodeby, William 181

P

Paca, William 83
Packington's Rents 106
de Paganis, Hugo 129
Page's Buildings 261
Paget, Lord 116
Palace of Westminster *1*, 4, *5*, 13
Palgrave Buildings 117
Palgrave's Head 117
Panyerman's Close 256

Paper Buildings 36, 89, *90*, 99, 100, 101, 215
Parliament *see* Palace of Westminster
Paston letters 92
Patent Office 190
Patent Office building 226
Paulet, Sir Amyas 148
de Payens, Hugues 129
Peasants' Revolt 41, 121, 147
Peel, Sir Robert, 4
Penn, William 172, 182
Pennefather, Alfred 22
Pennethorne, Sir James 180
Pension Books 246, 260
Pepys, Samuel 20, 40, 150, 151, 153, 159, 204, 207, 212, 261
Perceval, Spencer 199, 206
Peto, Henry 229
Philip II of Spain 42
Philippe IV (the Fair) 132, 133
Phillimore, Lord 120
Phoenix Fire Office 150
Pierce, Edward 37
Pinckney, Charles Cotesworth 84
Pinckney, Henry 151
Pipe Office 243, 253
Pitt, William 186, 214
Pitt, William (the younger) 199, 210
Plowden, Edmund 84, 122, 123
Plowden Buildings 81, 82, 84, 119, 122
Pomeroy, Frederick W. 145, 168, 171, 243
Pope, Alexander 51, 103, 129, 150, 157, 255
Pope's Head 144
Powell, Richard 103
Pownall, George 54
Press Association 158
Prince Henry's Room 150
Prior, Sir James 115
Prisons
 Newgate 165, 166, 223
 Sloman's 188

Privy Council
Judicial Committee 21
Privy Garden, 104
Probate and Divorce Court 13
Probate Registry and Wills Office 49
Prowse, Jeff 242
Prudential Assurance building 226, 227, *228*
Public Record Office 152, 180-181
building *176, 181, 180-181*
Museum 8
Pump Court 81, 90, 110, 111, 112, 126, 127
Punch Tavern 159
Purcell, Henry 138
Purefoy, Humphrey 241
Purefoy's Buildings 241
Pynson, Richard 153

Q
Quality Court 190
Queen Elizabeth Building 82
Queen's Counsel 197
Queen's Remembrancer 199
de Quincy, Thomas 127

R
Rackstrow's Museum of Natural Curiosities and Anatomical Figures 148
Radcliffe, Charles (Earl of Sussex) 238
Rainbow Tavern 150
Raleigh, Sir Walter 14, 96, 97, 124, 125, 126, 182
Randolph, Peyton 84
Raymond, Lord Robert 217, 247, 258
Raymond Buildings *257*, 258
Reade, Charles 196, 199
Recorder of London 168, 170
Register of Births, Marriages and Deaths 30
Requests Court 3
Reuters 158
Reynolds, Sir Joshua 29, 141, 157, 214, 220

Rich, Robert (second Earl of Warwick) 260
Richard I 223
Richard II 7, 182, 228
Richard III 190
Richard of Hastings 130
Richardson, Samuel 157
Riley, John 123
Rizzello, Michael, 66
Robertson, Tom 242
Robin Hood Court 51
Robinson, Jacob 144
Robson, T.J.F. 138
Rogers, Francis 101
Rogers, Samuel 101
Rolls Chapel 181, 183, 184, 195
Rolls Court 204
Rolls Gardens 152
Rolls Yard 199
Romilly, Sir Samuel 216, 253
Roosevelt, Franklyn D. 248
Roosevelt, Theodore 158
Rowe, Nicholas 148
Royal Academy 30
Royal College of Surgeons 220
Royal Courts of Justice 32, 47-74, 47, 63
Admiralty oar 68-*69*
Alfred's statue 72, 73
Bar Room *71*
Bear Garden 71
Chancery Division 74
clock tower *72-73*
Crypt Courts 64
demolitions required for 32, 51-2
design 52-56
Great Hall 56, 58-*60*, 63
inauguration 59-62
Janus clock, *72*
legal costume display 66, *67*, 68
legal prints exhibition 65
Lady Chief Justice of England's Court *66, 69*
Lord Russell statue *64*
main courts floor 69-*70*

277

Moses statue 74
Street memorial 58-59, *61*
Thomas More Building 58, 74
West Green Building 57, 67, 74
Royal Insurance Company 178
Royal Society 30
Rumpole of the Bailey 144
Russell, Francis (Earl of Bedford) 239
Russell, John 190
Russell of Killowen, LCJ 64, *64*, 115
Rutledge, Edward 83
Rutledge, John 84
Rye House plot 39, 42

S
Sacheverell, Dr Henry 233
Sackville, Thomas 95, 125
St Albans, Viscount (Francis Bacon) 188, 230, 239, 243, *244*, 245, 246, 255
St Andrew's, Holborn 138, 233
St Bride's 158-159, *161*
St Clement Danes 23, *37*, 49, 186
St Dunstan's-in-the-West 147, *152*, 179
St George's Inn 34, 121, 162
St Mary-le-Strand 12, 28-29
St Paul's Cathedral 162
St Peter's Sanctuary 16
St Sepulchre's, Newgate 162
St Stephen's Chapel 3, 4
St Stephen's clock tower (Westminster) 5
Saint-Gaudens, Augustus, 15
Sala, George Augustus, 145
Salisbury, Earl of (Robert Cecil) 250
Samuel Pepys Society museum *150*
Sanderson, William 126
Savage, James 122
Savoy 88
Savoy Hotel 28
Scarfe's Inn 177
Scarlett, James 104
Schmidt, Bernard 137
Schreider, Christopher 138

Scotland Yard 21
Scott, Clement 242
Scott, Sir George Gilbert 53, 54, 212, 253
Scott, Sir Richard 98, *99*
Scott, Sir Walter 179
Scroop's Court 234
Scrope's Inn, 155, 234
Seacoal Lane 162
Seddon, Frederick 169
Seddon, John 53
Selborne, first Earl (Lord Chancellor) 45, 59, 61-2, 214
Selden, John 99, 105, 137, 179
Serjeants' Inn 155, 156, 177
Serle, Henry 215, 217
Serle's Coffee House 217
Seymour, Edward (Duke of Somerset) 9, 27, 29
Shakespeare's will 183
Shakespeare, William 35, 41, 88, 89, 125, 152, 153, 249, 250
Sheldon, Gilbert 253
Sheppard, Jack 165
Sheridan, Richard Brinsley 101, 127, 141, 188
Ship tavern 51, 219
Shoe Lane 158, 195, 166
Shute, Robert 255
Shute's Buildings 255
Sidmouth, Viscount (Henry Addington) 199
Sidmouth, Viscount (Thomas Thynn) 117
Sidney, Sir Philip 125, 251
Simmonds, 149
Simonds, Viscount (Lord Chancellor) 208
Simpkinson, Sir Francis 218
Singer Sargent, John 214
Sir John Soane's Museum *220*
Six Clerks Inn 184
Skipworth, William 237
Smethwick(e), John 152
Smirke, Sir Robert 177

Smirke, Sydney 93, *96*
Smith, Adam 141
Smith, F.E. (Earl of Birkenhead) 248
Soane, Sir John 12, *220*
Society of Actuaries 226
Society of Knights Batchelor 180
Society of Merchants of the Staple 226
Somers, Sir John (Lord Chancellor) 123, 126
Somerset House 28, 29, *30, 31*
South Square 224, 240, *242, 243*
Southampton, First Earl of (Thomas Wriothesley) 10, 233, 250
Southampton Buildings 133, 190
Southampton House 190
Southey, Robert 179
Southwark Cathedral 12
Spencer, Herbert 31
Stafford, Henry (Duke of Buckingham) 9
Stanhope, Sir Edward 255
Stanhope's Buildings 243
Stanley, Thomas (Earl of Derby) 238
Staple Inn 224-227, *225, 227*
  south courtyard *227*
Staple Market 27
Stapleton Inn 38
Star Chamber 6, 7
  Court of 243
Starkie, Thomas 101
Steele, Sir Richard 51, 117, 150
Stirling, Samuel 42
Stone Building (Lincoln's Inn) 12, 185, 191, 199
Stone Building (Westminster) 12
Stowell, Lord Chancellor 123, 141
Strafford, Earl 191
Strand 27-45
Strand Inn 28
Strand Well 28
le Strange, Ebulo 195
Strange's Inn 195, 233
Straw, Jack 98
Street, George Edmund 44, 53, 54, 55, 58-59, 61, 71
Suffolk, Duke of (Charles Brandon) 238
Sulyard (gentleman) 196
Sumption, Lord 209
Sun 156
Sunday Express 158
Supreme Court of the United Kingdom, 15, 16, *17, 18-19*
Swift, Jonathan 41, 51, 148
Sydney, Sir Philip 183
Symond's Inn 34, 187

T

Talbot, Lord Chancellor 204
Talfourd, Sir Thomas Noon 179
Tanfield, Sir Laurence 106
Tanfield Court 107, 108
Tatersall's Buildings 243
Taylor, Sir Robert 209
Taylor, Tom 86, 87
Taylor, Sir William Francis Kyffin (Lord Maenan) 106
Taylor of Gosforth, Lord Peter 66, 98, 99
Templars 91, 127-36
  disbanding 131
  seizure of property 131
  see also Temple Church
Temple, 75-144
  Blitz damage 81, *82-83*
  see also Inner, Middle and Outer Temple
Temple Bar 27, 39, 40, 41-45, 52
  monument *44*, 147
  restored *43, 163*, 164
Temple Bridge 78, 80
Temple Church 12, *128*, 129, *134-135*, 190
  Blitz damage 137
  Call ceremony, *139*
  chapel royal 138
  memorials 136-137
  St Anne chapel 138
  St Thomas chapel 139

Temple Gardens 80, 81
Temple Pier 69
Temple Stairs 78, 79, 88, 148
Tenniel, Sir John 160
Tennyson, Alfred 87, 157, 213
Thackeray, William Makepeace 33, 35, 86, 89, 108, 115, 123, 127, 158, 188, 256
Thalben-Ball, George 138
Thatcher, Margaret 199, 206, 214
Thavies Inn 195, 228, 232-233
Thavies Inn House 233
Thesiger, Frederick (Lord Chelmsford) 103
Thomas à Becket (saint) 29, 190, 252
Thomas de Lincoln, serjeant 231
Thomas of Lancaster 195
Thomas More Building 58, 74
Thompson, John 227
Thornhill, Sir James 93
Thorpe, Jeremy 169
Thurlow, Edward (Lord Chancellor) 128
Thurlow, John (Lord Chancellor) 65, 188, 198, 201, 206, 207
Thursby, William 120
Tichborne claimant 115
The Times 157
Tolpuddle Martyrs 182
Tomes, Henry 239
Tonson, Jacob 51, 255
Took's Court 188
Torrigiano, Pietro 183
Tothill Fields 14
Tower Hill 9
Town Court House 15
Treasury Building 21
Trumpet tavern 52
Tucker, James 81
Tunis, Earl Alexander of 199
Turner, Sydney 81
Turner, Sir William 96
Turton, Sir John 248
Twain, Mark 158
Twisden's Buildings 110

Tyburn 166, 223
Tyler, Wat 41, 121, 147, 165
Tyndal-Atkinson, E. 122

U

Union Court 234
United States
   Abraham Lincoln, statue, 15
   American Bar Association 123, 248
   constitution, 83-84
Upjohn, Lord 201

V

Van der Wyngaerde, Antonio 101
Vanbrugh, Sir John 51
Vardy, John 12
Venables, George 106
de Vere, Edward (Earl of Oxford) 238
Verulam Buildings *255*, 256, 257
Vice-Chancellor 13
Vice-Chancellor's Court 13, 169
Victoria (Queen) 45, 59, 71, 206, 213, 218
Victoria Street 14
Vine Court 112
Voltaire 157

W

Wade's Buildings 243
Wake, Archbishop 252
Walker, Matthias 152
Wallace, Edgar 160
Wallace, Sir William 8
Waller Conspiracy 155
Waller, Edmund 201
Walpole, Horace 199
Walpole, Sir Robert 20, 51, 199
Walsingham, Sir Francis 261
Walton, Isaak 152, 176, 245
Waple, John 241
War of the Roses 88
Warbeck, Perkin 6, 9
Ward, Artemus 242
Warton, Thomas 141

Warwick Court 191, 224, 260
Warwick House 260
Waterhouse, Alfred 53, 54, 226
Waterman, George 42
Watkin-Wilkins, Sir Charles 113
Watling Street 165
Watts, G.F. 213, 214
Webb, Sydney 251
Weldon's coffee house 239
Wellington, Duke of 4, 217
Wesley, John 260
West, Benjamin 31
Westbury, Lord Chancellor 126
Westminster Abbey 3, 4, 5, 7, 14, 27
Westminster Cathedral 14
Westminster Guildhall 15
Westminster Hall *4, 5*, 6, 7, *8, 9, 10-11*, 23
Westminster Palace *1*, 4, *5*
Westmorland, Earl of (Henry Neville) 239
Whetstone Park 219
White Friars 133
White Hall (Court of Requests) 3
Whitefriars 12
Whitefriars Street 157
Whitgift, Archbishop 239, 252, 254
Whittington, Richard 170
Wig and Pen Club 38, *39*
Wilcocks booksellers 158
Wilde, Oscar 66, 168
Wildy's Bookshop 149, *151, 197, 217*
Wilkes, John 160
Wilkes obelisk 160
William the Conqueror 6
William II (William Rufus) 7
William III 94, 123, 184
William IV 4, 184, 185
William the Chamberlain 165
William of Wykeham 182
William, Prince of Wales, 126
Williams, Montagu QC 88
Wilton, Lord Grey of (Reginald de Grey) 237
Wine Office Court 84, 156, 157

Wolfit, Donald 126
de Wollore, David 178
Wolsey, Cardinal Thomas 113, 140, 148, 182, 191, 198, 249
Woolf of Barnes, Lord 98, *99*
Wordsworth, William 1, 141, 151, 182
Worthington, Sir Hubert 93
Wren, Sir Christopher 37, 42, 102, 111, 114, 117, 137, 148, 159, 206, 233
Wriothesley, Thomas (Lord Chancellor) 233, 250
Wyatt, Thomas 53
Wych Street 32, 162
Wymbush, Nicholas 184

Y
Ye Old Cock Tavern 151
Ye Olde Cheshire Cheese 157, *159*
Yeats, W.B. 158
Yelverton, Sir Christopher 248, 255